Enter The Light

Daniel J. Neiman

1st Revised Edition
reformatted with additional chapter subheadings

ISBN: **0615735193**
ISBN-13: **978-0615735191**

DEDICATION

To all those on a never ending mission to seek truth, I bow to you. To my college professor who told me to keep going and not stop, thank you. To all those who have supported me over the years, thank you. And to all my readers, blessings aplenty. Yours truly, Dan Neiman.

CONTENTS

INTRODUCTION   vii

1   WELCOME TO SUBJECTIVE REALITY: PART 1   1

-The rejection of valid scientific data due to a priori   2
beliefs about reality
     2
    Telepathy
    UFOs   6
    Near-death experiences   10
    Mediumship   22
    Astrology   28
    Intelligent Design   32

-Assessing the Situation   55

2   WELCOME TO SUBJECTIVE REALITY: PART 2   59

-The mind and the creation of reality   59
    The placebo effect   59
    Beyond the placebo effect   71
    Hypnosis and the far reaches of the mind   75
    Mind over matter   82
    When ideas become real   92
    Mental beliefs and our experience of reality   94
    Summing up: The mind and the shaping of reality   99

3   WELCOME TO MULTI-DIMENSIONAL REALITY   103

-From the physical to the other-dimensional   103
    Energetic phenomena during the transition to another   104
      dimension
    Visual phenomena during the transition   107
    Transition assistance   109

Lost time and the magic want   111
Dimensional travel continued   115

-Astonishing dimensional excursions   117
    Sequoyah Trueblood   117
    Neale Donald Walsch   118
    Barry Smith   120
    Remembering other-dimensional experiences   123

-Learning from other-dimensional experiences   124
    Chris meets Peco: A lesson in dimensionality   124
    Duane's NDE – telepathic communication   126
    More on telepathy   129
    Experiencing the mind of another   131

-Shaping the experience   133
    Believe!   133
    Co-creating with the deeper Self   134
    Not this time: When the deeper Self throws you a curve ball   135
    A further source of limitation: When two minds conflict   137
    What we've learned   138

-Experiencing higher consciousness   139
    Are we being used?   140

-The thought-directed nature of experience   142
    Giving shape to the unseen world   144
    The unseen world shaping this world   148
    Mental Influence   150
    The little creatures within   152

-Life after death   154

-The reality of other-dimensional experiences   167
    Physical effects of other-dimensional experiences   168
    Signs of crossing over   174
    It feels real!   178
    Mental Realities   179

Higher-dimensional beings are toying with us   184
Making meaning of our manipulation   189

4   METAPHYSICS AND THE FUTURE   191

-Comparing Worldviews   191
    Why it's important   194
    The choice is yours   195
    Why "evil" is not a problem   196

-The future of conscious development   201
    We are One   204
    The only time is NOW   206
    Moving Forward   207

CONCLUSION   210

APPENDIX – ON RANDOM MUTATION AND   219
NATURAL SELECTION

NOTES   228

SELECTED BIBLIOGRAPHY   255

INTRODUCTION

I consider myself a philosopher and a rationalist. For every belief I hold, there is evidence for it. I do not base anything on faith. If I believe in life after death, it's because I've seen compelling evidence to support that belief. If I believe that an Intelligent Consciousness creates and evolves the universe, again, there's evidence to support it. In this book I will present the evidence that leads me to believe as I do. I will present evidence that consciousness is fundamental, that material reality is a subjective creation of consciousness, and that life after death is a given. I will especially spend much time exploring the evidence for the existence of other dimensions which we can consciously experience, after death or beforehand.

It has taken me a long time to come to the beliefs that I now hold. I started as a standard Christian, but have long since left those beliefs behind. I disagree with much religious dogma for many of the same reasons atheists disagree with it, namely, because it is irrational. Take, for instance, the belief that Jesus died for the sins of humanity as some atonement to the devil, and that whoever believes in Jesus may go to heaven while those who reject him will be subjected to eternal damnation. It just doesn't make sense. When you consider that the majority of the time the religion you are born into is the one you will adopt, it would seem that one's place in the afterlife is determined by the conditions of their birth and the culture they grow up in. Not to mention the fact that God would need some sacrifice for our sins, sins which are inevitably part of human nature. To be subjected to eternal damnation or heaven based on the actions of just one short 70 or so year life, with varied circumstances, is a highly illogical concept and, as such, I reject it. Besides, I have sifted through hundreds of Near Death Experience reports and have found little evidence to support the traditional Christian view on the afterlife.

However, I equally reject the idea that we live just one short 70 or so year life and then die and simply cease to exist as a personality or conscious entity. This is equally as illogical to me. Consciousness being fundamental, and my body being a medium through which that consciousness experiences, it makes no sense that I would live only one life on Earth. It makes much more sense that I would continue to come back into other bodies and live multiple lives, male and female, in order to gain a variety of experience and learning. We'll get to the evidence for the fundamental nature of consciousness and life after death in the first chapter.

I've come to view reality as a subjective play of consciousness. There is no objective reality apart from Consciousness. The material world is a construction of consciousness. There is no material reality apart from our conscious perception of it. Reality is a creation of the mind and this is easily seen in other-dimensional experiences, which we'll talk about in chapter 3, but also seen in the workings of the physical universe. What's real is based on what we think is real, in other words, based on our subjective perception of reality. In the 1700s, for instance, meteorites were not real, at least, not in the sense that they were rocks that fell from the sky from outer space. If you thought such a thing you would have been derided and ridiculed by the scientists of the day. So, subjectively, in that time period they weren't real. They were either delusions or rocks born by the wind and heated by lightning. That's what they were until the scientists changed their minds about rocks falling from the sky and said, "Shit, wouldn't you know it, these things really are from outer space." Only then did meteorites, in the sense of rocks from outer space, become real. Now, the tendency is to say, "Well, they were real all along, the scientists were just wrong about them." You're trying to think objectively. But you can't do that. Reality is subjective, it's based on what we think about it. To the scientists of the 1700s meteorites were not real and you would be laughed at for asserting otherwise. Reality for them simply did not include such things. Reality for you, on the other hand, does include a belief in such things, and as such, meteorites are real to you. From your subjective perspective, you then project your ideas through all of time and demand that meteorites, as rocks crashing to Earth from outer space, must have always been real. Our beliefs color our perception of things. Imagine a future science that comes to a new realization that meteorites actually form in our upper atmosphere from the condensation of heavy elements, then fall to earth and simply look as if they came from outer space. Now you're the foolish one. There's always an underlying phenomenon, but our ideas and beliefs shape our perception of it and how we experience it. The same is true for apparitions of the dead. For some people, these apparitions are a clear indication that there is life after death. For others, they are hallucinations of the mind. Who's right? The answer is no one is right because reality is subjective. Subjective beliefs determine how we experience the world, and as such are fundamental to reality.

Everyone constructs a subjective belief system upon which they live and act. Everyone, in this regard, has their stop limit. For instance, one might say, "Ok, I'll admit that telepathy is real, but psychokinesis.... Ahhhhh......No, not gonna go there." Or you might say, "People seeing UFOs which can't be explained as a natural phenomenon I'll accept. But aliens abducting humans...... Ahhhhhh......No, not gonna go there. I can't accept that." Some people are really strict, "Wireless communication between computers is absolutely real, but telapthic communication between minds.... Ahhhhh.......No, not gonna touch that one." Even I myself find myself creating a limit to what I will believe. For instance, I wholeheartedly believe in regressing people under hypnosis to past lives and exploring past life causes for present problems. But one hypnotherapist talks about demons from Satan coming to people and causing their physical and emotional problems. Remember, I left religion behind, so this idea was just plain distasteful to me. I drew the line and said, "No way, I'm not gonna buy it. This is total bullshit." I threw that book aside and kept reading other material. But later I got to thinking: Am I really justified to say that's not real when she and her clients obviously are not making this up? They truly are experiencing the source of their emotional problems, or physical problems, as demons who have come into their bodies. The demons talk while the subject is under hypnosis and give their names and histories in some instances. There are many ways to interpret such a phenomenon, but it is definitely a real experience and they choose to believe in Satan and demons. So, I came to the understanding that this is their subjective reality. It's real. It might not be real to you, but it's real to a certain group of people, just like meteorites from outer-space might be real to you, but not to an 18th century scientist. As another example, telepathy is real to many people who have experienced it, but not real to many scientists who disbelieve in it and pass all telepathy claims off as delusion or coincidence.

In chapters one and two we will look deeper into this concept of subjective reality. We'll start by taking a look at science's rejection of anomalous data and then dig right in to the evidence for an intelligence involved in the evolution of life. We'll then dive into how our beliefs affect reality and what we experience. Chapter three will be all about extraordinary experiences people have in other dimensions, covering out-of-body experiences, lucid dreams, alien abductions, and Near-Death Experiences. Chapter four will be a discussion of metaphysics and metaphysical considerations. I'll also cover an outline of possible future evolution.

I've written this book because it is my passion. I'm driven from within. You could call me obsessed. I'm obsessed with researching the paranormal and looking for Truth. Let me tell you, it feels awesome to be obsessed with something. There's nothing better than understanding your purpose in life and putting yourself to the task with zeal. I'm driven, and have only just begun. This is my first book, but will not be my last. I will keep collecting and analyzing evidence until the day I die. It's what I love to do. I hope you love the result, which is this book. I hope to open your mind and expose you to new ideas. Whether or not you agree with me, I hope you take something from this book and enjoy reading it. With no further ado, turn the page. . .

1

WELCOME TO SUBJECTIVE REALITY: PART I

Just think about this world for a minute. How many diverse groups of people are there? People are spread all over this planet with widely differing belief systems and experiences of the world. People go on and on arguing for their version of reality over another's. Scientists are especially troubling in this regard, as they have become the new Church; the gatekeepers of reality. It is now the scientific establishment who gets to dictate what we believe as reality. Supposedly they are the objective, rational, harbingers of true reality, as opposed to that made up fiction of religion.

However, as I intend to show: *no one* or *no group of people* is "objective" or even can be. This is because we live in a subjective reality. In the next chapter we'll examine evidence for how we create our own experience based on what we believe and desire to experience. For now we'll examine the scientific establishment's resistance to the paranormal (or any data that doesn't fit within their present belief system) and the idea of an intelligence that forms and evolves the universe. We'll see that scientists have constructed a box of beliefs (worldview) that shapes their view of the world, and what's possible and not possible in that world. This belief in only material objects and energy blinds them to the true nature of reality even when the evidence for it is staring them in the face.

Don't get me wrong, I'm not opposed to science. Scientific experimentation is wonderful and has led to many advances. What I'm railing against is a certain *scientism* that has grown up around the halls of academia. It is a scientific fundamentalism that dictates what kinds of

1

theories are acceptable in science, and subsequently about what kinds of studies are acceptable to undertake. Any findings that might upset the dominate beliefs of the scientific establishment are attacked or just simply ignored.

It is not an environment that is open to any and all inquiry. Precisely the opposite, what you can and cannot believe is determined by the scientific establishment based on the dominating paradigm, or worldview, under which they operate. And by "scientific establishment" I don't mean all scientists, but the majority of scientists, especially the high ranking and influential ones. Things like telepathy, communicating with the dead, or a guiding intelligence underlying the universe, to name just a few, are not open for discussion. They are impossible based on the materialistic worldview of many scientists. Even when scientists study these things, their science is labeled pseudoscience and simply ignored by the establishment.

The rejection of valid scientific data due to a priori beliefs about reality

We live in the confines of the box of our beliefs about reality, trapped by a worldview whether it's a scientific or religious one; it doesn't matter. There may be "objective" facts. This person did this experiment and found this result. That's an objective fact. However, our beliefs come to define which facts we accept, which we ignore, which we ridicule, and which define our reality. Science is *no* exception to this rule.

As an example, just look at research into psychic phenomena performed in laboratories all around the world. Parapsychologists have been actively looking for evidence of the paranormal (think telepathy, clairvoyance, and telekinesis) for over 100 years. For over 100 years they've been setting up experiments and conducting tests for these things. And they've been finding statistically significant results.

Telepathy

Nowadays, a typical telepathy experiment operates on what is known as the ganzfeld protocol. This involves two people: a sender and a receiver. The receiver goes into an acoustically sealed room, dons a pair of headphones, and relaxes in a comfortable chair. Ping pong or tennis balls are halved and placed over the subjects eyes and a red light shines down from above. The receiver is then taken through a progressive relaxation routine for 15 minutes. Then for the next 30 minutes white noise is played through the headphones and the receiver is asked to articulate any thoughts or images that come to his/her mind.[1]

You see by the design of the experiment that the idea is to eliminate any outside sensory stimulation. All you can see is soft red light and all you can hear is white noise. So there's not much to stimulate the mind in this situation, which in theory makes one better able to pick up on subconscious images or ideas relayed by the sender. Because if telepathy is real it operates on a higher/deeper level of mind that we are usually not conscious of. Some people call this the subconscious mind, but we'll talk more about the multi-level nature of mind in the coming chapters.

In what's known as the autoganzfeld, which is the kind used today, a computer randomly chooses a picture or video clip from a vast library of such pictures and clips to show to the sender. The sender is in another room with a one-way audio speaker which allows him to hear the receiver, but the receiver cannot hear him. This is so the sender can receive feedback about what the receiver is mentally experiencing and make adjustments to his/her thought processes accordingly. For 30 minutes the sender concentrates on sending the picture or video clip to the receiver in the other room.

After the 30 minutes is up, the session ends and a set of 4 pictures or video clips, including the target one, is shown to the receiver who then has to guess which one the sender was trying to telepathically send to him/her. If it were merely a guess we should expect people to guess the right picture 25% of the time. However, as it turns out when the experiments are run the average hit rate is around 33%.[2]

You may think this is a relatively small effect and wonder why the hit rate is not much larger. But think about the fact that we are not taught to believe in such abilities, much less to utilize them. So, very few people have much practice with this ability, and not surprisingly telepathy is relatively foreign in our everyday experience. Another way of putting it is that our society's belief system, dominated as it is by the scientific establishment, does not include telepathy as real, much less important. In fact, the typical response is to fear or ignore such abilities even when they are experienced. Therefore, it is likely that there are strong mental blocks to experiencing such things. As we will look at more in the next chapter, our belief system shapes how we experience reality.

It is quite telling that when gifted artists were tested, their hit rate was found to be a much higher 47%.[3] So, people who often utilize their right brains and are very imaginative seem to be able to tap the subconscious much better than those that are predominantly left-brained. It would be interesting to see if they have a much higher belief in psychic awareness or if they have had more experience with this ability than the general population, who are the test subjects in normal ganzfeld experiments.

In any event, 33% is getting right one out of every three, a significant deviation from the chance expectation of one out of every four. In fact, Mario Beauregard, in his book *Brain Wars,* reports that "a meta-analysis of the replication studies [of the autoganzfeld] conducted by Radin, Bierman, Bem, and Parker has revealed a hit rate of 33.2 percent with odds against chance beyond a million billion to one."[4] That means that it's not just a fluke. The odds are astoundingly stacked against this result happening by chance. Telepathy is operating, not perfectly, but it's definitely there.

In actuality, today's telepathy experiments are just a formality, trying to prove under the strictest of conditions what has been experimentally verified by competent researchers for over 100 years. The great Armand-Marie-Jacques de Chastenet, Marquis de Puységur (really, could a name be longer?), for one, put a subject named Victor in a hypnotic state. From there Puységur was able to give unspoken mental commands to Victor, which he would dutifully obey. Paraspychological researcher Brian Inglis explains, "Victor would behave as he was willed to behave, talk as he was willed to talk; and if willed to stop talking, he would 'stay his thoughts, his phrases, in the middle of a word.'"[5] This was all done without speaking a single command, but through the transmission of Puységur's thoughts to the subject. Puységur explicitly states:

> "When he is magnetised [a form of hypnosis], he is no longer a simple peasant who can barely answer a question; he is something I cannot describe. I have no need to speak to him, I think in front of him and he understands and answers me. If somebody comes into the room, he sees him if I want him to, and speaks to him, saying what I want him to say, not always in the same words, but true to their meaning. When he wants to

say more than I consider fit to be heard, I stop his ideas and sentences in the middle of a word, and I change his mind completely."[6]

In complete rapport with his subject, who is himself in a higher sphere of mind, it is as if they are together of one single mind. Many other researchers also found that they could influence a subject under hypnosis mentally, even when they were separated by great distances to preclude any other type of influence.[7] There is really no other explanation for this type of phenomenon than a telepathic communication between hypnotizer and subject. In the past, it was sometimes attributed to a hypersensitivity on the subjects part, so that they could pick up subtle muscular clues or drafts of air and somehow deduce what was in the hypnotists mind. However, this type of explanation stretches credulity and cannot possibly be taken seriously, especially when the hypnotist is not even in the same room as the subject. We will explore the reaches and powers of the mind more fully in the next chapter, but this suffices to show that experimentation with telepathy is nothing new and in no way are the modern day ganzfeld experiments necessary to prove its existence. Telepathy has simply been demonstrated time and time again, as well as reported by people the world over, to be beyond doubt.

However, considering there are modern day experimental proofs of telepathy we should ask the question: Do you remember that New York Times article proclaiming how scientists have found telepathy and it will enter the school curriculum next year and be taught as an established principle to all grade school children? Probably not because it wasn't there. Do you remember learning about telepathy as a serious scientific study when you were in school? Again, I doubt it. Unless you took specialized classes in parapsychology in college you probably never heard a word about the subject. And if you did it was probably in a passing reference to "pseudoscience." As if the controlled laboratory experiments I described are somehow less scientific than normal experiments just because they study something that's not supposed to exist!

Indeed, telepathy is still excluded from most scientist's belief system even though the data is overwhelmingly in favor of it. The key point is that facts themselves don't matter, beliefs matter. When the facts don't fit into your belief system there are a few options: ignore them, try to explain them away, or change your belief system. The first is the easiest and most common, followed by the second and third. Let's take a look at some more examples, shall we? Ok, we shall.

UFOs

Astrophysicist and computer scientist Jacques Vallee studied the UFO phenomenon for many years and wrote a series of books on the subject from the 1960s up until the early 1990s. He was a very open minded man who wanted to understand what these UFOs were, if they were physically real, and how they affected human populations who came in contact with them. But to his surprise, his astronomer colleagues were for the most part only interested in ignoring the phenomenon. He complains:

> "On two occasions I have tracked some unknown objects, using small telescopes. A few of my astronomer colleagues made similar observations, and, after making inquiries, we became aware of sightings kept confidential by professional astronomers the world over. The objects we were tracking were not spectacular, but the reaction they elicited among French scientists fascinated me. Instead of asking if these seemingly maneuverable and "impossible" objects could be a manifestation of some advanced technology (and in some cases they may well have been terrestrial), they thought only of suppressing the records. They did this by denying every observation, by blaming it on airplanes or planets when the documentation was unassailable, and by destroying the data when it was demonstrated that no airplane could have behaved as the objects did."[8]

So much for objective scientific inquiry. I do have some sympathy for these astronomers who were suppressing, ignoring, and even destroying data because I realize that we live in such a close minded society, especially among mainstream scientists. I can just imagine one of these astronomers coming out and saying that he tracked a UFO by telescope and releasing the data that it couldn't have been a planet, airplane, or conventional phenomenon. This poor astronomer would be immediately subjected to ridicule by his colleagues who would propose some bullshit theory about what he saw (think swamp gas). If he were at a university, they might marginalize him and make sure he never gets tenure.[9] It's not easy to challenge the orthodoxy. It's much easier not to push the boundaries of belief, just better to stay quiet, shut up and do real science!

Sometimes scientists are even barred from publishing in a journal solely because their conclusions about the phenomenon are on the wrong side of the ideological fence. Such was the case with optical physicist Bruce Maccabee. He went to Kaikoura, New Zealand to investigate some well documented UFO sightings involving multiple witnesses, movie footage, and radar tracking. He spent a good month in Kaikoura analyzing the data and interviewing the witnesses. To his surprise "an article appeared in the *Journal of Atmospheric and Terrestrial Physics* concluding that refracted lights from Japanese squid boats were responsible for the sightings." Having done his own in depth research, Maccabee had reached the opposite conclusion, namely, that it was an unidentified phenomenon and couldn't be explained on the basis of mirages or other terrestrial phenomena. So, he decided to submit a rebuttal to the Journal explaining his position. UFO researcher Thomas Bullard sums up what happened nicely:

> "The editor rejected his article, saying it contained no 'real science,' in an apparent demonstration that a study based on extensive investigation did not merit publication if it arrived at an unacceptable answer, while a study based on nothing more than newspaper reports breezed into print as long as its results conformed to proper scientific opinion."[10]

Is this not the case with all belief systems though? You readily accept findings that fit nicely within your preexisting belief system even if the evidence is flimsy, while rejecting or ignoring strong evidence to the contrary. Science, the supposed objective arbiter of truth, turns out to be no different. It's not about the evidence. Belief system comes first, evidence second. Let's take a look at another UFO related scandal involving the Condon Committee, which was a group formed at the University of Colorado headed by physicist Dr. Edward Condon and commissioned by the Defense Department to study UFOs in the late 60s. Given a healthy sum of money to the tune of half a million dollars, their investigation into the UFO matter was strikingly short. Thomas Bullard reports that investigations started early in 1967 and wrapped up in the spring of 1968.[11] Another intriguing detail to clue us in to possible bias in the final outcome is that Condon, who "never thought very highly of the subject," made a public speech in January of 1967 stating, "that he thought there was nothing to UFOs—'but I'm not supposed to reach that conclusion for another year.'"[12] In a similar vein, Jacques Vallee tells us that within a year of beginning their study, "field investigations were nonexistent. Questionnaires were sent out to witnesses, but only one assistant was available to encode the results for the computer file. . ."[13] This prompted a minority faction of the committee to rebel and publish a memorandum to the effect that "the Condon Committee had never intended to look seriously into the UFO problem." Afterwards Dr. Condon fired the minority group and proceeded to run the project his way, which according to Vallee was essentially to not take the phenomenon seriously.[14] Of course, the final report stated that the official study of the UFO phenomenon should be abandoned.[15] But the more intriguing part of the scandal involves what happened to the committee's files afterwards. Were the files opened to the public and the scientific establishment for independent review? Far from it, Vallee reports that after the committee released their report stating that UFOs were not worthy of study, the University of Colorado locked up the project's files, which were later "transferred to a private home and were burned shortly thereafter."[16]

This last event is really telling that they were not serious about studying UFOs and UFO related events. It's fine if you want to conclude that there's nothing to the phenomenon. But the least you can do as a respectable body of scientists is release the data you've collected so that other scientists and scientific bodies can do their own analysis. For example, they could have said, "Here you go, take a look at these files and you'll see that it's just a bunch of hallucinating farmers and truck drivers staying up too late popping caffeine pills. (And probably smoking joints) Take a look; I'm sure you'll come to the same conclusion." Releasing the data and giving a statement like that would have been ok, although it would have pissed off farmers and truck drivers. But burn the data? Is this a scientific committee or a medieval Catholic Church?

In the 1700s people were also seeing things in the sky. Not only that, they were claiming that these rocks in the sky were falling to Earth. We call them meteorites today, but in the 1700s the suggestion of space rocks falling to Earth was just plain ludicrous. I can hear the scientists of the day wailing, "What kind of bullshit is this? Rocks! Falling from the sky! What are these peasants smoking?" Of course, the scientists of that time may have employed a slightly different linguistic style in their thought processes, but I think I've captured the meaning of what they would have thought.

It was in France that this whole fiasco came to a head. Thankfully, the scientists at the prestigious French Academy of Science were up to the task of putting these bullshit rumors of rocks falling from the sky to rest. So, in 1772 this prestigious group of distinguished pipe smoking scientists (I'm guessing on the pipe smoking) studied reports of rocks falling from the sky; what we now refer to as meteorites. What was their conclusion? You guessed it:

> "There are no such things as hot stones that have fallen from the sky because there are no stones in the sky to fall. Reports of the phenomenon must have other explanations--delusionary 'visions,' stones heated after being struck by lightning, stones borne aloft by whirlwinds or volcanic eruptions, and so forth."[17]

Here we come to the central problem; the problem which faced the prestigious French Academy. That is, how could it be possible? You see, they had no way to understand how meteorites *could* exist, as their scientific belief system was still primitive in terms of understanding space. If you had no conception of an asteroid belt or meteorites in space, how could you possibly believe in rocks falling from the sky? It just seemed so absurd at the time, so *impossible*.

The same is true for the astronomers tracking UFOs, or poor professor Condon who got himself balls-deep in UFO data and didn't know what to make of it. Science just can't fathom how an alien spacecraft would get here. The distances are too vast and wormholes require too much energy to create and keep open to be plausible. There's just no way to understand them. (And theorizing UFOs popping in from other dimensions is still way outside the box for most scientists to venture) It also doesn't help that aliens don't land on the White-House lawn like good aliens should. That, or immediately attack us and take over our planet like the movies suggest. Many scientists just can't wrap their heads around intelligent beings who would come here and not do one of these things. But you have to ask yourself: Are we really in a position to judge the actions of a higher intelligence? They may have a meta-logic all of their own. Instead of openly manifesting and giving us all the solutions to our problems, maybe they want to covertly guide us in ways that we are only beginning to piece together.

Telepathy and other psychic phenomena are no different. Scientists just can't fit it into what they know to be true. They have no idea how telepathy could exist. In fact, most scientists still think that the brain produces the mind as an epiphenomenon, or that the mind is reducible to neural firing in the brain. The former is the view that somehow the complex workings of the brain give rise to the mind, which exists as a secondary phenomenon not reducible to brain activity, but still dependent on it for existence. The latter is the view that all mental events are just patterns of neural activity in the brain; in other words, we can reduce the mind to the physical activity in the brain.[18] Both of these views require the brain for the mind to exist and neither can explain how one mind could transmit information directly to another mind. Since mind, in these views, is limited to a person's brain and nervous system functioning, how could one person's brain send a nerve (or neural) impulse across space to affect another person's brain?

So you see, we need a new belief system that can allow for what is now considered the paranormal. In order for science as a whole to accept the data, they need to be able to understand it within a broader system of thought. We need to have a belief system that makes the paranormal *normal*. Otherwise we'll go on living in our nice little box and fearing and ignoring major aspects of reality. In essence, we will stifle further advancement of knowledge by shunning the very phenomena we should be most interested in. We'll get to that larger belief system, but for now let's continue to look at how scientists ignore the data and try to explain it away.

Near-death experiences

Near-death experiences (NDEs) became a hot topic after the publication of Raymond Moody's book *Life after Life*. Since Moody laid out his findings of patients experiences of their consciousness leaving their body and traveling to the beyond, many more researchers have collected thousands of accounts of NDEs. If you take these experiences literally, they reveal that consciousness can leave the body, exist independently outside of the body, and travel to other dimensions. The biggest sense of proof we have regarding NDEs comes from what are known as veridical NDEs. These are NDEs where, after the person is revived, they report accurate details of what happened while they were unconscious or had a flat EEG. I've already reviewed some of this evidence in my 2010 paper, "A New View of Consciousness and Reality," but let's take a look at a couple more intriguing accounts of veridical NDEs.[19] The first account comes from Grandmaster of NDE Research (a title I've bestowed upon him) Kenneth Ring. It tells the story of a twenty-one-year-old U.S. soldier who was wounded in the Korean War and flown to Japan for surgery in 1952. Even though the experience happened many years prior to his relating it to Ring, "he still remembers the details of his operation vividly."

> "Spinal column surgery . . . Ineffective spinal anesthesia in midsurgery required rapid use of gas/shots from a panic situation. I heard later that the combination 'went green,' i.e. sour. I recall lapsing into unconsciousness (having been awake and alert during the first hour of surgery). I 'sensed' my heart stopping--thought, 'HEY, you guys are losing me.' The next moment I was 'floating' against the canvas roof of the O.R. tent, looking down on 'me' stretched out on the table, face down, still being operated on.
>
> The surgeon was alerted to cardiac arrest; several people shouted at once. A heavy, muscular black Air Force sergeant rushed in on call. 'I'm not clean, sir,' he said. 'To hell with that, flip this man over!' He waited for a second for the surgeon to pack the wound, then fork-lifted me onto my back. I clearly 'saw' an x-shaped scar on the top of the sergeant's scalp--even though my vision without glasses is 20/400. The medical team frantically worked on my body to resuscitate me. I saw the anesthesiologist (female, lieutenant, Air Force) wiping tears, shaking her head, saying, 'Oh shit, oh shit, he's gone!' I 'yelled' to her that I was still here, but she couldn't hear me. (Now I recall that my 'being' at the roof top had no form, no mouth--only consciousness, vivid, painless, unimpaired hearing and vision and thought.)
>
> I felt myself being sucked back. Many days later I regained consciousness. . . . Weeks later I spoke of my experience to my surgeon, hoping he wouldn't think I was crazy and declare me Section 8. Surprised that I could describe every detail of my 'death' and [be] aware of the black corpsman's x-shaped scar on his scalp, my doctor only shrugged and said, 'Well, nothing surprises me anymore.'"[20]

Of course this happened a long time ago and we don't have signed affidavits from the attending surgeon and scarred Air Force sergeant attesting to the fact that he did indeed perceive every detail accurately. So, it is just an anecdote. But, if we assume that the man is telling the truth and indeed did verify that his perceptions were accurate with the surgeon afterwards, then the case is very revealing concerning consciousness. As eminent NDE researcher and Cardiologist Pim Van Lommel points out, "research in both humans and animals has shown that during an induced cardiac arrest the loss of function of both the cerebral cortex and the brain stem results in unconsciousness within seconds."[21] And, "if the heartbeat is not immediately restored, the complete loss of all electrical activity in the cerebral cortex *always* results in a *flat* EEG after ten to twenty (a mean of fifteen) seconds."[22] Therefore, there should be no way his brain could have processed these detailed memories of what happened after he went into cardiac arrest. He would have been unconscious within seconds and after about 15 seconds, his EEG would have been flat. Therefore, in order for him to have experienced the things he did, his consciousness would have had to have been operating independently of his brain. If we accept the facts at face value, he was outside of his body in a pure conscious form just as he reports.

This case points to the theory that the brain is a mediator and filter of consciousness. Far from being the producer of consciousness, the brain/body acts as a tool consciousness uses to experience physical reality. Your consciousness, while alive, has to operate through the human body. We can compare the brain to a TV set. If I didn't know any better, I might mistakenly assume that the TV program exists inside the TV. But we all know that the TV program doesn't exist inside the TV any more than an internet website exists inside and is produced by my computer. The TV accesses the program and acts as a modulator, translating the signals into picture and sound. If I damage, say, the color module of my TV then I might get some weird looking programs. Once I had a TV which was getting old and every TV program was cast in a red glow, that is, until I gave it a good whack on the side and the color straightened out again. Something must have been wrong with the parts that process color. Then I got smart and bought a new Samsung TV. This one was HD and had much better picture quality than the other TV ever had in its long illustrious 15 years of sitting in my and other peoples living rooms.   The man in our previous NDE said his vision was vivid and clear while outside of his body, even though his vision was a pitiful 20/400 in real life. 20/400 vision is considered severe visual impairment by the optometry profession. Well, if we consider the brain/body system as just a modulator of consciousness, this is easily explained. His physical eyes and brain modules, which his consciousness used to process visual information while alive, were damaged, causing his bad vision, just as the parts of my old TV were damaged which led to the casting of every program in a red glow (until that good whack from my fist). But outside of the body, when his consciousness was not being modulated by the damaged brain/body system, he could see crystal clear as well as exercise other abilities of consciousness such as thinking and hearing. The same program that I used to watch on my shitty old TV comes in 10 times better on my HD Samsung. I can see the individual beads of sweat running down the faces of the actors as well as count every nose hair (not that I've tried). On my old TV, no way; much worse picture. It's the same exact program, just being modulated by different TV sets. The TV sets aren't producing the program, just processing it and relaying the picture and sound. So it is with the body/brain system. Our consciousness manifests through it and uses it to operate in the physical world. Some people's physical systems are damaged so they can't hear as well, or see as well, or think as well, etc... But there's actually nothing wrong with their consciousness. It's just the brain modules that are processing the information that are damaged.

It turns out, though, that it's not as simple as the picture I've painted for you. There's much more going on with the mind and mental powers to affect the physical. For instance, people suffering from multiple-personality disorder may have different vision and need different eye glasses for their various selves.[23] (More on the power of the mind in the next chapter) Also, there's some disagreement as to whether we need a brain at all to get by in the physical. I shit you not, a December 1980 issue of *Science* had an article entitled "Is Your Brain Really Necessary?" Sheffield University Professor John Lorber studied people with a rare condition called hydrocephalus, in which there is a problem in the developing brain regarding the circulation of cerebrospinal fluid. The ventricles in the brain become backed up with this fluid and expand, causing them to fill up significant portions of the head. According to *Science* magazine, this can lead to "a real loss of brain matter." One case investigated by Lorber was of a mathematics student at his university.

Lorber relates:

> "There's a young student at this university who has an IQ of 126, has gained a first-class honors degree in mathematics, and is socially completely normal. And yet the boy has virtually no brain. When we did a brain scan on him we saw that instead of the normal 4.5-centimeter thickness of brain tissue between the ventricles and the cortical surface, there was just a thin layer of mantle measuring a millimeter or so. His cranium is filled mainly with cerebrospinal fluid."[24]

Well, it seems consciousness doesn't need the brain to operate whether outside or inside the human body. This just goes to show you that mind (consciousness) is all-powerful and may overcome any physical limitation.

Another more documented case of a veridical NDE involves a man with dentures. This account was recounted to Dr. Pim Van Lommel by a nurse at a coronary care unit and was published in the prestigious medical journal *The Lancet*. With no further ado, here's the account as given by the nurse:

> "During the night shift the ambulance crew brings in a forty-four-year-old cyanotic [purplish-blue skin discoloration], comatose man. About an hour earlier he had been found in a public park by passers-by, who had initiated heart massage. After admission to the coronary care unit, he receives artificial respiration with a balloon and a mask as well as heart massage defibrillation. When I want to change the respiration method, when I want to intubate the patient, the patient turns out to have dentures in his mouth. Before intubating him, I remove the upper set of dentures and put it on the crash cart. Meanwhile we continue extensive resuscitation. After approximately ninety minutes, the patient has sufficient heart rhythm and blood pressure, but he's still ventilated and intubated, and he remains comatose. In this state he is transferred to the intensive care unit for further respiration.
> After more than a week in coma the patient returns to the coronary care unit, and I see him when I distribute the medication. As soon as he sees me he says, 'Oh, yes, but you, you know where my dentures are.' I'm flabbergasted. Then he tells me, 'Yes, you were there when they brought me into the

hospital, and you took my dentures out of my mouth and put them on that cart; it had all these bottles on it, and there was a sliding drawer underneath, and you put my teeth there.' I was all the more amazed because I remembered this happening when the man was in a deep coma and undergoing resuscitation.

After further questioning, it turned out that the patient had seen himself lying in bed and that he had watched from above how nursing staff and doctors had been busy resuscitating him. He was also able to give an accurate and detailed description of the small room where he had been resuscitated and of the appearance of those present. While watching this scene, he had been terrified that we were going to stop resuscitating and that he would die. And it's true that we had been extremely negative about the patient's prognosis due to his very poor condition when admitted. The patient tells me that he had been making desperate but unsuccessful attempts at letting us know that he was still alive and that we should continue resuscitating. He's deeply impressed by his experience and says he's no longer afraid of death."[25]

Again, in this case we have a man who is comatose and should not be capable of processing memories via the brain. In fact, in a later interview with the nurse by a researcher trying to verify the account, it was revealed that:

"B. [the patient] had not shown any sign whatsoever of being conscious at the time. He was clinically dead, period: no heartbeat, no breathing, no blood pressure, and 'cold as ice.' The ambulance personnel had tried to carry out some reanimation while driving to the hospital, but without result. Most important, immediately after B. entered the hospital, T.G. [the nurse] removed the dentures from B.'s mouth and intubated him before starting up the entire reanimation procedure. Therefore, as T.G. categorically stated, any 'normal' observation by the patient of his dentures being removed from his mouth was simply unthinkable"[26]

So here we have one of the strongest cases of veridical perception during a NDE on record. Again, unless this nurse is straight out lying his ass off, we have very good evidence that consciousness *does not need* the brain to exist, perceive the environment, think, and feel emotion. These experiences are merely mediated, or modulated, by the brain when alive. That's why we always see changes in brain activity whenever we think, feel emotion, or sense something, just like there's always changes in the electrical circuitry of our TV when it's processing TV programs. It's because we use the brain/body system to think, feel emotion, and perceive while alive in a physical body; in other words, our brain receives and processes our conscious thoughts, emotions and perceptions. But in fact, outside of our bodies we can think, feel emotion, and perceive much better than when inside the body. When consciousness has to work through the physical system, it seems that this physical system does more to limit consciousness.

So what has science got to say about such experiences? Are they ready to concede that "yep, consciousness exists without a body"? I think not! In fact, they've constructed so many theories to try and explain it away you would think they were whipping up cook book recipes. Let's see, just picking some of my favorites here, hmmm...., ah yes! Oxygen starvation; that's a good one. This theory hypothesizes that:

> "Lack of oxygen will cause random activity throughout the visual system, giving the impression of bright lights flashing in the middle of the visual field, where there are lots of cells, but fading out toward the periphery, where there are fewer. This, it is argued, will give the impression of a bright light at the end of a dark tunnel. As the oxygen level [in the brain] continues to fall and the brain's random activity increases, the bright light in the middle will get bigger and bigger, giving the impression of rushing through a tunnel toward a light. Eventually the whole visual field will seem to be light, giving the impression of having entered the light."[27]

Now *that* is a beautiful theory. Well constructed. Scientific sounding. I like it. And to Mr. Joe Blow who just fell off the turn-up truck it might sound like a good explanation of NDEs. But to any serious researcher into the experience, like myself, it looks like what it is: a desperate attempt by the scientific establishment to explain away a phenomenon that just can't be possible under the reigning materialistic paradigm that sees the brain as the producer of consciousness.

This oxygen deprivation theory attempts to explain one part of the experience while simply ignoring the other parts. Even if it could explain the tunnel and light experience, which I don't believe it can, it has no explanation for other significant parts of the experience, like the life review, meeting spiritual beings, experiencing being in another dimension, telepathic communication between the experiencer and other beings, and the out of body experience.[28] In order to account for other aspects of the NDE, other theories must be added to the mix. The oxygen deprivation scenario also does not account for NDEs where the person doesn't enter a tunnel and go to the light. Very often, there is only an out of body experience before the person is sucked back into their body without ever having a tunnel/light experience, as we saw with the Korean war soldier who had a NDE during spinal surgery.

So what other theories are there that might explain NDEs as nothing more than brain function or psychological aberrance? Well, a whole litany of them, including endorphins released to produce feelings of peace and calm, excessive carbon dioxide in the brain, temporal lobe seizures, fantasy and wishful thinking, dissociated states due to trauma, imaginative reconstructions of what was happening during resuscitation, semiconscious perception, and memories of birth.[29] Holy shit, I'm winded after saying all those. That's why I referred earlier to making cook book recipes. Take about 3 or 4 of the above theories, mix them up, set the oven to bake and wait 30 minutes and you've got yourself a full explanation of the near death experience (Ok, minus the oven and baking for 30 minutes)! And that's really what it takes, combining multiple theories to try and account for all of the aspects of the experience. For example, we could mix together the oxygen deprivation, endorphin, dissociated state, temporal lobe seizure, imaginative reconstruction, and wishful thinking theories. First, oxygen deprivation theory will take care of that pesky tunnel and Light experience; then, endorphins will explain the peace and calm that people feel; next, a dissociated state will produce a false sense of out-of-body experience; then, a temporal lobe seizure might explain the life review as some people report reproductions of past experience when they have these kinds of seizures; next, imaginative reconstruction will explain how they "remembered" what was going on in the room at the time they were unconscious and had their NDE, and finally we'll throw in some wishful thinking for those that experience meeting past loved ones or a being of light.

Wow, I did it! I explained NDEs. Damn that feels good. Of course I'm being sarcastic now. But that just shows you how many assumptions materialistic science has to make in order to come up with a full theory of NDEs. They have to assume all of these elements (or some other combination) are present in people who are dying.

In the final analysis, we just need to use simple reasoning skills to show that it doesn't matter what NDE recipe you decide to make, you will fail to provide any comprehensive explanation of the experience. Take the life review for example. Many people during their life review will not only experience their entire life over again, but will be aided in this review by a spiritual being (being of light), and they will experience not just their thoughts and actions during the events reviewed, but also the thoughts and feelings of others involved in those events.[30] They clearly learn a great deal from the review, especially regarding how their actions in life affected others. And you have to ask yourself, if this were just a temporal lobe seizure reproducing old memories, why include the being of light? Why experience the thoughts and feelings of other people involved? These elements are certainly not what you would expect if your brain was just cycling through memories. Even an imaginative reconstruction would be unlikely to include the thoughts and feelings of others, as this is so alien to our everyday experience.

I mentioned before that I didn't think the oxygen deprivation theory could explain the experience of "The Light" in NDEs. In NDEs, "The Light" is not experienced as some purely visual phenomenon. Near Death Experiencers (NDErs) report experiencing a profound sense of oneness with this Light. It is an ecstatic reunion with "the Source," or what some NDErs call "Home." While immersed in this Light there are wonderful feelings of love and peace, a sense of knowing all things and understanding existence, and being in a timeless state of pure consciousness. NDErs also report communicating telepathically with it.[31] These are not things that can be explained on the basis of it being a purely visual phenomenon based on the random firing of neurons in the visual cortex.

What it comes down to is this: A person having a NDE is DYING! Their brain is *shutting down* due to the lack of oxygen flow when the heart stops. If the experience is mediated by the brain, is it really logical to believe that they have lucid, coherent and meaningful experiences during this time? Wouldn't it be more logical to experience disorientation, fragmented memory, confusion, and fear? But instead, NDErs time and time again report an enhanced consciousness--the exact opposite of what should be happening if indeed these experiences are a result of brain functioning. They report vivid perception as well as enhanced abilities, such as the ability to be in more than one place at once, 360 degree panoramic vision, and the ability to see through walls.[32]

I'm going to leave it at that and quote one final extraordinary NDE that really shows that we're dealing with something that can't be explained away by materialistic science.

> "When I was a young, single woman living in my hometown of London, England, I was admitted to Memorial Hospital with severe complications following a failed attempted abortion which I had done in my apartment bathroom. Being raised Catholic, I sought to handle the unwanted pregnancy secretly and alone. After losing a great deal of blood and feeling very cold, I called for an ambulance to take me to the hospital.
>
> As soon as I was rushed into the emergency room, I recalled all the staff running into my room bringing carts with equipment, bottles, pumps, needles, bandages, tubes, etc. From the navel down I was drenched with blood and very weak. I was in a life threatening, very critical condition. As the blood drained from my body so did my will to live.
>
> I heard a 'pop' sound and suddenly the pain stopped. I felt calm for the first time in 3 months since learning of my pregnancy by a man who had lied to me telling me he loved me and wanted to marry me but who had a wife and 5 children in another city. I had a very clear view of my body as they ferociously worked on me, hooking up a transfusion and other tubes. I recalled thinking that I just wished they would stop. I looked horrible and my color was very bad. I was embarrassed to be the cause of all the panic. I had sinned and didn't deserve to live. The fact that I was having these thoughts from within inches of the ceiling didn't bother me or confuse me as much as sensing the stress I was causing among those below me. I also know I was totally conscious even though I had heard a nurse, the only one in a blue smock, tell the doctors I had lost consciousness soon after entering the emergency room. I was very aware of every detail of the events and the room.
>
> I was aware of a tunnel which appeared suddenly, and I was being pulled into it. I was happy to be away from that tense scene below. I floated toward the tunnel and passed right

through a ceiling fan and then the ceiling. The blackness of the tunnel was churning and I began to gather speed. I was curious about my present body or form and looked at my arms and hands. They seemed to be expanding and emitting a slight glow. I felt a rush of air and a low droning noise like a vibration as I gained speed heading for a bright light far in the distance. As I proceeded at a faster rate, I felt there was a presence with me that kept me calm and emitted both love and wisdom. I didn't see anyone, but I felt the essence of my grandpa who had died when I was 13. I was aware of his comforting presence but saw or heard nothing.

I finally came to the end and floated into a place which was overwhelmed by a radiant white light that seemed to embody all the concepts of love. A love which was unconditional and like a mother has for a child. It was definitely a warm joyful presence, the same one that drew me into the tunnel in the first place. It seemed like a giant force field or energy that radiated all the good and noble emotions known to man. I had given up the ways of the Catholic Church as soon as I left parochial school at 17, feeling that I had been released from an unyielding prison and was far from religious, but I knew in my heart that this was God. Words can't describe my awe in this presence. It seemed like I became part of The Light and then the Light became part of me. We were one. I suddenly understood, without question, how interconnected we all are with each other, God and all life forms in the Universe.

At that time, I recall wondering if I would be punished for murdering my child and in doing so, kill myself as well. I could tell He knew my every thought and feeling. The next thing I knew I was seeing a sleeping baby I knew to be me. I watched with fascination as I saw the highlights of each stage of my life. It was like seeing a circular movie screen and many different scenes flashing by at tremendous speeds. Somehow I was able to see and grasp not only what was happening, but the feelings I was experiencing at the time as well as the emotions I caused in others. I watched and felt my mother's shame as she bore me out of wedlock right up to the elation of love and the crushing pain of rejection and betrayal. I understood the fear and insecurities of the man that caused my pain and his own guilt upon breaking up with me upon learning of my pregnancy. I felt every good or bad deed I had ever done and its consequences upon others. It was a difficult time for me, but I was supported by unconditional love and weathered the painful parts.

I was asked telepathically about whether I wanted to stay or return to my former life in the 'Earth School'. I fell to my knees in order to show my desire to stay with Him. He showed me a beautiful shiny bubble which floated next to me. In it I saw a tiny baby nursing at a breast. The baby became a toddler and began walking toward me still inside the bubble. Then the image of a young boy turned into a teenager and he continued to age until he was a full grown man. Who is that? I asked. Your son Michael, was the reply. I recall feeling very relieved that I hadn't destroyed his chance at life. A flood of fearful thoughts crowded into my mind. I wasn't even married and could barely support myself, how could I raise a son? Could he ever forget or forgive me for trying to abort him at four months into life? How could I ever do this alone without help? I saw a flash of myself with a man I knew to be my future husband and he was holding the 2 year old boy I saw in the picture. For the first time, I allowed myself to feel love for the baby I was carrying. All the embarrassment, complications and hardships I had used to rationalize my abortion seemed very weak and selfish.

Suddenly, I was popped back into my body and searing pain tore through my lower body. The same nurse in the blue smock was giving me a shot and telling me to relax that the pain medication would soon begin to take effect. It seemed as if I had not been unconscious for more than a few minutes yet my visit to the 'Other Side' seemed to last hours.

While out of my body in the E. R., I noticed a red label on the side of the blade of a ceiling fan facing the top of the ceiling. When I was taken to the recovery room, I was told that my baby was saved. I said, " yes, I know". I asked if someone would please listen to my incredible experience and was told that they had no time. My doctors said it was a miracle that he was able to save the baby along with myself. He said he thought he'd lost us on two occasions. I tried to tell him about my experience but he was called away. His parting smile, left no doubt that he felt he was wasting his time listening to the drug induced ramblings of a crazy woman. My mother arrived later, with 'religious' reinforcements trying to get a confession of sins. I was mildly amused when a Nun appeared and began to pray for me, asking God to forgive me. I knew I was already forgiven. My punishment came from my own emotions of guilt and shame that I experienced so painfully during the bubble movie review of my former life. Only one nurse in the hospital listened to me. She did so after I told her a few details of what she had said to the doctors and nurses while I was unconscious. She told of hearing of others who had been brought back from the brink of death, with similar tales. I finally convinced her to get a tall ladder and see for herself the red sticker whose appearance I described in great detail on the hidden side of the emergency room ceiling fan. The nurse and an orderly saw the sticker, confirming all the details of its appearance I described. I knew what I knew, but I felt better that at least two people believed me. I never mentioned this experience again until now.

I went ahead with my life optimistically, with a whole new attitude and delivered a healthy baby boy 5 months later, and I named him Michael. The damages I had done to myself prevented further pregnancies but the psychic and love bond I experienced with Michael is truly a cherished 'gift' from Beyond.

The experience remains as real and vivid now as it did 34 years ago and changed my life in many spiritually uplifting ways."[33]

Imaginative reconstruction? Wishful thinking? The last flickerings of a dying brain? I don't think so. Usually the critics just ignore these kinds of cases because "that just can't be possible." Look, you can always find a way to ignore evidence. You can always assume that these people are just making shit up. But once you look at hundreds of NDEs (as I have) and see the same kind of extraordinary experiences it's hard to believe in the "making shit up" hypothesis or any of the other "scientific" reductive NDE theories I listed earlier.

Mediumship

Studying evidence for life after death and paranormal phenomena is nothing new. Over a hundred years ago eminent researchers like Alfred Russell Wallace, co-founder of the theory of evolution, and Harvard psychologist William James were studying mediums and becoming convinced of their authentic abilities.[34] In modern times, most people know mediums from the famous ones with TV shows like John Edward. A typical medium today will sit or stand in front of an audience and wait until a spirit comes through for one of the audience members. Then they will call out something like, "In the back corner here, does anyone know a John or James, maybe Jeffrey. He's a young male and I'm sensing some kind of illness, like cancer." And you can bet the skeptics just have a heyday with this kind of stuff. It's easy to say that they are being too vague or too general and that surely someone in the audience knows someone with a name that starts with "J" and who died of some illness. Now, the mistake in thinking with these skeptics is that just because it could plausibly sometimes be done with trickery doesn't mean it always is. One example comes from a registered nurse named Sarah. She had a sister who died of cancer. Her sister, Debbie, was never able to accept the fact that she was going to die. She became increasingly uncomfortable and agitated in her final days before passing away. This was difficult for her family, of course, but it also took a toll on the family Doctor, Brett, who had worked hard to help save her life. Dr. Robin Kelly reports:

> "Two years after Debbie's death, Sarah, who describes herself as open-minded but healthily skeptical, visited a psychic medium. She didn't know what would happen. To her surprise, the medium did make contact with someone -- named Debsie -- a pet name Sarah had used since Debbie was a toddler. Sarah was intrigued, but even more so as Debbie proceeded to tell her to reassure Brett that he was a good doctor and that he 'shouldn't give it all away.'
>
> To help convince Brett that this message was indeed from Debbie, she asked Sarah, through the medium, to tell him about the clutch repair he had just done on his car, and about that new pink shirt he had bought -- the one his wife had taken such a dislike to.
>
> Debbie, Sarah told me, had always been mischievous.
>
> Before the session with the medium ended, Debbie again stressed that 'Dr Brett' should not give up, and that his skills and compassion were very special. She also reassured Sarah that her own (Debbie's) 'cancer had gone,' and that she was 'truly at peace.'
>
> The following day, Sarah phoned Brett, who was confounded by the information she gave him. *His car had indeed just come back from the auto repair shop with a brand new clutch. He could only imagine that Sarah had been talking to his wife about this and the pink shirt -- the very shirt only a few days*

before she had described as being 'Just Awful!'

Sarah then passed on Debbie's message of encouragement -- and it was then that Brett admitted at the time of Debbie's illness he had indeed toyed with the idea of giving up general practice, feeling dispirited and inadequate.

Sarah wasn't exactly sure just how Brett had eventually responded to all this information -- but is delighted that eight years later he is continuing to run a thriving practice."[35]

The making shit up hypothesis aside, here we have a case of verifiable accurate information relayed to the medium that the medium could not have otherwise known. We're not talking generalizations here ("I'm getting something with his car. Did he have any car trouble recently?"), no, we're talking specific information about the clutch being repaired and a pink shirt which his wife disliked. Neither the medium nor Sarah should have had access to this kind of information. This example is just one of many where a medium gave information, supposedly coming from a deceased individual, pertaining to facts that were specific and couldn't have been known by the medium.[36]

Now, in James's and Wallace's day mediums were doing far more than giving readings from deceased spirits. They were doing that of course, but they were also producing all kinds of "spirit phenomena," which included ectoplasmic materializations and moving objects in the room without physical contact.[37] Here again, the skeptics will assume that these things *must* be due to trickery. Then they will see if they can reproduce the phenomenon using such trickery or find a medium caught using such trickery, and then proceed to conclude that such trickery is always the case. But consider one of the eminent researchers in the 19th century, co-discoverer of the theory of evolution by natural selection, the great naturalist Alfred Russell Wallace. He was well versed on the scientific method and certainly no slouch on the skeptical side of things. But after a number of experiences with mediums and his own experimentations to rule out trickery, he became convinced of the existence of spiritual phenomena.[38] That is, he believed that the spirit (mind) could be disembodied and could act upon matter.[39] Of course, such views were scorned by the scientists of his day, leading author Guy Lyon Playfair to speculate that he "would be regarded today as a much greater man than he is if he had not, among other things, become a Spiritualist, claimed to have been present when thirty-seven flowers materialized out of thin air, and to have helped levitate the furniture in his own home."[40] You wonder why in Biology class there's a whole lot of talk about Darwin and just a little blip about Wallace. Well, one of the reasons may be that Darwin stayed well within the scientific belief system of his day, but Wallace went well outside that box of consensus, including the view that there is a superior intelligence that has guided evolution.[41] (We'll be discussing this in detail soon) Concerning Wallace's conversion to a spiritualistic belief, he wrote:

> "Up to the time when I first became acquainted with the facts of Spiritualism [. . .] I was so thorough and confirmed a materialist that I could not at that time find a place in my mind for the conception of spiritual existence, or for any other agencies in the universe than matter and force. Facts, however, are stubborn things. My curiosity was at first excited by some slight but inexplicable phenomena occurring in a friend's family, and my desire for knowledge and love of truth forced me to continue the inquiry. The facts became more and more assured, more and more varied, more and more removed from anything that modern science taught or modern philosophy speculated on. The facts beat me. They compelled me to accept them as facts long before I could accept the spiritual explanation of them; there was at that time 'no place in my fabric of thought into which it could be fitted.' By slow degrees a place was made; but it was made, not by any preconceived or theoretical opinions, but by the continuous action of fact after fact, which could not be got rid of in any other way."[42]

Wallace complained, among other things, that the skeptics who write off such phenomena--like the levitation of furniture through "spiritual" agency or messages conveyed from the deceased--had not devoted any serious study to it, citing one author who attended a total of only five séances (most of them failures) and subsequently wrote off the phenomena as entirely fraudulent.[43] William James, too, complained of this failure of scientists to seriously consider mediumistic phenomena and study them sufficiently. A quote from James is telling:

> ". . . I invite eight of my scientific colleagues severally to come to my house at their own time, and sit with a medium for whom the evidence already published in our "Proceedings" had been most noteworthy. Although it means at worst the waste

of the hour for each, five of them decline the adventure. I then beg the "Commission" connected with the chair of a certain learned psychologist in a neighbouring university to examine the same medium, whom Mr. Hodgson and I offer at our own expense to send and leave with them. They also have to be excused from any such entanglement. I advise another psychological friend to look into this medium's case, but he replies that it is useless; for if he should get such results as I report, he would (being suggestible) simply believe himself hallucinated. . . . This friend of mine writes *ex cathedra* on the subject of psychical research, declaring (I need hardly add) that there is nothing in it;. . . and one of the five colleagues who declined my invitation is widely quoted as an effective critic of our evidence. So runs the world away!"[44]

Here is one of the most prestigious and influential psychologists of his day getting stiffed by his colleagues when it comes to psychical research. Even though James had an open mind and was willing to bend his belief system to fit the evidence he was getting from mediums, his colleagues wanted nothing of it. Even though they were supposedly scientists and psychologists who you would think should be most interested in the advancement of science and finding truth, all they really seemed interested in was protecting their belief system. James says they ridiculed the subject without doing any direct research or agreeing to sit with a medium! I guess, why research something that can't, *a priori*, be real?

Wallace saw much the same thing James did regarding the scientists of his day and wrote:

"They are so firmly convinced, on *a priori* grounds, that the more remarkable phenomena said to happen do not really happen, that they will back their conviction against the direct testimony of any body of men, preferring to believe that they are all the victims of some mysterious delusion whenever imposture is out of the question. To influence persons in this frame of mind, it is evident that more personal testimony to isolated facts is utterly useless. They have, to use the admirable expression of Dr. Carpenter, 'no place in the existing fabric of their thought into which such facts can be fitted.' It is necessary, therefore, to modify the 'fabric of thought' itself;"[45]

Wallace's point here is critical and one which I will come back to time and time again in this chapter. What he is saying is that you need a belief system which can incorporate the facts before you accept those facts. Facts alone mean nothing. They can be explained away or ignored. Without the proper belief system in place, no amount of facts will convince you of the reality of the phenomenon. When one is wedded to a materialistic belief system, for instance, the facts--of tables rising up into the air and moving around without mechanical or physical intervention, and of accurate information about the deceased being produced by a medium--are simply not possible. There must be another explanation, such as trickery, deceit, delusion, you name it. Anything but the acceptance of the facts as reported. As James in the earlier quote mentions a psychologist friend who would simply believe himself hallucinated if he encountered authentic mediumistic phenomena, a person who holds a belief system that absolutely excludes certain phenomena from possibility will never be convinced by the weight of the facts alone. Facts, then, only serve to influence someone towards a certain belief system. But unless one is willing to adopt a belief system which supports such facts, the facts themselves will remain on the fringe: ignored, down-played, ridiculed, and swept under the carpet. In essence, the facts won't matter.

The situation isn't any different today as it was in Wallace's day. Psychiatrist, consciousness researcher, and one of the founders of transpersonal psychology, Stanislav Grof explains an informal meeting he had with famed astronomer Carl Sagan. Sagan had asked for the meeting in order to have "a session of open confrontation and discuss theoretical issues related to this discipline [transpersonal psychology]."[46] At one point during the meeting Grof explained to Sagan a case of veridical out-of-body perception during a NDE. This case was reported by Cardiologist Michael Sabom in his book, *Recollections of Death,* and involves a man who was resuscitated after undergoing cardiac arrest. This man, after reporting having watched the details of his resuscitation while disembodied, "was able to reconstruct to Michael Sabom's surprise the entire procedure, including the movements of the little hands on the measuring devices in correlation with the interventions of the surgical team." Grof says,

"Having described this case to Carl, I asked him how he would explain this event in the context of the worldview to which he subscribed. He paused for a while, and then he said assertively: 'This, of course, did not happen!' I shook my head incredulously, not believing what I just had heard. 'What do you mean, this did not happen? Cardiosurgeon Michael Sabom reported this in his book based on the research he had conducted with his patients. What is your explanation for what I have just described to you? What do you think all this is about?' I asked. This time the pause was even longer; Carl was clearly thinking very hard, struggling to find the answer. 'I'll tell you,' he finally broke the long silence. 'There are many cardiosurgeons in the world. Nobody would have known the guy. So he made up a wild story to attract attention to himself. It's a PR trick!' [. . .] I saw that Carl was willing to question the integrity and sanity of his scientific colleagues before considering that his belief system might require revision or modification to fit the new data. He was so convinced that he knew what the universe was like and what could not happen in it that he did not feel the slightest inclination to examine the challenging data."[47]

"So runs the world away" as James so eloquently put it. Does Sagan here not sound just a bit like a young earth creationist who, when confronted with scientific evidence that radiometric dating of the oldest known rocks show the Earth to be over 4 billion years old, puts up his hands and says "that of course is not true! The scientists obviously have faulty dating methods because that just cannot be true." (Or they are being deceived by God) Well, ignoring the facts is a sin in my book whether you're a young earth creationist or one of the most prestigious and well respected scientists in the world.

Concerning psychic phenomena, Chris Carter points out in his book, *Science and Psychic Phenomena*, that "for the most part, skeptics have simply criticized from the sidelines and have produced no experimental research of their own."[48]

Astrology

A telling example of one reason skeptics may decide not to do research but instead just criticize is given in Carter's book. It has to do with The Committee for Scientific Investigation of Claims of the

Paranormal (CSICOP). This is an organization created by scientists in the 1970s to objectively and impartially examine claims of the paranormal.[49] Remarkably, Carter reports that there's been only one scientific investigation undertaken by the committee.[50] Ever since this first investigation they've just criticized the work of others, and I think you will clearly see why after we find out the results.[51] Their one and only investigation involved the claim by French psychologists Michel and Françoise Gauquelin that "significantly more world-class athletes were born when Mars was rising or transiting." This is the so-called "Mars effect" which lends support to at least one aspect of astrology. As Carter points out:

> "The Gauquelins' results showed that 22 percent of European sports champions were born with Mars rising or transiting. Since the Gauquelins divided the sky into twelve sectors, according to pure chance the probability of Mars being in any two sectors at one's time of birth is 2/12 or 17 percent, well below the 22 percent reported. With a sample size of 2,088 sports champions, the odds are millions-to-one against these results occurring by chance."[52]

Well, CSICOP couldn't have any of this hocus-pocus. They decided to put the Gauquelins to the test and compare their sample of athletes with a control group of non sports champions that were "born about the same time and place as the champions." They figured maybe all people in general showed this trend towards Mars rising or transiting at the time of birth. For example, one theory put forth by a CSICOP member was that Mars is more likely to be rising or transiting in the morning hours, which he suspected is when a greater number of people are born.[53]

As it turns out, the skeptics were wrong. 17 percent of the control group showed Mars either rising or transiting at the time of birth which is exactly what is expected by chance and well below the 22 percent reported for world-class athletes.[54] So did CSICOP concede that we truly do have evidence for astrology? Of course not. It's members were already wedded to a particular belief system which only sought to disprove claims of the paranormal. So they resorted to another famous tactic of scientists who don't want to face the facts and alter their belief system. They just manipulated the statistics.

First they excluded female athletes, and then subdivided the remaining sample of male athlete champions by geographical locale.[55] And of course when you get a smaller and smaller sample it's difficult to prove anything statistically. If I flip a coin four times and three times it comes up heads and once tails, then technically I have a result that deviates from the expected outcome of 50% heads and 50% tails. But it's not statistically significant because of the low number of flips. It could easily be due to chance and not some manipulation of the coin. But if I flip it 1,000 times and 750 times the coin comes up heads, then that kind of result becomes more convincing that something is influencing the coin, like the wind or the way I'm flipping it, and it's not due to chance. What the CSICOP members did was just reduce the sample size of athletes by the methods mentioned and then claim that they didn't get statistically significant results, except for Paris where there is a bigger population and the sample size of athletes would have been larger. For other geographical locales, the sample size was just too small to be significant statistically.

Obviously you see the flaw here. The whole purpose of the study was to see if the champions scored the same as a matched sample of non-champions in the occurrence of Mars rising or transiting at the time of birth. Since the non-champions scored at chance levels and the champions scored at a higher percentage, the results are in favor of a definite effect of the planet Mars on winning championships, or being a championship level athlete. You can't then pick apart the data, reduce the size of the sample and then claim "see, it's not statistically significant." That's as good as saying, "Fuck you and your statistics. I'll make the results conform to my belief system." In other words, "I can't be wrong no matter what the facts are." To be fair, this statistical hack job was orchestrated by a few members of the CSICOP organization, and not all members agreed. Indeed, Carter reports that several of the members resigned in disgust after the hack job paper was published by CSICOP members in *The Humanist* magazine.[56]

The astrological theory is that Mars is associated with traits such as war, aggression, assertion, and action.[57] The idea is that these traits would help someone win sports championships. Depending on the position of Mars relative to Earth at the time you are born, it may or may not be a dominant influence in your life. Astrology is a complex science which I can't say I fully understand and there are many different interpretative methods. But as author Keiron Le Grice explains:

"The method employed to analyze and interpret the
archetypal dynamics of human experience in terms of the
positions of the planets is based on a consideration of the
geometric alignment -- the specific angle of relationship --
formed between the different planets in their respective orbits.
The meaning of every planetary alignment or 'aspect' depends
both upon the archetypal characteristics associated with the
planets involved and the particular angle of relationship
between the planets. As in the Pythagorean view, in astrology
principles of number and geometry are recognized as
fundamental to the deep structure and organization of the
cosmos, and these numeric principles are reflected in the
geometric relationships between the planets."[58]

Astrology, therefore, tries to connect the outer universe of the stars
and planets to the inner world of the human psyche, suggesting a very
deep order and structure to not only the cosmos, but to one's psychology
as well. It amazes me how scientific and mathematical astrology appears
to be, yet it is not embraced by mainstream scientists.[59] Even though its
entire basis is on mathematical relationships between the planets and
seeing how those alignments tend to reflect certain traits in human
psychology, it is still considered just *pseudoscience,* which is as good in
scientific circles as saying "it's bullshit." Maybe you could argue that the
psychological categories are too broad and could apply to anyone.
However, mostly we're dealing with specific archetypal principles; Mars
represents war and aggression, Venus represents beauty and desire, etc...
The reason I think science doesn't embrace astrology, even if there's
evidence for it, is because they can't understand how such a relationship
between the inner and outer *could* be possible.

We still live in a world very much based on Newton's ideas of an
objectively existing outer world apart from ourselves. What we are now
beginning to understand is that the outer is in a sense a mirror of the
inner world. This doesn't mean that the planets affect us through some
sort of energy transfer, although there could be subtle energies which
emanate from the planets and affect us psychologically. It's certainly a
possibility. But this relationship between the positions of the planets and
the dynamics of the human psyche could also be a sign that the universe
is orchestrated by a deeper intelligence. That our psychological dynamics
unfold in accordance with the movement of the spheres gives one that

sense of awe and wonder of an ordered universe guided by a supreme intelligence. We have a sense of some divine plan and unfolding beyond our limited understanding.

Intelligent Design

But dare mention an intelligence involved in the formation/evolution of the universe, or of the natural world, as a scientist and you might just get kicked out the front door with walking papers in hand. Hypothesizing an underlying intelligence responsible for the formation of the universe or of biological evolution is pure blasphemy in science. Just ask evolutionary biologist Richard Sternberg. In 2004, he was a staff scientist at the Smithsonian National Museum of Natural History and editor of the journal *Proceedings of the Biological Society of Washington*.[60] That's when he was sent a paper by Steven Meyer entitled "The Origin of Biological Information and the Higher Taxonomic Categories"[61] This was a paper which argued for intelligent design as the best explanation for the novel animal phyla that exploded onto the scene during the "Cambrian Explosion." Sternberg sent it out for review and the reviewers found no reason to reject the paper, but did say that the conclusions about intelligent design reached by Meyer would ignite controversy. Apart from that, criticisms of specific points in the paper were given by the reviewers, so Sternberg sent the paper back to Meyer with the criticisms. Meyer then sent the paper back to Sternberg with point-by-point answers to all of the criticisms and made additions to the paper where necessary to address them. Sternberg, apparently impressed with this and finding it worthy of publication, decided to do just that and published it in the aforementioned Journal.[62]

Oh boy did the scientific community get pissed off. Sternberg describes how he received many criticisms of the paper by people who "refused to read such 'pseudoscientific' or 'creationist' nonsense." The Biological Society of Washington, for whom he was editor of their journal, was even pushed "to issue a statement that implied editorial malfeasance." Furthermore, there was an attempt to have him fired from the Smithsonian National Museum, and after that didn't work he was severely harassed.[63] Sternberg explains the harassment as follows:

"The Chair of the Invertebrate Zoology Department in the

museum told me not just that I was on the wrong side of the
political spectrum and thus a threat to many, but that if
anything went wrong in the museum--a manuscript missing, a
purse lost or stolen: anything awry--I was going to be blamed.
My research was severely curtailed and placed under the
supervision of an opponent, who was given complete control
over what I could and could not do, and what I could and could
not write and publish. My keys were demanded from me, and I
was ordered not to go back to my office--which permitted the
museum then to blame me for not coming in to my office on a
regular basis and adding alcohol to the specimen jars that
remained in there. I could go on and on. It was surreal--like a
David Lynch adaptation of a Kafka novel."[64]

Considering this harsh reaction to the idea of intelligent design, we
will now turn to a full discussion of the evolutionary debate. Most people
know modern evolutionary theory has its theoretical foundations in the
theories of Charles Darwin. Darwin was a brilliant man who saw that
animals could change over time and show considerable in-species
variation. Darwinian disciple Richard Dawkins gives one example of dogs,
which all descended from the wolf.[65] There are over 200 breeds of dogs
varying vastly from the little chiwawa that you keep in your purse (not
that I recommend this practice) to the Great Dane weighing over 120
pounds (try putting that in your purse). But unlike dog breeding, Darwin
suggested that there was no need for an intelligence to explain the
variation among living forms. The environment itself could affect great
changes in organisms. Any mutation, or change, in an organism that
would confer a survival advantage would inevitably lead that organism to
produce more offspring than its less capable predecessors. It could be a
mutation that makes the organism faster, better able to digest food, or
even more attractive to the opposite sex; anything that helps it to survive
better. Thereby, nature would select the best traits and over millions of
years organisms would evolve, diverge and develop into the variety of
forms we see today.[66]

As it turns out, this idea was not only revolutionary in a biological
sense, but also had great cultural ramifications as well. Culturally it was
used to justify the practice of Eugenics.[67] This is the forced sterilization of
"undesirable" groups of people, or in Hitler's case the extermination of
those people. I'm not saying Darwin would approve of such practices, only

that his ideas of survival of the fittest were used to justify those practices. The "undesirables", whether handicapped, mentally challenged, Jew, Catholic, dark-skinned etc... were thought to be less evolved than the dominant group and/or less fit to survive. Based on Darwin's principle of survival of the fittest, it was up to the stronger race of people to weed out the weaklings. These days we abhor such practices, and for good reasons. But nevertheless Darwin's theory does suggest that it's all about survival of the fittest, the nasty struggle for survival. No need for love in such a world.

Nonetheless, Darwin's idea of natural selection acting on random mutations to account for the divergence and evolution of all life was a brilliant idea that seemed to explain how life forms could evolve without any intelligence involved in the process. But we need to preface that last statement. More accurate is that his idea was brilliant *for the time period in which he lived.* We can compare Darwin's theory in biology to Newton's laws of physics as laid down in the *Principia*. In Newton's own time, his ideas, too, were revolutionary and of tremendous importance for the advancement of science. However, as we gained more knowledge we learned that his theory did not hold in all situations. It was only partially true. Einstein's theory of relativity and quantum mechanics ended up superseding Newton's theories about the nature of the world. Newton's laws still have their place and we still use them, but they don't give us a complete and accurate view of reality.

In a similar vein, we know today much more about the biological complexity of organisms than we did in Darwin's day. In fact, around the time Darwin wrote *On the Origin of Species* biologists thought the cell was a relatively simple entity. Ernst Haeckel famously called the cells "homogeneous and structureless globules of protoplasm."[68] Having no idea of the complexities of the cell, it was easy for biologists in those days to fathom a natural process randomly changing cells and over time producing novel structures within the animal. They had no idea of the information rich systems and molecular machinery within the cell we know about today. They had no idea that to produce novel structures within an organism you would need new proteins, protein machines, and cell types which all require massive amounts of information rich genetic code to be inserted into the DNA. Hell, biologists in Darwin's day didn't even know about DNA. So it's not surprising that Darwin's theory caught on as it did. At the time, it did seem to fit the available data, or at least it seemed plausible.

The real surprise is that the theory wasn't superseded by a higher law of intelligent causation after the information rich code in DNA was discovered (we'll talk about why in a minute). The theory of random mutation and natural selection should have been kept, but reduced to a limited sphere of activity, just as Newton's theories were kept but reduced in scope after the introduction of relativity and quantum mechanics.[69] Instead Darwin's theory was kept intact and it was proposed that random mutations in the DNA code caused the changes in organisms that were later selected (or weeded out) by the environment. The problem of how random mutations could create the kind of complex specified information needed to evolve life has been for the most part ignored.

Today, we know the cell is vastly more complex than envisioned by biologists in Darwin's day. Australian Biologist Michael Denton compares the cell to an enormous automated factory the size of a large city:

> "On the surface of the cell we would see millions of openings, like the portholes of a vast space ship, opening and closing to allow a continual stream of materials to flow in and out. If we were to enter one of these openings we would find ourselves in a world of supreme technology and bewildering complexity. We would see endless highly organized corridors and conduits branching in every direction away from the perimeter of the cell, some leading to the central memory bank in the nucleus and others to assembly plants and processing units. The nucleus itself would be a vast spherical chamber more than a kilometer in diameter, resembling a geodesic dome inside of which we would see, all neatly stacked together in ordered arrays, the miles of coiled chains of the DNA molecule.... We would notice that the simplest of the functional components of the cell, the protein molecules, were, astonishingly, complex pieces of molecular machinery.... Yet the life of the cell depends on the integrated activities of thousands, certainly tens, and probably hundreds of thousands of different protein molecules."[70]

Far from a blob of structure-less protoplasm, we see that the cell actually resembles a huge automated factory with thousands of protein workers coordinating together to perform jobs in the cell. As we will explore soon enough, to create such a massively coherent system requires information, and not just any information, but the kind of information found in written language or computer code: specified information.[71] That means the information is arranged in a complex and highly specified manner. Just like the letters of the English language need to be arranged in specific orders to convey meaningful information, so too do the nucleotide bases need to be arranged to code for functional proteins. We'll get to a full explanation in due time. For now, let's get back to Meyer's paper which threw the editor of the journal which allowed it to be published into a firestorm of controversy.

Meyer's main argument in the paper published in the *Proceedings of the Biological Society* and another one co-authored with Marcus Ross, Paul Nelson, and Paul Chien, is that many of the major animal body plans (he estimates between 47.5% and 85.7% depending on how you interpret the data) first appear fully formed in a narrow five to ten million year time frame.[72] This is during what was coined the "Cambrian Explosion" because of the sudden appearance of animals in the fossil record; that is, sudden by geological standards.[73]

As Meyer points out, "During this event, at least nineteen, and as many as thirty-five (of forty total), phyla made their first appearance on earth. Phyla constitute the highest biological categories in the animal kingdom, with each phylum exhibiting a unique architecture, blueprint, or structural body plan."[74]

He goes on to argue that these animals were drastically more complex than their Precambrian predecessors and would have required great leaps of "specified information" in the genetic code to account for the new structures and cell types that arise in them. He explains:

> "Studies of modern animals suggest that the sponges that appeared in the late Precambrian, for example, would have required five cell types, whereas the more complex animals that appeared in the Cambrian (e.g., arthropods) would have required fifty or more cell types. Functionally more complex animals require more cell types to perform their more diverse functions. New cell types require many new and specialized proteins. New proteins, in turn, require new genetic information. Thus an increase in the number of cell types implies (at a minimum) a considerable increase in the amount of specified genetic information."[75]

To understand his argument fully, one needs to understand the nature of information in the genetic code. The nucleotide bases (Adenine, Cytosine, Thymine, and Guanine) are located along the sugar-phosphate backbone of the DNA double helix and operate like a digital code. In the DNA molecule you have chemical bonds joining the phosphates and sugars together, as well as chemical bonds joining each nucleotide base to a sugar. However, there are no chemical bonds between the individual nucleotide bases. Furthermore, the chemical bond between the nucleotide base and the sugar it attaches to is the same in every case. So, any sugar attachment site can accept any one of the bases.[76] What this means is that, as computer expert and Chemist Donald Johnson points out, "DNA is an ideal information storage system."[77] The reason is because the bases can be arranged in any order along the sugar-phosphate backbone of the DNA molecule. There is no law determining their order and there isn't any affinity of one base to be next to another.[78] Indeed, if there were then DNA would not be a good information storage device because it would exhibit a repeating pattern, thereby inhibiting the kind of functional information needed to produce proteins and control the processes of the body.

As far as protein coding is concerned, the DNA bases are arranged in three base blocks (like letters arranged into words), called codons. Each codon codes for a specific amino acid or represents a stop codon which signifies the end of the protein coding sequence.[79] There are 20 different standard amino acids, which can be thought of as like a protein making alphabet. Just like the English alphabet has 26 letters that are put together in specified arrangements to make a meaningful sentence, the 20 different amino acids are linked together in specified arrangements to construct a functional protein. So, based on the DNA code words (codons), amino acids are linked together in a specific order and then the completed chain of amino acids folds into a three dimensional shape and is released in the cell to do its job.[80]

However, we now know that DNA is highly more complex than this simple picture of encoding for proteins. "Only 1.5% of the 3.2 billion base pairs of the human genome encode protein, yet those 31,000 or so genes specify 100,000 to 200,000 distinct proteins."[81] First of all, this shows us that only a small portion of DNA encodes for proteins. Other regions of DNA, once thought to be "junk" DNA, have been found to function in various ways, including regulating DNA replication, marking sites for programmed rearrangements of genetic material, and controlling RNA processing, editing, and splicing.[82] Commenting on the function of the non-coding regions of DNA, Meyer states that "the nonprotein-coding DNA directs the use of other information in the genome, just as an operating system directs the use of the information contained in various application programs stored in a computer."[83] Also, we see that there are many more proteins than there are protein coding genes. It turns out that overlapping genes can encode for multiple different proteins depending on where (which nucleotide) the protein coding sequence is initiated. In other words, by starting in a different position within the gene sequence different codons will result and a different protein will be built.[84] So the same gene(s) can code for multiple proteins. On top of that, sections of code from various parts of the DNA molecule can be spliced together to form the protein coding sequence, "sometimes joining messages that were separated by thousands of nucleotides."[85] You can imagine the sophistication and precision of execution necessary for such a multilayered complex system of information.

There is also a still emerging branch of genetics called Epigenetics. This field looks at how DNA expression is controlled, like how a gene is turned on or turned off. What they've found is that there are all kinds of chemical tags and markers placed on and around the DNA. Epigeneticists are still working to figure out how this system works. So far, it's been shown that these chemical "tags" can lock down a section of DNA so that it is not opened up and copied. Conversely, when the tags are removed the DNA is open and ready to be unwound and copied.[86] It's kind of like locking and unlocking file drawers in a file cabinet. This is helpful in understanding why all cells in the body can have the exact same genetic information housed in their nucleus, but function very differently. What seems to happen is that a cell's system of tagging closes off the sections of DNA that are not useful to that particular cell, so that only the proteins and other control information that particular cell needs will be open for transcribing (copying and using).[87] Again, this is an informational system, informing the protein machinery that is constantly buzzing up and down the DNA molecule what sections to read and copy and which not to read. It's information on top of information. It's a highly sophisticated and complex system of information.

Steven Meyer, in an interview with radio host George Noory, tells the story of a colleague of his who was an architect level programmer at

Microsoft. He came to work at the Biologic Institute, where Meyer works, to work with molecular biologists to create an artificial genetic code simulating how the information in DNA directs the synthesis of proteins. One day he came into Meyer's office and laid a book on his desk called "Design Patterns," a standard manual for software engineers. In it, he showed Meyer how software engineers use these different design strategies, like strategies for error correction, hierarchical filing, distributive storage and retrieval of data sets, etc.... He then told Meyer that, "When I see what's going on inside the information processing system in life, I get an eerie feeling that someone has figured all this out before us." The cell uses all of these different design patterns, he explained, but in the cell they are being executed with an 8.0, 9.0, 10.0 elegance. It's the same basic logic, only executed with a precision way beyond our current capabilities in computers.[88]

Meyer's colleague is not the only one to make this comparison between DNA and computer software. Geneticist Craig Venter, lecturing at Trinity college in Dublin, Ireland told the crowd,

> "All living cells that we know of on this planet are 'DNA software'-driven biological machines comprised of hundreds of thousands of protein robots, coded for by the DNA, that carry out precise functions. We are now using computer software to design new DNA software."[89]

New Scientist magazine, which reported on Venter's lecture, continued, "The digital and biological worlds are becoming interchangeable, he added, describing how scientists now simply send each other the information to make DIY biological material rather than sending the material itself." It's easy to see here that DNA is an information molecule operating on the basis of a digital code. This information directs the protein machinery of the body. It's highly analogous to computer software which directs the machinery of robots or computers. In fact, Venter says the two worlds are interchangeable. At the very least, this should make us pause and wonder how the hell this happened and how our own computer software, which we intelligently write, could mimic the software already in place in our own biological bodies.   As I explained before, the twenty different standard amino acids are like an alphabet that is used to construct the thousands of proteins that do the work in the cell. As Steven Meyer, in his masterpiece

Signature in the Cell, describes:

> "Proteins build cellular machines and structures, they carry
> and deliver cellular materials, and they catalyze chemical
> reactions that the cell needs to stay alive. Proteins also process
> genetic information. To accomplish this critical work, a typical
> cell uses thousands of different kinds of proteins. And each
> protein has a distinctive shape related to its function, just as
> the different tools in a carpenter's toolbox have different
> shapes related to their functions."[90]

This specific shape that proteins must have in order to do their job
depends on a specific arrangement of amino acids, which in turn depends
on a specific arrangement of DNA bases along the backbone of the double
helix. This information is complex in that it doesn't follow a repeating
pattern. It is specified in the sense that a specific arrangement of amino
acids is necessary to produce a specifically shaped protein that has a
specific function within the cell. Proteins are hundreds, sometimes
thousands, of amino acids in length and each protein is specialized for a
specific function. That's a lot of amino acids that need to be arranged
properly!

A Protein, remember, is made by linking together amino acids in a
long chain and then folding into a three dimensional precise shape in
order to do its job. Meyer states that "though proteins tolerate a range of
possible amino acids at some sites, functional proteins are still extremely
rare within the whole set of possible amino-acid sequences."[91] For
instance, Molecular Biologist Douglas Axe calculated that for a simple
protein of 150 amino acids, the probability of finding a sequence of amino
acids of that length capable of folding into a stable functional protein is a
mere 1 in 10^{74}.[92] What that means is that finding functional proteins by
linking amino acids together at random is *extremely* unlikely. In essence
then, the amino acid "alphabet" operates in the production of functional
proteins much as our own alphabet operates in the production of
meaningful sentences. Take all the letters in my previous sentence and
see how many different combinations of those letters would produce a
meaningful sentence. There might be a few combinations that work to
produce a meaningful sentence, but the vast majority of combinations of
those letters would produce pure gibberish; a meaningless string of
nonsense that no English speaker would be able to understand. It's the

same situation for finding functional proteins by linking together amino acids. Most combinations of the amino acids will produce "junk" that can't fold into a protein and function within a cell.[93] So, the central question is: where does this highly complex functional information found in DNA and proteins come from? To borrow a term from my philosopher friend David Chalmers (actually we've never met, but I consider him a friend in spirit), the problem of how new complex functional code gets inserted into the DNA molecule in order to build new proteins and complex cellular systems is the "hard problem" of evolutionary biology.

As Donald Johnson points out, "In examining any complex functional information where the source of the information is known, it invariably (no known exceptions) resulted from a source other than chance and/or necessity."[94] What is this source other than chance and/or necessity? In one word: Intelligence. Humans write novels and computer code. Humans arrange material parts in specific highly complex arrangements to perform functions, such as constructing an automobile or computer. Meyer states that "intelligence is the *only known cause* of complex functionally integrated information-processing systems" like those found in DNA.[95] You don't need to be a genius to figure out that random mutations will just not allow for the generation of such highly complex information. Forget about the natural selection component, random mutations will simply not be able to produce the complex information to be selected.[96] Nor will some fixed law or set of laws produce such information. The only explanation left, which we know works, is intelligent causation.

But mainstream biologists just have a pissy-fit when you try to invoke intelligence. They whine and say, "But it's not science. We can't just throw in the towel and say ok, we can't figure it out so God must have done it. Those God of the gaps arguments just aren't what science is all about, namely, trying to explain things from natural causes." Arch skeptic Michael Shermer is especially adamant on this point that science only deals with natural explanations. He says we cannot invoke anything supernatural as an explanation in science; that's just not science. He says it's not testable, that we can do no experiment to test for a deity. Invoking intelligence as a cause in nature is, in his words, "a conversation stopper."[97]

What Shermer and others consistently fail to understand is that this is not a "God of the gaps" argument. We're not saying we can't figure out how it works so God must have done it. Quite the contrary, we know exactly how this kind of highly specified information is produced, and it's not tornadoes sweeping through junk yards and piecing together airplanes from the parts, nor is it getting a bunch of chemicals together in a pond and striking them with lightning. It's not an argument from what we don't know. It's precisely an argument from what we do know. We know that intelligent agents produce highly complex and information rich systems. Like I said before, humans write information rich novels and computer software all the time. We see the same kind of information in DNA.

If I find a computer buried in the ground, can I not say that an intelligence created it? Do I have to assume that the parts somehow gathered together in the sand and organized themselves? In fact, despite their differences computers are an ideal analogy to living cells. A computer is built with precisely manufactured parts with specific functions, and those parts are arranged in a precise manner to allow the computer to function as a whole system. Likewise, living cells are built of precisely manufactured parts called proteins that have specific functions and are arranged in a precise manner for the cell to function as a whole. Neither the cell's protein parts nor the parts in a computer are manufactured by, arranged by, or directed by some natural law or force. Quite the contrary, intelligently written computer code, or software, directs the hardware of a computer, while the code contained within DNA, or DNA software--which bears the same specified complexity as computer software code--is used to direct the protein machinery of the cell. The main difference is that a computer is made of metal and other manufactured parts that don't move around for the most part, while cells are made of chemical and "biological" parts that do move around. However, the same principles of design and operation are present in both systems. For one we infer an intelligent creator, but for the other we somehow think a natural process responsible. I don't want to say that scientists are stupid, but I will say that they are blinded by a false paradigm that simply doesn't allow them to think in terms of intelligently designed biological systems.

By now you should readily see the illogical nature of Shermer's argument. When you see something, in nature or engineering, that has consistently and only been shown to be due to intelligent causation, then why not concede the obvious? So, why don't biologists concede this point? It's the same problem the French Academy of Sciences in 1772 had with claims of rocks falling from the sky or the scientists of today have with accepting telepathy or UFOs as real. They can't conceive of *how* it would be possible. They don't yet have the worldview necessary to accept these things. They are still trapped in the box of materialism which says that the universe is full of purposeless, unguided energy and matter. They have yet to expand their belief system out of this box. It seems that in order to see, one needs to have the right set of beliefs. Data alone will not convince people. Remember, you can always ignore data or try to explain it away. Until these scientists expand their box (belief set) to include mind and conscious intelligence as fundamental to the nature of the universe, they will hold back the progress of science, and indeed human evolution itself.

The reason Darwinian theory still holds prominence today is because natural selection acting on random mutations of the genetic code is simply the best explanation on the table, without positing a guiding intelligence. There simply are no other theories that can explain the hard problem of biological evolution.[98] And if you rule out an intelligence in the emergence and evolution of life *a priori*, then you unnecessarily limit your options. People don't buy Darwinian explanations for the evolution of life because the evidence overwhelmingly supports it, but simply because there's nowhere else to turn. If we rule out an intelligence operating in nature, then we are left struggling to fit the facts with a faulty theory, and at the same time blinding ourselves from seeing the true nature of reality. It provides comfort for those atheists who think that proposing a supreme intelligence behind the universe would be tantamount to ending science. They say that we must only speak of 'natural' causes. We cannot invoke the supernatural. But what a pitiful understanding of the world they imply. They know not nature and they know not themselves. For it is consciousness and intelligence that is the key to unlocking the secrets of nature. To think that blind, unconscious, random processes of a purely unguided material world created all of the organized galaxies in the universe, all of the life forms on earth, a self-aware consciousness as found in humans, art, culture, desires, yearning, poetry, emotion, language... To not see intelligence at work in the universe is to be but a blind man without a stick.

One of the main arguments, you will remember, against an intelligence responsible for the information in DNA is that it's a science stopper. "Ok, so God did it. So what? Where does that get us? How does that help us do science?" They say we can't make any predictions from that viewpoint. But that's completely not true. As Steven Meyer points out in his book, we can make many predictions if we assume intelligent causation in biological systems. It predicts that we should find the use of design strategies and logic in the information processing systems of cells that mirrors or exceeds that used by engineers.[99] We already have anecdotal evidence that this is true from Steven Meyer's software engineering colleague discussed previously. Another prediction is that the fossil record should show "a top-down, rather than bottom-up, pattern of appearance of new fossil forms."[100] Here we already have evidence, as discussed earlier, that many, if not most, of the major animal phyla appear fully formed with no clear morphological antecedents during the Cambrian explosion, in a mere miniscule time window of 5-10 million years.[101] Finally, studies of structures that were once thought to be bad designs in life "should reveal either (a) reasons for the designs that show a hidden functional logic or (b) evidence of decay of originally good designs."[102] Indeed, I can think of two perfect examples.

One example of what was once thought to be useless, but now known to have vital functions is the misnamed "junk dna," which scientists once thought constituted up to 97% of the entire DNA molecule. That's a lot of "junk," and certainly not what we would expect if it were intelligently designed. But, low and behold, scientists are constantly finding out that it really isn't junk; it's functional.[103] Scientists working on the ENCODE project, which is a project to explore and identify the functions of the human genome, reported in a press release that "the genome contains very little unused sequences and, in fact, is a complex, interwoven network. In this network, genes are just one of many types of DNA sequences that have a functional impact."[104] Indeed, in the first major paper published by the project, which examined roughly 1% of the total genome, it was found that between 74 and 93 percent of the DNA sequences analyzed were opened up and copied routinely onto RNA molecules. The RNA molecules then use the code for various functions, like building proteins, regulation and maintenance of cell processes, or directing the processing of other genetic information.[105] Recently, another paper was published by the ENCODE project which looked at genome expression across 147 different cell types. This paper also found that most DNA is functional. They found functions for 80% of DNA, and the Lead

Analysis Coordinator of the project stated that it was likely that by looking at genome expression in more cell types, functions would be found for the other 20% of DNA.[106] Far from being a few functional protein encoding genes surrounded by vast amounts of junk, the human genome is a vast integrated network of information vital to maintaining and controlling the processes of the human body.

Another example of what was once thought to be useless but now known to be functional is the appendix. For years doctors and scientists considered the appendix to be useless and found no reason why it should be in the human body. Many considered it a vestigial organ. That is, one left over from our ancestors that we have since lost the need for.[107] Therefore, it was thought to no longer function or have any use inside of our bodies. In fact, it was routinely taken out "during other abdominal surgeries to prevent any possibility of a later attack of appendicitis."[108] However, now we know that the appendix plays an important role in immune function. Quoting Loren G. Martin, Professor of Physiology at Oklahoma State University, "the appendix has been shown to function as a lymphoid organ, assisting with the maturation of B lymphocytes (one variety of white blood cell) and in the production of the class of antibodies known as immunoglobulin A (IgA) antibodies."[109]

Indeed, if scientists had been coming from a design perspective all along we probably would have figured out the function of the appendix a long time ago. A design perspective would have clued us in that there should be a function to every part of the body and this would have spurred research into those things for which there was no known function to try and find a function for them.

You see, intelligent design is far from a "science stopper" as Michael Shermer asserts. Finding the function of the appendix is an example of how science could have progressed much faster if they had adopted an intelligent design perspective.

With an intelligent design perspective, science still goes on as normal. We still study life and still find out more information about how life works. The only difference is how we approach the study. From an intelligent design perspective we might take a look at a software engineering manual and try to find the same design patterns at work in the cell. From a non-intelligent design perspective, we might study the cell and find those design patterns, but it would be an accidental find because we wouldn't be actively looking for them. From an intelligent design perspective we would actively study the non-coding regions of DNA (most of which was, and still is, thought to be junk) to try and find functions for those regions. From a non-intelligent design perspective, again, we might occasionally run across such functions, but we wouldn't be actively looking for them. You see, the only thing that changes in science from an intelligent design perspective is how we approach the study of life.

But I would like to posit that there are even more dramatic and lofty predictions that we can make based on the theory of intelligent design. That's right, no pussyfooting around for this author! I'm shooting for the big conclusions, so let's talk about the *real* predictions of intelligent design. If we assume that there's an intelligent consciousness (mind) responsible for the formation and evolution of the universe, then the biggest prediction I can think of is that we could communicate with this intelligence. If there's a higher consciousness forming the world around us, then we, as conscious beings, should be able to communicate with it and affect natural processes. How? Through our own minds of course; Mind-to-Mind. That's right, by communicating with this intelligent source, we could quite possibly direct our own evolution or any other natural process. Indeed, this is the basis of prayer. And if you don't think human minds can direct the processes of the natural world, go talk to former talk radio host Art Bell. He describes how on the air he performed experiments to affect the weather. He would have his listening audience (which constituted millions of people) either focus on creating rain for areas that were in severe droughts and for which there was no rain expected, or try and reduce the amount of rain for areas that were getting too much rain. Describing these experiments years later, Art relates, "We made rain happen where there weren't even clouds. Rain wasn't even anywhere near the forecast. Within hours, actually in some cases minutes of doing what we did here on the air we made rain. We did that, in several geographic locations in the US and Canada. These experiments began to kind of scare me."[110]

Did his and his audience members' minds really effect processes in the natural world, or was it a fluke? Coincidence? Keep in mind that communication with the forces of nature has been a common belief of shamanistic cultures worldwide. So, what Art Bell was able to do is not an isolated case. In fact, highly respected western academics such as psychiatrist Stanislav Grof and mythologist Joseph Campbell have been shocked to see shamans perform rain ceremonies in areas suffering from a severe drought, only to be pouring down rain when they were finished.[111] If everything is a creation of a higher intelligent consciousness of which our minds are a part of, then it makes sense that our minds should be able to communicate with that intelligence. Not just that, but we should also be able to affect other minds through our focused intent. That brings us to our next, more scientific, experiment in using consciousness to direct the world.

This time we're not trying to change the weather, but human action. From July 7th to July 30th, 1993 approximately 4,000 individuals gathered in the nation's capital, Washington D.C., to practice transcendental meditation with the intent of increasing coherence and reducing stress in the district. The variable they used to determine if this was effective or not was the incidence of violent crime, including homicide, rape, aggravated assault, and robbery. Temperature was used as a control variable since "average weekly temperature was significantly correlated with homicides, rapes, and assaults (HRA crimes), as has also been found in previous research." What they found was a significant correlation between the size of the meditation group and the decrease in violent crimes in the area. The size of the meditation group ranged from the first week with over 500 people participating to the final week by which time there were just shy of 4,000 participants. By the final week of the program, there was a 23.3% decrease in violent crimes in the district. This decrease was not found to be due to changes in police staffing or to seasonal cycles and trends. Furthermore, "no significant decrease was found in any of the prior five years during this period of time, indicating that this effect was not due to the specific time of year."[112] It seems that consciousness truly can have an effect on the outside world, whether it's affecting material processes such as the weather or other minds.

Another astounding prediction based on an intelligence underlying the universe, which I've already alluded to, is that we are a part of this intelligence, i.e. this intelligence is us at a deeper level of mind. I could keep going: If the universe of matter arises from the operations of a consciousness we could predict that there is life after death, and that our consciousness is not dependent upon matter to exist. In other words, intelligent, aware consciousness is pre-existent of any material/informational realm such as our physical universe. In such a view, consciousness becomes fundamental. Matter arises from the operations of consciousness, not the other way around. Now we're outside the box.

Before taking a trip further outside the box (don't worry, we will), let's come back and examine some more of the arguments that supposedly show that evolution doesn't need a designer. Let's start with a typical argument for and against intelligent design of biological systems. (I think you know which team I'm on but I'll try to be fair in presenting the other side's arguments.)

Biologist Michael Behe introduced the idea of "irreducible complexity." This is the idea that some molecular machines have many individual parts (proteins) that make them up. You cannot build these machines through a stepwise process because the machine won't function until you have all the parts in place. It would be like building a car starting from just the frame. If you slowly add parts to the frame, you won't have anything functional (an operational car) for a long time. Since natural selection is not oriented towards a future goal there would be no reason for natural selection to keep these non-functional pieces long enough for a functional system to arise.

In two books on the subject, *Darwin's Black Box* and *The Edge of Evolution,* Behe describes the bacterial flagellum which is a molecular machine used to help cells move around. Behe refers to it as similar to an outboard motor bacteria use to swim around.[113] He explains how the flagellum is constructed from several dozen different kinds of protein parts and can be broken down into three main subsystems: "the base (which contains the motor), the 'hook' (which acts as a universal joint), and the filament (which is the propeller). Within each subsystem, however, are multiple precision-made parts [proteins]."[114] In a nutshell, what we have here is an example of integrated complexity, whereby a number of independent protein parts fit together to create a molecular machine with a specific function within the cell. There are a number of different such molecular machines that do various jobs within the cell. What Behe effectively argues is that for these multiple-protein machines, if any of the parts in the machine are missing it becomes non-functional.[115] Therefore, it could not have arisen in a step by step evolutionary process. Instead, the entire system had to be designed and implemented as a whole.

So, how do the intelligent design haters address this fundamental problem? Well, big wig biologist Ken Miller comes to the rescue. In a video lecture, he describes how there just happens to exist a precursor system to the bacterial flagellum that uses just 10 proteins in the base of the flagellum. [116] This is called the type III secretory system, which Miller describes as a molecular syringe used by certain "nasty" bacteria to inject toxic proteins into our cells. He then goes on to drop another bombshell on the intelligent design movement claiming that almost all of the other proteins used to make the bacterial flagellum "are strongly homologous to other proteins that have functions elsewhere in the cell."[117]

First of all, it's not surprising that similar types of proteins might be used in many different systems within the cell. After all, bolts used in the construction of my car might be "strongly homologous" to bolts used to put together my desk at home or bolts used in other types of machines. Sharing parts is common practice in mechanical machines, so why not in biological ones? Also, I have to wonder the degree to which all of these precisely manufactured proteins that make up the flagellum are homologous to other proteins with different functions. Considering the vast number of proteins that function within a cell (thousands), it's probably not hard to find two that share some similarities. I could look through a book and find two sentences that shared a lot of the same words and say, "Those sentences are strongly homologous." However, the sentences would also have differences and be used in different contexts, so the meaning would not be the same. In the case of a living cell, each protein is specifically structured and designed to perform its specific function, whether that function is forming the structure of the cell's propulsion system, transporting cellular materials, or just catalyzing a necessary chemical reaction. There might be another protein, somewhere in the vast ensemble of proteins that do jobs in the cell, which looks similar to another, but the function and context of the respective proteins may differ and we cannot assert that one evolved from another.

Secondly, just because you've shown one other molecular machine that uses 10 of the dozens of parts of the bacterial flagellum doesn't help in explaining how all the other parts got there later on to perform an entirely different function. There's even a debate about whether the type III secretory system originated before or after the flagellum. [118] It may in fact turn out that the type III secretory system is a devolved system from the original flagellum.

So really Miller has proven nothing here except to himself. The story makes sense to him. If I raised the argument to Miller that he still has the problem of how all of these "homologous" proteins from various parts of the cell came together fortuitously to be able to operate as the cell's propulsion system, he would probably just hand wave it and say it's not a big deal and that although we don't know at this point that eventually we'll have the knowledge about other precursor systems and how all the parts came together in a stepwise Darwinian fashion. But we have much reason to beware of such arguments since, as Behe argues, currently "there is *no* evidence that Darwinian processes can take the multiple, coherent steps needed to build new molecular machinery, the kind of machinery that fills the cell."[119] In essence, there is no molecular machine that biologists can explain the origin of through a step by step Darwinian process. The best biologists can do is show less complex systems that evolve into more complex systems. Then they infer that each step was accomplished via an unguided process. But that inference is simply a bias based on their view of the world as devoid of intelligence. There is no actual evidence that each step was accomplished by random mutation and natural selection. They can't show a process by which the DNA code could have been randomly mutated to produce the new proteins and regulatory processes necessary for the evolution of more complex structures from less complex structures. The informational requirements for each step, I would argue, demand an intelligence. As we've seen, even to produce the information for one novel protein via a random search is highly unlikely.

In the case of the flagellum, Ken Miller has shown a *possible* precursor, but by no means has he explained how the completed flagellum was created through a step by step Darwinian style process.[120] Ken Miller showing that the base of the flagellum can be used in a different context is like me showing that the frame and wheels of my car could be used to make a horse and buggy carriage. There's a *long* way to go from making a horse and buggy carriage to building a car, and a slew of precisely engineered complex parts that need to be fitted together in just the right way. Well, the situation is no different whether we're talking about automobile parts or protein parts. Both require precise specification to perform their jobs and both need to be integrated into a complex system where each individual part fits together to perform the overall function of the machine.

Molecular machines are mysterious enough in their own right, but consider the fact that often many of these protein complexes will work in tandem in a step by step process to perform a certain function. Protein synthesis is a perfect example. When the cell needs a certain type of protein, how does this protein get made? The answer is in a step by step process known as protein synthesis. First, a protein complex, or machine, called a polymerase has to go and unwind the tightly wound strands of DNA to produce a single stranded copy of the DNA message. This copy, called a messenger RNA (mRNA) transcript is then released from the polymerase and goes through the nuclear pore complex which controls the flow of material in and out of the cell's nucleus. Then the mRNA transcript arrives at another protein machine, called a Ribosome. This is where the mRNA transcript gets translated into a chain of amino acids based on the instructions copied from the DNA. After the chain of amino acids is completed this chain goes into a barrel shaped machine to get folded into a precise shape necessary to perform its function in the cell. Finally, the finished protein is released to do its job in the cell.[121] This process is complex, requiring the use of multiple precisely engineered protein machines. Also, it is integrated requiring the coordination of those machines to get the job done.

If you have a polymerase to unwind the DNA and make a copy, but don't have the ribosome to translate the code into a sequence of amino acids, then you're shit out of luck when it comes to making a protein. Then again, if the barrel machine for folding the completed amino acid strand is missing then you won't get a functional protein. So, unless you have all the steps in the process, the system won't work. You may be able to simplify the process a little, like by removing the barrel machine and having the amino acid chains self-fold, but you've still got a multi-part system with the polymerase, nuclear pore complex, and ribosome all doing their jobs to ensure the final protein gets made. This kind of step by step integrated process requiring the coordinated actions of multiple protein machines is not the kind of system we would expect to come about through a chance or random process with no intelligent guidance. It is precisely the kind of process we would expect to be guided and implemented by an intelligence.

Another evolutionary argument deals with the fossil record. Scientists will point to constructions of fossils that seem to show a gradual process of evolution of one life form into another. They then jump from the fossil record to the explanation that it's a natural, successive, undirected process. However, there is no such conclusion that can be made because just because we see animals over time morphing and changing does not mean that this is an undirected process.[122] In fact, based on what we've learned about the digital code in DNA, it *can't* be.

And as a quick analogy let's image some future Earth where modern man has been wiped out and a new intelligent species has arisen. One day, an archeologist digs up an ancient (to them) car. Let's assume this first car dug up is an 84' Chevy Nova (my favorite, and yes I am trying to be funny). This future species has no idea what this thing is, but they find most of the parts and put it in a museum, reconstructing what the original must have looked like as best they can. Well, they think this is interesting but don't make too much of it until later when many more cars are dug up, maybe a 1992 Nissan Maxima, a 1999 Oldsmobile Intrigue, a 2004 Ford Mustang, and the big prize, a 2012 Lamborghini. Now, they have 5 different cars on display and can see a kind of evolution in design and parts with the 84' Chevy Nova seeming quite primitive compared to the later 92' Maxima, which looks primitive compared to the 99' Oldsmobile, which in turn looks a little less sophisticated than the 04' Mustang, which is less sophisticated than the 2012 Lamborghini. "My God!" they say. This must be due to an evolutionary process, and not understanding that there were intelligent species upon the Earth long ago, they try to postulate some natural explanation. So they come up with a theory of how there were volcanic eruptions which heated and fused the pieces of metal together and violent wind storms tightened the bolts in place and the cars evolved in some undirected natural process. And if anyone doubts them, they can come look for themselves at the gradual, successive evolution of the cars which obviously supports their theory of a natural unguided process that made the cars. And if you still doubt, they will point to obvious design flaws in the construction, or things that could have been designed better (especially in the Chevy Nova, right), which obviously no intelligent species would have included. Now, I realize this is a purely hypothetical example as the cars would probably have just rusted away by the time this later species came about. But, these are basically the same arguments you find in modern evolutionary theory.

Let's take a real evolutionary example of whale evolution. The modern evolutionary story goes that whales evolved from land mammals.[123] A common debate in this regard would be a mainstream biologist pointing to a chart showing an ancient land mammal and showing how it morphs slowly into a whale over time (according to the fossil record), going through many successive changes. There you have it, a gradual evolution with slight modifications at each stage followed by natural selection until you get a whole new animal. No designer is necessary. What they fail to recognize is the informational requirements needed to make these changes.[124] You see, it's not quite as simple as they make it out to be. A whale is adapted to a completely different environment than a land mammal, requiring major structural changes such as moving the testes from the outside of the body to the inside, a ball vertebra to allow the tail to move up and down, the reorganization of kidney tissues to allow for taking in salt water, forelimbs transformed into flippers, reduction of the hind limbs, novel muscle systems for the blow hole, modified mammary glands to be able to nurse the young under water, and a lot more.[125] Many of these changes would require new cell types which require new kinds of protein and machinery. Therefore, you would need vast amounts of new "specified information" inserted into the DNA to account for these changes.

Transitions or no transitions, we're back to Steven Meyer's argument in the paper he published that got Richard Sternberg into so much trouble: Where did the information come from to build these new animals? When you look at the basic elements of life, proteins (which in turn conglomerate into complex molecular machines) and DNA, and how proteins are coded for, you clearly see that the only way to meet this informational requirement is for there to be an intelligence underlying life that can "write" the new DNA code which allows for the production of new proteins, molecular machines, and cell types needed to create novel structures within organisms. I argue, then, that there's a superior consciousness that forms the material world and guides its evolution. We're back to the idea that consciousness forms matter, not the other way around. Intelligent consciousness is the primary "stuff" of reality that forms the material.

As an analogy to creating new animal life forms from pre-existing ones, let's say I'm writing a multi-chapter book. Each chapter is 20 pages long and represents a new animal life form in our analogy. Let's say I write the first chapter and then I want to make a new chapter. Well, to create that new chapter I need paragraph upon paragraph of meaningful English text that fits together into a coherent and meaningful story. In the animal life form you need novel functional genetic code that codes for the novel proteins, protein machines, and cell types, which then fit together to form a coherent and functional animal. How am I going to get that meaningful information?

Well, if I attach the neo-Darwinian theory to my book example, all I have to do is start randomly changing letters around in my last chapter until I get different meaningful sentences, select each new meaningful sentence until I get new meaningful paragraphs until finally I have a brand new book chapter. This would be akin to randomly mutating DNA until you get new functional proteins, select each new functional protein until you get new functional molecular machines which will finally be arranged into new functional cell types. But, as you may already intuit, the problem is that each step of the process would be more and more difficult, and be more and more unlikely to occur in an undirected process. In fact, the probability of creating just one novel meaningful sentence, or functional protein, by random mutation is very low.

Sure, if you have a future goal in mind of a new molecular machine that can operate in a new type of cell, then you can select only those new proteins that would go into building such a machine and intelligently arrange the DNA in accordance with this goal. But if you're just randomly mutating DNA code until new proteins are formed, it is highly unlikely that you will get just the right combination of new proteins that magically come together to create a new molecular machine. In our analogy, If I randomly mutate the sentences in my last chapter, then I might get a few new sentences after many, many mutations, but it is highly unlikely that these new sentences would then come together to form a coherent meaningful paragraph. It is much more likely that these new sentences would have nothing to do with each other, and although in and of themselves the sentences might be meaningful, they could not come together to form a paragraph of text that fits together in a meaningful way.

But alas, I'm going to give the other side some slack and say that they are right. What are you doing Daniel? How can you say Ken Miller and Michael Shermer are right? Are you crazy? Ok, calm down and let me explain. In their world, they are right. That is, subjectively they are right. Remember a long way back I was trying to point out that belief system structures our perception of reality. Well, the Ken Millers of the world and the Michael Shermers truly experience the world as a completely natural process, lacking any inherent intelligence. They look at the evidence and interpret it subjectively to support their views. When confronted with the information problem, they either ignore it or hand wave it and say we don't know of the exact Darwinian undirected step by step process through which these proteins and molecular machines have evolved, but someday science will understand it. This classic defer until later argument reminds me of a child trying to put a square block into a round hole. You see his obvious mistake and try to point out to him, "No Timmy, that doesn't go there. That goes over here in the square hole." However, before you can demonstrate how to put the block through the square hole, the child grabs the block out of your hand and, with a linguistic skill far beyond his age, says, "No, it goes in this hole. Just give me more time and I'll figure out how to get it in here."

Assessing the situation

It all comes down to one's subjective beliefs about reality. It's no different than a scientist reading a report of someone who says they saw their deceased grandmother appear to them in a vision to say goodbye just minutes after they died, before the person even knew they were dead. The scientist, whose belief system prohibits such things, laughs and says "oh, people and their hallucinations." Again, you can always ignore or explain away evidence that doesn't fit within your present belief system. As another example, say one day you go frolicking in a field in Ireland and see a fairy. You're like, "holy shit balls, I've gotta get a picture of this." So you pull out your camera and take a picture before the fairy fades away like a phantom. When you go to load your pictures onto the computer you see the fairy in the picture just as you photographed it. Its face and outline can clearly be seen. Finally, proof that fairies exist! Oh, how magical. So you send it off to a university and say, "You guys have to look at this. This is evidence that fairies exist." You wait a few months and never hear back from the university. So, you call up the university and say, "Hey I sent you that fairy picture to examine, what happened?" The voice on the other end hesitantly replies, "Ah, Oh yes I think I remember something about that. Look we're really not interested in investigating this." Incredulous, you say, "Why? This could be a landmark discovery validating the belief in fairies of generations of Europeans." The voice on the other end replies, "Ah, that sounds nice but we're still not interested and this is obviously a fake picture. What are you in it for the money?"

You see where this is going. The scientific community, even if after examination of the picture couldn't themselves see how it could be the result of fraud, would still assume that it *must* be fraudulent. You have the picture. You know it's real and that you really did see a fairy and take a picture of it. It's valid evidence to you and others who accept a belief in fairies, but to people who don't believe in fairies it's not. So, they would just ignore the evidence. Every group of people does this. They readily accept evidence that supports their belief system and ignore evidence that doesn't.

Even when confronted with valid scientific data of telepathy, it's easy enough to explain it away. Common explanations against the scientific evidence of telepathy, which we explored earlier, include the file drawer problem. This is when you postulate that the studies that show evidence for telepathy are overshadowed by a massive amount of non-significant studies that never get published but simply sit in a file-drawer in some parapsychologists laboratory.[126] You don't have to actually produce evidence that this massive pile of non-significant studies actually exists. In fact, Dean Radin has pointed out the absurdity of this explanation by calculating just how many unreported studies showing a chance result would be required to nullify the results of the published studies. At a ratio of 15 unpublished studies for every published study, and considering the time it takes to perform a ganzfeld experiment, this explanation for the positive results is highly unlikely.[127] It's simply a comfortable rationalization for someone who wants to ignore the evidence and stay locked in their nice little box of what's possible and what's not. If the above explanation doesn't work, there's always another way to explain away the data--collusion between experimenter and subject, study flaws, cherry picking studies for meta-analysis in order to show a chance result, ignoring sample size during a meta-analysis, etc...[128] Sometimes the criticisms are valid, but mostly they use these explanations to rationalize their disbelief in the phenomenon. And In their subjective perception of the world telepathy indeed does not exist.

We subjectively interpret the world and the data we receive based on our prior beliefs, which are often subconscious beliefs. These are things we have been taught over and over about the nature of reality through social conditioning and the educational system. We are all conditioned to define reality in a certain way. We structure our world based on those beliefs and erect fences defining its boundaries; what's real and not real, what can and cannot happen. However, if we are fundamentally intelligent, aware consciousness with an unlimited supply of energy and potential, I think it's time we take down the fence, or at least expand it. Reality can be what we want it to be, but first we have to believe.

There's a certain fear at work here as well. There's great fear for some people of allowing paranormal phenomena into their belief system because of what it might lead to. Once you widen the box, where do you set the perimeter? The famous psychologist Sigmund Freud faced this conundrum in regards to telepathy. Freud found plenty of evidence that telepathy was real, but could not bring himself to publicly admit it until late in life.[129] The J. Newton Rayzor Chair of Philosophy and Religious Thought (my old job--joking) at Rice University, Jeffrey Kripal writes that:

> "Freud's colleague and biographer Ernest Jones was concerned that such a development [telepathy being admitted into psychoanalytic theory] would end in 'the essential claim of the occultists,' namely, 'that mental processes can be independent of the human body.' For his part, Freud could finally not bring himself to allow such dangerous things into public debate."[130]

Sounds a little bit like the gateway drug theory. You know, the one that says if you smoke a joint it will lead to harder drugs like cocaine and heroin. Well, if we let telepathy into acceptance in science, then "my God," that could lead to clairvoyance, out of body travel, telekinesis, and eventually maybe even pyramid power. "No no, that's too much now. Let's keep the box closed. It's just too risky." You see, it's the fear of going off the deep end and not being able to stop the fall. Our logical, rational, egoistic minds need boundaries to exist. We need to set the perimeter of the fence somewhere.

Well, I'm not afraid of the deep end of the ocean. I trust in myself and my rationality to weave through its waters and erect a deeper, truer belief system that can account for anomalous phenomena. I'm interested in Truth, and no less. So the question is, are *you* ready? If so, then stick with me as we weave our way through the expansion of reality that is taking place on a global level. Don't worry, you won't be alone. Millions of people have directly experienced phenomena which have opened the doors to a larger reality. We're going to look at what they've experienced, the knowledge they've brought back from those experiences, and how those experiences are shaping a new vision of reality. We're going to explore reality, expand the box, extend the fence, and find out what is possible and what isn't. And here's a hint: throw out the word impossible. You're not going to need it anymore. Before we do that though, we're going to examine how belief affects reality and delve into the depths of the mind to try and formulate a theory of mind and reality creation.

2

WELCOME TO SUBJECTIVE REALITY: PART II

Never allow authority, conceit, habit or the fear of ridicule to make us indifferent, much less to make us hostile to truth. --John Elliotson

The mind and the creation of reality

There's a mysterious power that humans possess. It is the power of thought to shape not only the lens through which we see the world, but to shape the world itself. That's what we will be exploring in this chapter. This is new territory. We're outside the waters of traditional science. We're into the "damned" data that science shoos away and relegates to the pseudoscience pile. The "that can't possibly be true" pile. The "Oh shit! That's scary" pile. It's what Charles Fort called the data of the damned. But in order to really find truth and not just stay within the safe confines of current scientific dogma, we *must* acknowledge and come to terms with this data.

The placebo effect

First, we're going to start with a pretty well known phenomenon called "the placebo effect." This is a medical term referring to any non-active medical agent, like an injection of distilled water, that the patient believes is actually a medical treatment. There are literally vast amounts of data that have piled up regarding this phenomenon and it has become so common these days that Mario Beauregard remarks, "Today, high placebo responses are ruining several clinical drug trials and threatening the financial health of pharmaceutical giants, which in the 1990s were more profitable than major oil companies."[1] Fewer and fewer drugs are being approved these days because they fail to do better than placebos. Could this be due to the aggressive advertisement and marketing campaigns perpetrated by the drug companies? Is this not increasing people's beliefs in the effectiveness of drugs to heal their ills? I think that's exactly what's going on. The drug culture has spawned a population of people who are indoctrinated with the belief that drugs are the answer to their problems.

But do the drugs actually work? In some instances the answer seems to be a resounding no. That is, they don't work apart from your belief in them. In a landmark book exposing the hugely profitable psychiatric drug industry, psychology professor Irving Kirsch argues that the major psychiatric drugs used in the treatment of depression are no better than placebos. These drugs, like Prozac, Zoloft, and Effexor have been marketed for years and approved by the FDA, but an analysis of the actual clinical trials used to test the drugs reveals something striking. Kirsch and his colleague Guy Sapirstein began by taking a look at 38 clinical trials involving a range of antidepressants that had been published in scientific journals.[2] In what is called a meta-analysis, they pooled together the results of these studies and looked at the overall effects of taking the drug, taking a placebo, receiving psychotherapy, or receiving no treatment at all. What they found was that there were large effects in the improvement of symptoms in all of the groups except for the no treatment group.[3] In other words, people in each group got significantly better whether they were taking a placebo, an actual drug, or receiving psychotherapy. But the other thing they found was that taking a placebo was 75% as effective as taking an actual antidepressant drug.[4] This finding held even when analyzing the data for each specific class of drug separately. In other words, it doesn't matter which type of antidepressant was analyzed, they all turned out to be only 25% better than a placebo.[5]

Well, you might say, "Ok 75%, but the drug is still doing something. After all, it accounts for the other 25% of improvement." But Kirsch then considers another interesting finding that can be found by looking at the data. It turns out that drugs that are not even for the treatment of depression do just as well as antidepressants in the clinical trials. These other drugs include sedatives, stimulants, anti-psychotic drugs, barbiturates, and even a synthetic thyroid hormone "given to depressed patients who did not have a thyroid disorder."[6] This got the curiosity module in Kirsch's brain firing. What is this about? It doesn't seem to matter what kind of drug you give people. It will cure depression! Well, Kirsch knew there had to be an answer.

He asked himself the simple question, "What do all these diverse drugs have in common that they do not share with inert placebos?"[7] He came to the conclusion that the only thing they had in common was the presence of easily noticeable side effects. The clinical data showed that whereas there was little difference between placebo and actual drug in the alleviation of symptoms of depression, there was a substantial difference in the presence of side effects. This was a major clue to figuring out where the 25% benefit over placebos actually comes from. If it was from the physiological mechanism of the drug, then we shouldn't see such consistency across drugs that have such different properties. But, Kirsch reasoned, if the difference was because of side effects, then the 25% greater improvement in the people taking the actual drug could just be due to the fact that side effects clue drug study patients into the fact that they are taking the actual drug. Therefore, their belief that they are taking an actual drug and should get better increases.

What happens is that in a double-blind clinical trial neither the doctor giving the drugs to a patient nor the patient knows which group they are in: placebo or actual drug. However, if a patient experiences some of the well-known side effects of the drug, such as dry mouth, nausea, sexual dysfunction, etc..., then they will have a stronger belief that they are taking an actual drug, and therefore show more improvement in the alleviation of their symptoms. This is exactly what seems to be the case. For instance, in one large study where doctors and their patients were asked to guess which condition they were in before being told at the end of the trial, 80% of patients and 87% of their doctors were able to correctly guess whether they were receiving placebo or actual drug.[8] And it's not due to the fact that drug recipients were getting better and placebo recipients weren't. We've already seen that both groups show significant improvement in the alleviation of depression. In fact, the average difference between placebo and actual drug groups is only 2 points on a 51 point scale used to assess one's level of depression in clinical trials.[9] Then, how were the patients and doctors guessing correctly about which group they were in at such a high percentage? Again, the answer is because people taking the actual drug were experiencing side effects of the medication at a much higher rate than those on placebos.

One other finding that convinced Kirsch that antidepressant drugs are nothing more than "enhanced placebos" was the finding that for the mildly and moderately depressed patients there was no statistically significant difference between placebo and actual drug. Only for the severely depressed was the difference significant.[10] It's not that the effect of the drug becomes bigger in more severely depressed patients, just that the placebo response weakens. In other words, the severely depressed show just as much improvement as moderately depressed individuals when taking the actual drug, but less improvement than moderately depressed people when taking a placebo. Kirsch muses that this is because patients who are severely depressed "are much more likely to have been on antidepressant medication before, and they know what it feels like."[11] In other words, they are accustomed to the usual side effects of antidepressants, and if these side effects suddenly disappear then they will know that they aren't taking the actual medication and are instead in the placebo group. Also, severely depressed patients are more likely to receive higher doses of the medication which means more and greater severity of side effects.

After explaining these findings in his book, *The Emporer's New Drugs,* Kirsch then goes on a full out assault on the chemical imbalance theory of depression. We're talking AK47s blazing, all out attack. The chemical imbalance theory is the one you may have heard from your doctor or on TV commercials claiming that depression is caused by an imbalance of chemicals, such as serotonin, in the brain. Kirsch explains how the theory of chemical imbalance as a cause of depression was originally formed based on clinical experience and the testimony of experts regarding certain drugs that were said to alleviate depression. In short, drugs that increased the levels of neurotransmitters in the brain, such as serotonin and norepinephrine, were said to be useful in the alleviation of depression. However, a drug called reserpine that was thought to decrease the availability of neurotransmitters in the brain was said to make people severely depressed. Remember though, this was based on the testimony of doctors and not on placebo controlled studies.[12] After carefully controlled clinical trials were performed it was found that reserpine did not induce depression, but actually alleviated it. Since it was thought that this drug reduced neurotransmitter levels, this should have been a blow to the theory. However, by the time these clinical trials were done, the chemical imbalance theory was already widely accepted and so these studies were ignored.[13] Science? Ignoring data? You don't say?

Another blow to the theory came when clinicians tried to rapidly reduce levels of either serotonin, norepinephrine, or dopamine in healthy volunteers. If a chemical imbalance was the cause of depression, then we should find that these volunteers become depressed once their neurotransmitter levels are reduced. However, experimentally reducing these neurotransmitters was found to have no effect on the mood of healthy volunteers who had never had a problem with depression.[14] Finally, too many drugs work with the same overall response rate. Drugs that increase levels of neurotransmitters work as well as drugs that decrease their levels.[15] After exploring all of this evidence, Kirsch concludes:

> "The chemical-imbalance theory rode to fame on the basis of uncontrolled case reports of improvement on some drugs and deterioration on others, while contrary data – some of it from carefully controlled studies – were simply ignored. Later attempts to test the theory by experimentally reducing serotonin or norepinephrine in healthy volunteers disproved the theory completely. [. . .] The chemical-imbalance theory is dead in the water, and its resuscitation seems an unlikely possibility."[16]

What he's really suggesting here is that an entire medical industry, that of treating depression, is based on a myth. A myth. The theory about how the treatment works is incorrect and the treatment itself is entirely a placebo effect. It reminds one of the claims of 18th century mesmerist Franz Anton Mesmer. He believed in an invisible magnetic fluid that permeated the universe. If one got sick, he mused, it must be because of an imbalance (there's that word again) of this mysterious magnetic fluid in the person's body. There were many things he did to cure his patients. One famous technique was to stare into their eyes, producing something similar to a hypnotic state, and make magnetic passes with his hand on their body. This involved touching them, supposedly to channel the magnetic fluid into their body.[17] Other techniques involved having his patients stand under a magnetized tree or drink magnetized water.[18] He also used more elaborate methods, such as making his patients sit around a large wooden tub filled with water that was "magnetized." They would hold onto angled rods sticking out through holes in the lid of the tub, while "Mesmer and his assistants would stroll around waving metal wands, which they would point at individual patients while giving them a 'mesmeric' stare in the eyes and sometimes also laying their hands on them."[19]

After reporting great success with these methods, he was investigated by a Royal Commission established by Louis XVI, which found that his success was due to nothing more than imagination and belief.[20] In essence, mesmeric healing sounded great, had a semi-scientific theory to go along with it, and even worked. But it was all a myth, albeit a useful one. Today, it seems, we've just updated our myths to match our more technical understanding of the body. The results are still in many cases based on expectation, possibly even enhanced by our elaborate theories of how things are supposed to work which further instantiate our belief in the effectiveness of the procedure.

Now you must be thinking, "Ok, this is no big deal. Depression is a mental phenomenon susceptible to people's expectations. It was all in their minds in the first place. But surely physical problems such as cancer, tumors and other physical ailments aren't susceptible to the placebo effect." Think again.

Let's start with a placebo-controlled trial of Parkinson's disease. This is "a degenerative neurological disorder characterized by muscle rigidity, tremor, and a slowing of physical movement."[21] Here we have a physically based disorder, although ironically you could say it's "all in their heads." In any event, it's not the type of thing you would expect pure expectation to cure. The surgical trial in question was performed in 2004 at the University of Denver. It "was designed to determine the effectiveness of transplantation of human embryonic dopamine neurons into the brains of individuals with advanced Parkinson's disease."[22] Eighteen patients received the placebo surgery, which involved enacting the same procedure as used in the actual surgery but with empty needles that did not penetrate the brain. Twelve other patients received actual implantation of embryonic dopamine neurons. The results showed that the only factor that determined success of the treatment was whether or not the patients believed they had been in the actual surgery group. Those who believed in the treatment, regardless of what condition they had actually been in, reported greater quality of life a year after surgery than those who believed they had received placebo surgery. The actual implantation of dopamine neurons had no effect.[23]

Another physical condition that has been successfully treated by placebo surgery is osteoarthritis of the knee, "a joint disease that causes the cartilage between the bones to wear away."[24] In his book *Brain Wars,* Mario Beauregard reports the results of a double blind placebo controlled study involving 180 patients undergoing surgery of the knee for treatment of this condition. The surgery, called arthroscopy, was and is commonly practiced. One procedure involves making an incision and rinsing out the joint to flush out the bad cartilage from the healthy tissue. Another procedure involves rinsing the joint as well as scraping the rough surfaces. [25] In this study, one third of the patients were given the rinsing procedure, one-third the rinsing and scraping, and one-third a placebo surgery.

The placebo surgery mimicked the actions of the real surgery without any actual rinsing or scraping of the joint being done. Incisions were still made in the knee so that there would be scarring afterwards and look exactly as if surgery had been done. Additionally, during the placebo surgery the surgeon also "manipulated the knee as if arthroscopy were being performed" and "saline was splashed to simulate the sounds of lavage."[26]

The results indicated that in the short term after surgery, the placebo group fared much better than either of the two actual surgery groups. Two weeks after surgery, placebo recipients reported significantly less pain and more improvement on a test of walking and climbing stairs than the actual surgery groups. One year later the placebo group still performed better on a test of walking and climbing stairs than the group who received both rinsing and scraping. After two years, the differences between the groups were no longer significant and all groups fared about the same.[27]

This study suggests a couple of things. One is that scraping the joint may actually cause damage which can persist up to a year. Another is that this surgery is totally worthless. The improvement reported by patients is completely based on their belief that they will get better. The theory upon which it was based and thought to work turns out to be a myth. It seems were back in the 18th century again, just with an updated medical mythology.

Another instance of recent medical mythology involves the condition known as angina pectoris, which is chest pain related to coronary artery disease. It occurs when the heart doesn't get enough oxygen due to a blocking or narrowing of the arteries. In the 1950s this was treated with a surgical procedure called mammary ligation, which involved completely blocking off some of the coronary arteries. The theory (myth) was that once some of the affected arteries were blocked off, the blood would then find alternate routes to the heart.[28] Irving Kirsch reports that "clinical experience indicated that mammary ligation was very effective in the treatment of angina, with success rates as high as 85 percent."[29] But when later skeptical researchers tested it against a placebo surgery it was found that the placebo surgery was equally as effective. Here again, the placebo surgery made it look like an actual surgery had taken place, when in fact none had. The patients were cut open to expose the arteries and then sewn back up without any work having been done to the affected arteries.[30] Once it was shown that the surgery was no better than a placebo the procedure fell out of favor and is no longer performed. In a related vein, Dr. Herbert Benson looked at many treatments for this very same condition that were once thought to be effective but later discarded by the medical profession as utterly worthless. What he found should not surprise us at this point. When given what would later be deemed a "useless" treatment, patients nevertheless "displayed objective improvement—greater endurance in exercise tests, less use of nitroglycerin, and improved results on the electrocardiogram."[31]

With osteoarthritis, Parkinson's disease, and coronary artery disease we're dealing with real debilitating *physical* conditions, not psychological states such as depression. In each case, objective improvement is seen regarding quality of life, the ability to walk up and down stairs, or exercise. That's right, real *physical* improvement. What we're dealing with is the mind's ability to affect the physical. What are the limits to such an ability? And is it just confined to the physical matter inside our bodies?

Unfortunately, not every type of medical treatment has been subjected to a placebo controlled test, but there are case reports of remarkable placebo effects in cases where none would have been expected. One case involved a man suffering from an advanced stage of lymph node cancer. He had "large tumor masses, the size of oranges" in his neck, groin, chest, and abdomen. "His spleen and liver were huge, and between thirty and sixty ounces of fluid had to be drawn from his chest every other day just to enable him to breathe."[32] His prognosis was bleak and he was not expected to live more than a couple of weeks. But then the patient learned about a new cancer drug that was, to his lucky surprise, being tested by his treating physician. He begged his doctor to give him this new wonder drug, called Krebiozen.

His physician agreed and injected him with the drug on a Friday. Astonishingly, his tumors "melted like snowballs on a hot stove." By the following Monday, he was up walking around, joking with the nurses and in tremendously better shape. After another ten days of treatment he was completely cured and discharged from the hospital. Two months went by and then the patient read a story in the newspaper which said that research had determined that the treatment he received was not an effective treatment. His spirits plunged and with it the tumors came back. He was now back in the hands of his doctor, who was smart enough to realize that he had gotten better based on his belief in the treatment. So, he resorted to tricking the patient. He told the patient in a confident voice that the Krebiozen he had received before was from a bad batch which had deteriorated before it was injected into him, but now he had just received a new batch of drug which was "super-refined, double strength" and capable of curing him. The patient readily agreed to this new "miracle cure," and the doctor gave him a "super-refined, double strength" injection of -- distilled water. "Again the tumor masses melted, chest fluid disappeared, and within a few days he walked out of the hospital fully recovered and symptom free."[33]

Although cured by the second placebo treatment the story does end tragically. The patient ended up reading the final report about the drug, Krebiozen, which he had originally received and thought he got again in a new super refined form the second time. Well, the final verdict after the clinical testing was that it was totally ineffective in the treatment of cancer. The patient died just days later after being readmitted to the hospital.[34]

The amazing thing suggested by this case is that the mind alone is capable of healing cancer and tumors, even in a late stage where the odds of overcoming the disease seem slim to none. Literally, based on an idea, a thought, expectation--whatever you want to call it, some mental power--he "melted away" cancerous tumors. Wow. It's starting to look like there's not much the mind can't do when it comes to bodily function and affecting the physical matter of the body. If pure belief can effect a cure of the magnitude we've just seen, then we're dealing with a very powerful phenomenon. Also, this case makes you wonder if a typical chemo-therapy cancer treatment would do better than a placebo. The problem is that you'd have to find a placebo that mimicked the side effects of the chemo, and I don't know what kind of placebo could make your hair fall out as well as give you a bad case of nausea. This is necessary because, as we've learned, if the side effects aren't present then it would be all too easy for patients to realize if they had actually been given chemo, which would bias their expectations. I'm not saying for sure that placebo chemotherapy would do as well as actual chemotherapy, but based on the cases we've reviewed thus far -- I sure am curious.

To really drive this point home that there are no limits to what the mind is capable of when it comes to affecting the body, I want to present two more "miraculous" case reports that have been well documented. The first involves a devout Catholic man named Pierre de Rudder. He had the unfortunate accident of being in the way of a falling tree. The tree crushed his leg causing a compound fracture. As Astrophysicist and paranormal researcher Jacques Vallee reports, the aftermath wasn't pretty:

> "A surgeon, Dr Affenaer, had had to remove a piece of bone that had broken away and had inserted itself in the tissues. The bones were thus separated by a space of over one inch, and the patient had endured endless suffering during the *eight years* that had elapsed since the accident."[35]

His doctors informed him that there was nothing they could do short of amputating his leg, which he adamantly refused. He "was almost unable to move, even with the help of crutches," but managed to persuade his employer to pay for a trip for him to go to "the shrine of Our Lady of Lourdes in Oostacker, Belgium."[36] This is a religious shrine where many miracles were said to have occurred. Rudder was deeply convinced that he would be cured and no one was able to persuade him that it was better to stay home rather than attempt the trip in such a poor condition. Rudders opinion on the matter was matter of fact: "'Others have been cured in Oostacker,' said Rudder. 'So why not me?'"[37]

After arriving at the holy sanctuary and praying, "he felt deeply moved, overwhelmed by a strange feeling. Beside himself, he rose, went through the crowd, and knelt before the statue . . . Then he suddenly realized what he had done!" He then proceeded to walk, crutch free, around the cave in a joyous mood. When his wife saw this she actually fainted from the shock. After all, this is a man who for the past eight years hadn't been able to walk without crutches. Upon examination the following morning, it was found that the bones in his leg were no longer broken. "The bones were completely smooth at the place where they had been broken." Rudder suffered no more and went on to live for twenty-three more years walking normally. Even more, an autopsy on his exhumed body after his death showed that the bones that had been separated by the over one inch gap were now fused together by a "piece of healthy white bone, over one inch long, which connects the two sections still showing the traces of breakage."[38]

This is a case that was attested to by multiple doctors and witnesses. Here we have an instance of the mind, whether God's or his doesn't matter, creating new bone matter seemingly instantly. The mind--manifesting matter--controlling the material world. Have we heard this before? Oh shit, I think we did in the last chapter. Wouldn't you know, we're back to the same conclusion as before. Interesting.

Our next case involves healing via the use of hypnosis and teaches us a very important lesson about the nature of mental healing. There's something about the level of belief that seems to make a difference. Specifically, it suggests that there needs to be a firm conviction and the absence of doubt.

Such was the case with skilled hypnotist and anesthetist Dr. Albert Mason in the early 1950s. There was a patient named John who was born with a genetic disease called congenital ichthyosis.[39] This is a nasty skin disease in which the skin is covered by a hard, thick, in-elastic, black substance that causes painful cracking of the skin.[40] After receiving unsuccessful plastic surgery to try and alleviate the condition, a young Doctor Mason with plenty of swagger and confidence thought something along the lines of, "Shit, this ain't nothing but a bunch of warts covering his body. I know warts can be cured by hypnosis. I'll take care of this." So, with full conviction that hypnosis would work he put John under hypnosis and, focusing on just one arm, instructed "him that the skin on that arm would heal and turn into healthy, pink skin."[41]

Sure enough his subconscious mind took this confident suggestion hook, line, and sinker, and set to work to create his experience in accord with it. Within five days the rigid, black horny casing on his arm fell off to reveal pink, soft, healthy skin underneath. Within ten days from the hypnotic treatment the entire arm from shoulder to wrist was completely clear.[42] Dr. Mason thought John's surgeon, who had tried unsuccessful skin grafts to treat him, might want to see John's arm of new healthy skin. Upon seeing John and his amazing healthy skin, "the surgeon's jaw dropped" and he exclaimed "Jesus Christ! Do you know what you've done?" The surgeon told him about the disease and suggested Mason do some research on it. What he found out was that the disease was structural and organic. Specifically, "John's skin had no oil-forming glands that would enable its outer layers to flake off and renew themselves."[43] In other words, there was no way he should have been able to grow new skin. Medically, a cure was deemed at the time impossible. Mason had done something that should not be physically possible. Somehow, the programs in John's DNA had been altered to fix the genetic deficiency!

Mason continued to work on John to help clear the rest of his skin, but the seeds of doubt were already in his mind due to the new information he had recently acquired. No longer was he under the confident impression that it was just a bad case of warts that could easily be treated with hypnosis. Now, he knew it to be something far more serious. After trying to hypnotically cure other patients of the disease he found he was unable to work his previous magic. As biologist Bruce Lipton reports:

> "Mason attributes his failure [to replicate his results] to his own belief about the treatment. When Mason treated the new patients he couldn't replicate his cocky attitude as a young physician thinking he was treating a bad case of warts. After that first patient, Mason was fully aware that he was treating what everyone in the medical establishment knew to be a congenital, 'incurable' disease. Mason tried to pretend that he was upbeat about the prognosis, but he told the Discovery Health Channel, 'I was acting.'"[44]

In the absence of doubt, Mason pulled off the miraculous. But once that twinge of doubt entered into his mind, it completely destroyed his ability to do what he had just done! This is amazing and it brings to mind what Jesus says in the bible: "I tell you the truth, if you have faith and don't doubt, you can do things like this and much more. You can even say to this mountain, 'May you be lifted up and thrown into the sea,' and it will happen."[45] Consider also that the level of belief plays a central role in the standard medical placebo controlled trials. A more expensive placebo will work better than a less expensive one. A brand-name placebo will work better than one presented as a generic drug. A placebo given four times per day will work better than one given only twice a day.[46] A placebo pill is less effective than a placebo injection, which is less effective than a placebo surgery.[47] The only thing that changes in each case is the level of expectation of a cure. These different placebos simply come with differing levels of belief in their effectiveness based on societal conditioning.

Beyond the placebo effect

It makes you wonder: Do we somehow circumscribe reality with our deeply held convictions and thoughts? Do we somehow play a role in determining how reality operates? Consider the next case of a timely Shamanic intervention in the life of a man who was in dire circumstances and told by the medical profession that nothing could be done for him (we've heard that one before). Investigative journalist and author, Guy Lyon Playfair, relates the story of a man who, two days before his wedding day, happened to fall from a building and suffer severe internal injuries. "He was taken to the hospital and X-rayed, after which his bride-to-be was told there was nothing to be done for him. He was not expected to live more than a few hours."[48] Sounds something like the extreme case of the man with the cancerous tumors, whose story we reviewed before, who was given only two weeks to live. Well, there was no "miracle drug" available for this man, but luckily the mother of the bride had heard of a great Chukchee Shaman in a nearby village. Distraught and having nowhere else to turn, the mother, daughter, and a friend of the daughter decided to take the groom-to-be there.

They set off and arrived at a village of skin covered huts about four hours after the accident had occurred. Amazingly, although they hadn't told anyone about their impromptu trip, when they arrived to see the Shaman they found him waiting for them as if he knew they were coming. After asking the women for the price of five dogs and, refusing any further payment, he quickly got to work. And I hope you'll agree that it is quite an interesting form of treatment (but rather gruesome). I'm sorry in advance to any animal lovers. You may want to skip the following quote. I will quote directly now, as Playfair does a wonderful job of describing what happened:

"The three women sat and watched in silence as the shaman undressed the patient and rubbed his body with what smelled like blubber oil. Then -- I apologise to animal lovers, who are not going to like this -- he took the first dog, killed it, ripped out its organs and placed the kidneys, spleen and lungs on the corresponding areas of the man's body, which he then wrapped in a bearskin. He removed this about three quarters of an hour later to reveal what Ilieva [the bride's friend] described as 'something like thin oil-paper' where the dog's organs had been. She had the impression that 'some kind of exchange between these organs and the patient's body' had taken place. The shaman went through this grisly ritual four more times, and each time it seemed that the dog's organs had undergone less of a change, until after the fifth application they remained almost unaltered. Mercifully, the patient was still unconscious.

Next, the village healer poured some kind of mushroom soup into the man's mouth and drank some himself. Then he rubbed more blubbery stuff into the patient's skin, wrapped him up once more in the bearskin, and announced that he would sleep for four hours. He then repeated that if the patient woke up, he would be all right. But he would never know what had happened, and should not be told."[49]

Yeah, because he might shit his pants if he knew what happened! Fortunately, he did wake up and the women took him straight back to the hospital where he was X-rayed again and found to be completely cured. This shaman had a belief system, probably one that involved spiritual forces. His belief system and the methods he used to heal this man's internal injuries would be laughed at by most scientists. They would consider his beliefs and methods superstitious, primitive, shall I use the term—myth. But they worked! And as we've seen, even many of the practices of today's medical profession are based on myths. Myths that nonetheless work, but not because they are somehow objectively true, but because people strongly believe in those myths. This is what the placebo effect is all about, belief. If many of today's modern medical treatments are not better than a placebo, that means they are really based on the power of belief.

Consider the germ theory in medicine. This is the theory which states that bacteria and viruses cause disease, an idea that is firmly entrenched in modern medical theory; one which not many people today would question. Well, one well known critic of this idea when it was first formulated decided to prove that this idea was wrong. He was so convinced in the inaccuracy of this idea that "he brazenly wolfed down a glass of water laced with *vibrio cholerae,* the bacterium Koch [one of the creators of germ theory] believed caused cholera. To everyone's astonishment, the man was completely unaffected by the virulent pathogen."[50] Nevertheless, germ theory was accepted, and this critic's little experiment was simply brushed aside with a shrug of the shoulders and the thought, "Huh, that's strange." Which of course is how all paranormal phenomena, or any phenomenon that doesn't fit into current accepted scientific thinking, is dealt with.

This is not an isolated case either. In Brazil, mediums are commonly known to enter into what's called "trance possession." During this time, their bodies are said to be possessed by the gods while their own conscious awareness is somehow removed from the body or otherwise disabled.[51] During this time they can drink several liters of brandy without getting drunk, even though in a normal state of consciousness "they would be unable to tolerate such quantities of alcohol." In addition, they show heightened senses and psychic ability. They can also physically exert themselves without loss of energy. The reason, they report, is because it is the God in them who drinks the alcohol, exerts energy, and speaks of things unknown to the person channeling the God.[52] Respected psychiatrist and founder of the branch of transpersonal psychology, Stanislav Grof was fortunate enough to witness such a spectacle and saw firsthand as these mediums ingested copious amounts of alcohol while under possession. They drank "large bottles of aquavit, a strong distillate with about 45% alcohol, without showing any signs of motor instability." He was surprised, too, when one medium was able to tell him about specific things he was worried about at the time, and also made statements about his wife's gynecological problems and sadness over losing custody of her two children who were living in Hawaii with their father. This was information that his only connection to the medium, his guide Sergio, had no knowledge of.[53] Again, regardless of what you think about trance possession, we have facts here that can't be denied. Based on a belief that it's the God who is drinking the alcohol and not them, these people do not show the slightest signs of drunkenness even after ingesting large amounts of alcohol. Also, they can exert themselves extensively without showing loss of energy, again, because a God is somehow exerting themselves through them so their own energies are conserved. Somehow when it comes to the body, a strong enough idea can literally create that reality and overturn the laws by which reality normally operates. Finally, by channeling this other dimensional metaphysical "God" they somehow have access to knowledge outside of their sensory channels or knowledge base.

Another example of a belief system which leads to reality acting in a subjective way can be seen in the Kahunas of Hawaii. They regularly take strolls across molten lava after invoking the gods for protection. In one incredible and somewhat humorous instance, a curious but skeptical man named Brigham was promised by three Kahunas that they would perform the feat for him. They even said that they would "confer their fire immunity on him if he wanted to join them, and he bravely agreed." However, upon seeing the lava flow that "was so hot that patches of incandescence still coursed through its surface," he quickly decided it was better not to follow the Kahuna's across. "Fuck that shit!" he was probably thinking. Anyway, those are my words, not his. He watched the first Kahuna stroll across the barely hardened molten rock without harm. Then he stood up to watch the next and was surprised to get a hard push from behind. This "forced him to break into a run to keep from falling face first onto the incandescent rock." Suffice it to say, he ran like there was pack of wolves behind him. When he reached the other side he was amazed to see that "one of his boots had burned off and his socks were on fire. But, miraculously, his feet were completely unharmed."[54] Seeing his shocked expression, the Kahuna's, who knew all along that no harm would come to him, just laughed their asses off. Oh, silly primitive white man. When will he ever learn?

This case is especially interesting because it's nearly impossible to debunk and say, "Oh, the coals weren't really that hot. He's exaggerating." It's pretty hard to exaggerate your boot burning off and your socks catching on fire. Based on a belief in one's spiritual protection against the burning embers, these people do not get burned.

If you're confused right now, don't worry. This is confusing stuff for a Westerner who is trained to believe that reality is objective. You know, like, water boils at 100 degrees Celsius and if I touch a hot stove with my bare hand it will burn my skin -- every time, guaranteed. That's the view of reality that's pushed through our heads from day one. But it's wrong, it's dead wrong and we've seen example after example of why it's wrong. We somehow mold reality with our thoughts. Through our thoughts we somehow determine how the physical world acts and behaves. This is a great mystery, one that needs to be carefully examined. So far we've been looking at how the mind can influence the body, but can the mind extend its reach outside of the body? That's the question we ponder next.

Hypnosis and the far reaches of the mind

Our old friend from the 19th Century, Alfred Russell Wallace, did plenty of experimentation using hypnosis. One of the interesting things he tried was to induce hypnotic transference. This is when you hypnotize someone and tell them that they will experience whatever you experience. It's effectively a coupling of two minds so that they are "in phase," or entangled. For example, Wallace, who we met in the last chapter, experimented with hypnotic transference by making "a chain of several persons." He was at one end and the subject under hypnosis was at the other end. Wallace describes how,

> "When, in perfect silence, I was pinched or pricked, he would immediately put his hand to the corresponding part of his own body, and complain of being pinched or pricked too. If I put a lump of sugar or salt in my mouth, he immediately went through the action of sucking, and soon showed by gestures and words of the most expressive nature what it was I was tasting. I have never to this day been satisfied with any of the explanations given of this fact by our physiologists for they resolve themselves into this, that the boy neither felt nor tasted anything, but acquired a knowledge of what I was feeling and tasting by a preternatural acuteness of hearing. That he had any such preternatural acuteness was, however, contrary to all my experience, and the experiment was tried so as expressly to prevent his gaining any knowledge of what I felt or touched by means of the ordinary senses."[55]

This sort of hypnotic transference is not uncommon. All that needs to be done is to make a suggestion to the entranced individual that they will they will taste everything that you taste. You can then proceed to put any number of substances into your mouth, all the while hidden from the subject. And the subject will react appropriately to the taste, whether it's sweet watermelon or sour milk.[56]

Another fascinating experiment involving hypnosis and the mind's access to information outside the reach of the normal senses was reported by Grandmaster of New Age Thought (a title I've bestowed upon him), Michael Talbot. What happened was that Talbot's father hired a professional hypnotist to entertain some friends. After checking the susceptibility of a number of people at the gathering to hypnosis, an individual named Tom was chosen as the subject. Tom was a close friend of Talbot's father and had never met the hypnotist before. After fooling around a bit and, among other things, making Tom believe there was a giraffe in the room, the hypnotist finished his performance by telling Tom that when he came out of trance his daughter would be completely invisible to him. The hypnotist then had his daughter Laura stand directly in front of the chair in which he was sitting. Tom was awakened and asked if he could see her. Here's where it gets interesting:

> "Tom looked around the room and his gaze appeared to pass right through his giggling daughter. 'No,' he replied. The hypnotist asked Tom if he was certain, and again, despite Laura's rising giggles, he answered no. Then the hypnotist went behind Laura so he was hidden from Tom's view and pulled an object out of his pocket. He kept the object carefully concealed so that no one in the room could see it, and pressed it against the small of Laura's back. He asked Tom to identify the object. Tom leaned forward as if staring directly through Laura's stomach and said that it was a watch. The hypnotist nodded and asked if Tom could read the watch's inscription. Tom squinted as if struggling to make out the writing and recited both the name of the watch's owner (which happened to be a person unknown to any of us in the room) and the message. The hypnotist then revealed that the object was indeed a watch and passed it around the room so that everyone could see that Tom had read its inscription correctly.
>
> When I talked to Tom afterward, he said that his daughter had been absolutely invisible to him. All he had seen was the hypnotist standing and holding a watch cupped in the palm of his hand. Had the hypnotist let him leave without telling him what was going on, he never would have known he wasn't perceiving normal consensus reality."[57]

One interesting question which comes up in a case like this is if Tom heard his daughter's giggling. He was only instructed that she would be invisible, which deals only with sight. So, there's nothing in the hypnotic suggestion to suggest that he wouldn't be able to hear her. But in the account he only looks around the room and says he can't see his daughter, making no mention of hearing her voice. So, we are left wondering. But it could just be that many people in the room were laughing so that his daughter's laughing just blended in with theirs. Also, maybe he heard his daughter laugh and just didn't recognize it as her, thinking it was someone else in the room. This wouldn't be hard to believe because upon not seeing his daughter he would have thought it impossible to be hearing her laugh. And so he would have ascribed the laughing to others in the room, who probably were laughing as well.

In any case, the more interesting thing about this experience is that not only was his daughter invisible, he could actually see through her. The inscription on the watch should have been outside of the reach of his vision, blocked by the body of his daughter standing right in front of him. His mind somehow still had access to the information. This "mind reach" was also the case with super-psychic Alexis Didier. In an altered state of consciousness, he was able to accurately describe distant places.

In one remarkable encounter, he was tested and asked by the test practitioner, a Rev. Chauncey Hare Townshend, to visit Townshend's house in thought. Alexis then asked Mr. Townshend which house he should visit because Townshend in fact had two houses. Townshend advised Alexis to visit his house in the country. A brief moment later, Alexis declared "I am there!" He proceeded to describe the layout of the house and surrounding area in detail. He was also able to enter the house in his mind and accurately describe the paintings he saw hanging on Mr. Townshends wall. He correctly identified that "they were all modern paintings, except for two, one of the sea and one of a religious subject."[58] He then went on to describe in detail the religious painting, exclaiming "There are three figures in the picture--an old man, a woman, and a child." Furthermore, he described the scene that was taking place in the picture, that "of Saint Ann in the process of teaching the Virgin Mary to read." Also, he described the rough and bumpy black marble base that the painting was done on, saying that it was "a blackish-gray stone substance that was bumpy."[59] These, of course, are all facts that he could not have known. Either he was telepathically receiving the information from Townshend's own mind or he was somehow receiving the information clairvoyantly. Whatever the case may be, we have evidence that his mind was receiving information about a distant place through some mental channel.

Another interesting fact about this experience is that Townshend believed that his belief in Alexis's powers actually contributed to the success of the experiment. "He had no doubt that, had he been impatient or distrustful, 'Alexis would have lost his clairvoyance, and perhaps attempted to supply it by guessing.'"[60] Parapsychological researcher Brian Inglis, too, noted this difficulty of psychics to perform in front of skeptics, stating, "Like many earlier clairvoyants Alexis found difficulty in performing before hostile sceptics."[61] Famed author Charles Dickens wrote about Alexis, "He fails in a crowd, but is marvellous before a few."[62] It seems that for Alexis to perform there needed to be a rapport between him and his questioner. If this were not there, he found it difficult to display his clairvoyant powers. There needs to be some agreement of wills, it seems, between the person asking for the information and the clairvoyant. One's mind needs to be sufficiently open before this kind of rapport can take place. A completely closed mind is in a sense saying, "I do not want to see this work. I do not want to experience this." Well, this kind of skeptic may just get his wish, not because the phenomenon isn't real but because he refuses to open himself to the possibility that it is-- refusing to enter into a reciprocal relationship with the psychic. The psychic's own mental state also enters into the equation. One psychic noted, "The more I wish, the less I can do."[63] Another said, "When not anxious to see, I can see most clearly."[64] So, another possible reason psychics may not be able to perform as well in front of a skeptical audience is that they know they are being tested and become too anxious, eager, and nervous for the clairvoyance to operate. If you are too eager, it's like saying, "Oh, please, please let it work." This kind of thought pattern implies doubt that it may not happen. Better is to have a kind of confident expectant belief, not caring whether it happens or not but being confident that it will and just letting go, letting it happen.   We still need to tease out exactly how these psychic processes within the mind work. Does another person's doubt or resistance create a mental block in the psychic's mind thereby inhibiting his ability, or does a skeptical audience make a psychic nervous and too eager to please for the faculty to operate? In regards to this kind of psychic phenomenon, I do believe that the skeptical intentions of one mind can affect another, but only in so much as to cause the other to doubt or fear. It's not that the skeptic somehow has power over the clairvoyant's mind, only that the clairvoyant, influenced by the skeptical intentions of the observer, begins to doubt himself and is unable to be relaxed and comfortable enough to practice his clairvoyance. If it were the case that the skeptic's intention itself mentally blocked the psychic from performing, then we should never be able to see a skeptic turn into a believer upon experiencing the phenomenon firsthand. However, there are many cases of this kind where former skeptics have been forced by the evidence presented before their very eyes to recant and accept the reality of the phenomenon.[65] This assessment agrees with the findings of another investigator into mediumistic phenomena who noted that hostile skepticism could inhibit the medium, but detached or sheer ignorant skepticism did not affect the medium's abilities.[66] In any event, there is still much we need to learn about the interplay of minds and higher level psychic phenomena.

Finally, concerning the far reaches of consciousness, we should not overlook the work of Psychiatrist Stanislav Grof. He for years has worked with people in altered states of consciousness, first back in the 1960s with LSD and then moving on to his own method for inducing altered states called *Holotropic Breathwork*. Many times he ran into instances where his patients experienced information that they could not have acquired in ordinary life. For instance one woman, who had suffered from serious bouts of depression for four years leading up to her participation in a Holotropic Breathwork workshop, began in an altered state of consciousness to chant a prayer in a language Grof did not understand. After ending the session and coming back to normal consciousness, she said "that she had felt an irresistible urge to do what she did. She did not understand what had happened and indicated that she had absolutely no idea what language she was using in her chant." Luckily, there happened to be a psychoanalyst named Carlos from Buenos Aires who was also participating in the group. He had studied the Sephardic language as a personal hobby for many years. This language "is a combination of medieval Spanish and Hebrew" and the woman who spoke it "was not Jewish and did not know any Hebrew or Spanish." If not for Carlos the group would have never known what she was saying or if it was even a real language that came out of her mouth. But as luck had it, Carlos was able to understand and translate the prayer, which was translated as: "I am suffering, and I will always suffer. I am crying, and I will always cry. I am praying, and I will always pray."[67]

A slightly more interesting experience related by Grof is of a an Australian therapist named Graham Farrant who experienced becoming a sperm cell racing towards the ovum. Before you laugh, consider the fact that he gained information about this process that was at the time not known. Medical schools at the time taught that the sperm attacked and penetrated a passive ovum, but he experienced firsthand what medical researchers were later to acknowledge, "that the ovum cooperated by sending out an extension of its cytoplasm and engulfing him [the sperm]."[68] He relates that:

"My consciousness became less and less differentiated, and I started experiencing a strange excitement that was dissimilar to anything I have ever felt in my life. The middle part of my back was generating rhythmical pulses, and I had the feeling of being propelled through space and time toward some unknown goal; I had a very vague sense of what the final destination might be, but the mission appeared to be one of utmost importance.

After some time, I was able to recognize to my great surprise that I was a spermatozoid and that the regular explosive pulses were the beats of a biological pacemaker that were transmitted to my long flagella, which was flashing in vibratory movements. I was involved in a hectic super-race toward the source of some chemical messages that had an enticing and irresistible quality. By then I realized (using the information I had as an educated human adult) that the goal was to reach, penetrate, and fertilize the egg. In spite of the fact that this whole scene seemed absurd and ridiculous to my scientific mind, I could not resist getting involved in this strange race with all seriousness and great expenditure of energy.

[. . .] The excitement of this race was growing every second and the hectic pace seemed to increase to such a degree that it felt like the flight of a spaceship approaching the speed of light. Then came the culmination in the form of a triumphant implosion and ecstatic fusion with the egg. Shortly before the moment of conception, my consciousness was alternating between the speeding sperm and the egg experiencing strong excitement and expectation of a vaguely defined, but overwhelming event. At the moment of conception, the two

units of consciousness merged and I became both of these
germinal cells at once."[69]

What these cases really suggest is that the mind has no limits. It is
not localized in one's body and brain. The mind is non-local, somehow
everywhere at once. We only experience a small portion of this greater
sphere of Mind, but when under hypnosis or in an altered state of
consciousness we may access information from this larger sphere. This
supports the "Mind at Large" hypothesis proposed in modern times by
Aldous Huxley. He came to see that the mind is potentially infinite, having
access to all time and place. What we experience on a day to day basis
within the confines of our brain and body is just a small sliver of Mind at
Large. The brain is a reducing valve through which this Mind at Large is
funneled and reduced.[70] The same thoughts are presented by near-death
experience researcher and Cardiologist Pim Van Lommel in a more up to
date scientific way when he states:

> "In this new approach, complete and endless consciousness
> with retrievable memories has its origins in a nonlocal space in
> the form of indestructible and not directly observable wave
> functions. These wave functions, which store all aspects of
> consciousness in the form of information, are always present in
> and around the body (nonlocally). The brain and the body
> merely function as a relay station receiving part of the overall
> consciousness in the form of measurable and constantly
> changing electromagnetic fields."[71]

Here he's invoking quantum physics principles to explain the nature
of consciousness and its relationship to the brain. Quantum physics is a
mystical branch of science in which particles cannot be said to exist
before they are observed, or measured. More specifically, unless a
conscious being has access to information about the particle, such as its
speed, momentum, or direction of spin, the particle does not exist in any
discreet localized way.[72] Quantum physics says that the only thing we can
say exists before a measurement is taken is the particle's wave function.
Now, the obvious question to ask is, "Ok, what's a wave function?" Well,
it's a mathematical description of the particle. It's sometimes useful to
think of it as like a water wave or a sound wave traveling through space,
but as a physicist told me via email: "We could say that there are
probability waves flying all around us, but that sort of metaphysical

existence seems very different than that of a real water wave. I can touch water, but I can't run my hands through a stream of probability."[73] That is, the wave function of a particle is simply a probability distribution containing information about a particle. It is not the particle itself. The particle doesn't exist until a conscious being tries to obtain information about it, either through a conscious observation or a measurement of some sort.

When we get down to the subatomic realm reality slips through our fingers—escapes our grasp. At this level of reality we can no longer define reality in any definite sense, only in a mathematical abstract way. The physical particles aren't there, not physically anyway. What is there is non-physical information which becomes physical through some mystical process involving consciousness. Oooh…. Spooky. Spooky, but evidently true. Our minds play a part not only in how reality behaves, but also in its physical creation. We can now reverse the stipulation of modern scientific thinking from matter is fundamental and mind an epiphenomenon to mind is fundamental and matter an epiphenomenon.

Mind over matter

If this is all true and not just some New Age bullshit, then the mind should be able to exert a direct influence on matter. Mind, after all, creates it. If Mind at Large creates the material universe and we are part of that Mind, then we should be able to influence physical "matter" purely through mental operations. It may even have something to do with that funny little thing called belief, or expectation, that we found so dramatically influenced the placebo effect.

There are some laboratory experiments involving telekinesis, or the manipulation of matter through purely mental exertion. But I don't even really want to talk about them because they are way too boring. However, I will mention them just for the sake of completeness. In these experiments, such as ones performed by Helmut Schmidt, a random number generator is used to randomly generate binary numbers (1's and 0's) based on the purely random process of radioactive decay. Schmidt used a binary flipper that constantly alternated between two positions (0 or 1). An electron emitted from a radioactive substance (like Strontium-90) would cause the flipper to stop in one of the two positions. When this happened the user would get feedback about which position (0 or 1) the binary flipper stopped at in any number of ways. For instance, sometimes they would see lights arranged in a circle and if the flipper stopped in one position it would cause the lights to move clockwise, but if it stopped in the other position the lights would move counterclockwise. Or in some cases headphones were used and the user experienced clicks in either the left or right ear.[74]

During the random number generation the subject tries to will a certain result, such as the lights moving counterclockwise or more clicks in the right ear. Remember, since the emission of electrons during radioactive decay is a purely random process, these clicks in the left or right ear, or the direction of movement of lights on the screen, should be purely random meaning that we should get 50% of each result. Well wouldn't you know it, when people try to influence the results they can— barely. With odds against chance of over a trillion to one, the combined experimental data show that subjects get an overall hit rate of 51% in the desired direction when the expected outcome is 50%. In contrast, control studies without a subject intending a result are clearly within chance levels with odds against chance of only two to one.[75] In other words, study participants are able to bias the outcome in a desired direction (such as more clicks in the left ear) through their concentrated intent. That means they were able to exert some control over when an electron emitted from the radioactive isotope. The effect is indeed a small one, but it is statistically significant over many many trials. This means we can rule out chance as a probable explanation.

Oh my god is that boring though. Just describing it I was falling asleep. And their pitiful results just speak to the fact that this is so dull. My God, design some more interesting experiments. However, I do apologize to the researchers involved because, in all seriousness, their work is a preliminary first step that lets us know telekinesis is real and worth investigating. But you've got to do better than a circle of lights on a computer screen. Let's fucking make some shit happen already. I'm not interested in making a few electrons emit from an atom at a particular time in order to make a circle of lights move clockwise instead of counterclockwise. Who gives a shit? What they ought to be doing is something people give a shit about, like making a sexy woman/handsome guy appear on the screen. That would be more interesting. Replace that circle of moving lights with one picture people really like to see (the hot guy or girl) and another they absolutely don't want to see (their mother dying). Now you'll get some results. But anyway, what I was going to say is, "Let's do some *real* telekinesis." Screw this boring computer shit. Let's get some tables in the air, chairs flying around the room, scare the cat, maybe piss our pants a little—real fucking telekinesis. Yeah! Are you with me? Well let's get to it then!

Unfortunately, there are no modern day laboratory table levitation experiments, maybe because the researchers would be laughed at for even attempting such a thing. No scientist is going to get grant money or funding to study something very few people believe is even possible, much less worth investigating. However, there were attempts under well controlled conditions to verify the phenomenon in the 19th and early 20th centuries, when mediumship and table levitation were in vogue. One attempt was by Dr. Robert Hare, a former professor of Chemistry at the University of Pennsylvania. Without going into detail, he designed experiments to rule out the possibility of any physical pressure being applied to the table by the medium in order to ensure that it was truly a psychokinetic force and not the medium moving the table himself. His results were positive and showed that a force was being applied that was not from a known physical source. However, upon publishing these experiments he was immediately derided by his colleagues and accused of fraud.[76] In essence, his research was ignored. Not too big of a surprise for us, is it? Same old story of science ignoring evidence. Happens every day.

Even such scientific luminaries as William Crookes--who discovered the metallic element thallium and invented the Crookes Tube, which was a precursor to the cathode ray tube and was used to discover X-rays-- investigated psychokinetic phenomena, including table levitation, and found them to be authentic and not the result of trickery. His paper on the subject was rejected by the Royal Society of London, of which he was a distinguished member, showing that when even the most well respected scientist opposes orthodoxy or steps too far out of the box, the scientific establishment will with religious fervor oppose him.[77] And Crookes was not alone. Mediums who could produce psychokinetic phenomena were repeatedly tested by men of science and found to be genuine. Measures such as strip searching the medium and pre-inspecting the room of the séance were routinely applied. Furthermore, the medium's hands and feet were held by the investigators while they witnessed the levitations, sometimes in well-lit séances so they could clearly see what was going on.[78]

Some of the most impressive experiments of this kind were conducted in Paris by a formidable team of scientists headed by Sorbonne Professor Jules Courtier, and including director of the Laboratory of Biological Physics Jacques-Arsène d'Arsonval, University of Paris professors Pierre and Marie Curie, Henri Bergson, Charles Richet, and others. They conducted experiments with mediums in the early 20th century taking great care to prevent against fraud and delusion. They wired up the tables in the room so that any movement would be detected and recorded by machines kept in a separate laboratory. Not only the movements, but the source of the movement could be detected by the machines. They also recorded every sound made in the room. Still, they got results. When testing the famous medium Eusapia Palladino it was reported:

> "The table in front of her had moved when her feet were being held, and her hands withdrawn from it. First, two table legs, then three, rose, even when one of the investigators actually sat on it. Then the table levitated, all four legs off the floor, while Palladino's feet were controlled and her hands were resting on the heads of witnesses on each side of her; and remained for a few seconds floating about thirty centimeters above the floor. When the group stood holding hands above it, the table hoisted itself so high that its legs almost came out of the sheaths which had been designed to prevent any interference with them; its movements being recorded by the group of observers, and by the recording machines in the other room."[79]

Unless we want to suggest fraud on the part of a group of highly respected scientists and professors, we have clear evidence of a psychokinetic effect. And just to be clear, the phenomena produced by gifted mediums was not limited to the movement of tables. Sometimes a music instrument would play when no one was near it. All manner of objects in the room were floated through the air.[80] Sometimes objects in the room would act as if they were living creatures infused with spirit, such as a violin which rubbed up against the playwright Victorien Sardou during a session with Palladino. He says, "after an unsuccessful effort to climb higher than my knee, this apparently living creature fell with a bang upon the floor."[81] Other incredible things included disembodied hands seen floating around which could be grasped and held only to melt away in one's hand.[82] Sometimes a full person would materialize.[83] Also, objects were moved from another room to the séance room while the doors were locked.[84]

Investigative journalist and author Guy Lyon Playfair found out about table levitation firsthand from long time table levitation practitioner and clinical psychologist Kenneth J. Batcheldor. Batcheldor explained to Playfair that "in most cases, the table will start to move due to UMA [unconscious muscular activity]."[85] Then, the unjustified belief that something paranormal is taking place releases the PK (Psychokinetic) force, which always tends to be repressed by conscious or unconscious doubts.[86] In other words, sometimes the trick is necessary to generate the belief that it is real. That conviction then generates real psychokinesis. Our doubts need to be swept aside to produce moments of total faith for the phenomenon to manifest.

Have you ever heard the phrase, "You've got to believe in order to see."? Well, if we co-create reality with Mind at Large, or Source Consciousness as I like to call it, then it makes sense that reality in some sense may conform to that which we wish, through our beliefs, to experience. But if we doubt, that doubt is information that we don't want that experience. This, though, is a hard sell because we all know that you can experience things you don't believe in. So all we can really say is that if you enter into the belief system that allows for the reality of a phenomenon/experience then it's more likely to be experienced. And in this regard, too, we may have to take into account different levels of mind. For instance, some authors posit a conscious mind, subconscious mind, and superconscious mind. Each level of our mind has more and more power to shape our reality. A good example is the case of Tom we looked at before. Remember, he was hypnotized and made to believe that his daughter was invisible. Well, in a normal conscious state if we told Tom, "Hey bro, your daughter's invisible," he would just laugh and say, "No she's not you silly goose, I can see her right over there." But somehow by putting him into a different, shall we say higher, state of consciousness the hypnotist was able to tell him basically the same thing, but this time his experience actually reflected the belief. He really couldn't see his daughter after coming back to his normal conscious awake self, all because of a belief implanted at a higher level of his mind. So, we may have to ask, "Just how deeply convicted is your belief/disbelief?" And, "Is there any resistance/doubt in your mind at any level?" With any psychic phenomenon, too, it only takes one person to believe and produce the phenomenon for others to see. We know this is the case because back in the 19th century when mediums were regularly giving demonstrations of their abilities to produce materializations and movements of objects without physical intervention, they regularly submitted to test conditions and produced the phenomenon to skeptical observers, like William Crookes or Alfred Russell Wallace. So one's disbelief will only inhibit the phenomenon when only they or a group of other disbelievers is trying to make the phenomenon happen. But as long as one person in the group has a strong belief, and isn't himself made to doubt or become nervous because of the presence of skeptics, then it can manifest. I realize, too, that what I just wrote, although it makes perfect sense, is an oxymoron. Think about it, a group of all disbelievers trying to produce something they all don't believe is possible. What a highly unlikely situation! Ultimately, though, belief itself may not be a prerequisite since higher levels of mind, or beings in a higher dimension, have their own agency. However, due to our co-creative nature with reality, I cannot put down the idea that our beliefs, or disbeliefs, do have an effect on what we experience and what is real for us, so that doubt may be a hindrance to certain types of phenomena.

Before I describe a table levitation session involving Playfair and Batcheldor, I would like to joke around again for a minute, because by this time in the book you know I like to be funny. I like table levitation because it just sounds like a great idea. I want to get together with some friends, sit in a circle around my table with the lights off, and see if I can conjure up some spirits to move the damn thing and scare the piss out of my friends. Wow, couldn't think of a better idea myself. I just wonder who thought up this idea? Some guy just sitting at home, thinking "Man, this table is fucking boring -- just sitting there like that. I've gotta see if I can't get this damn thing to lift up in the air, vibrate, and move around the house. Maybe scare the cat with it or some shit." Alright, so maybe the phenomenon didn't actually get started that way. Actually, the movement of objects without physical contact has long been known to be an aspect of poltergeist cases. It is a real phenomenon attested to by many people and it is an example of an effect of mind on physical objects in the natural world.

This phenomenon, sometimes referred to as table-tilting, usually involves people sitting down around a table with their hands placed on top. There may be a concentrated wish or a spoken command for the table to move. Often times spiritual forces are summoned to move the table -- the method is not so much important as the belief that it can and will happen. It's also often done in semi or complete darkness. This again, helps one to believe by calming the doubts of the rational mind. After all, when it's over you can always blame the movements on your friends or find some other conventional rational explanation. Interestingly though, the phenomenon didn't always occur as a result of people's expectations. On some occasions people sat around a table expecting the "spirits" to respond to their inquiries with raps, or knockings, on the table. They were then surprised when the table began to tilt up and respond with movements.[87] This just shows you that higher levels of mind, which must control the phenomenon, can sometimes be unpredictable and give us new information and experiences.

Some influential people became convinced of its reality, such as Judge John Worth Edmonds of the New York Appeal Court. He attended one séance that was lit by burning lamps so that he could see everything that went on. There he saw a heavy mahogany table "levitate, swaying backwards and forwards even when they tried to stop it."[88] Everyone drew back and the table could clearly be seen suspended in the air without anyone around it to lift it. Edmonds, being a respected and highly regarded judge in New York, gave credence to the idea that these kinds of "impossibilities" could happen. So, after hearing of his accounts, the Governor of Wisconsin, Nathaniel Tallmadge decided it might be worth a look. He went to a séance and reported that, "a table moved when nobody was near it, and then levitated six inches off the floor while he was sitting on it."[89] There are thousands of such testimonials by people who witnessed telekinesis first hand, including the aforementioned scientific luminaries Alfred Russell Wallace and William Crookes, and of course the team in Paris.

The experiment I will describe involved four people including Playfair, Batcheldor, and two others. After experimenting with a smaller table, they decided to bring out a bigger table, described as "a circular monster four feet in diameter, weighing 46 pounds. It had a wooden top about an inch thick, and stout metal legs that slanted outwards, making it extremely difficult to tilt naturally." In darkness as they sat with their hands resting on top of the table, it began to vibrate and "tilt up and down with quite alarming force."[90] Playfair then decided to sit on the table and see if the phenomenon continued. It did. The table continued to vibrate, slide around, and tilt up on two legs with him sitting on it. This being a little uncomfortable and alarming, Playfair decided to get off and return to his chair. He placed his hands back onto the wobbling table when it began to actually levitate off of the floor.

"Then, with a thunderous crash, the table flung itself over on its side. If my foot had been in the wrong place, it would have been turned to strawberry jam," said Playfair. Alarmed by this he decided to get out of the way for awhile and retreat to the couch. Others also took measures to protect themselves. Then...

> "A few moments later, after some miscellaneous knocks and bangs, the table gave a violent jump. Batcheldor was ready for that one. He had his small pocket torch in his hand and switched it on briefly, just long enough for all of us to see that none of us had a hand or a foot within reach of the table. It was a skilful demonstration of Batcheldor's methods of verifying the phenomena discreetly and unexpectedly. It was the first time he had used his torch that evening and it came on almost at the moment the table hit the floor, to reveal Bill, Brian and me behind our chairs, with Batcheldor himself holding his torch. So who picked up the table?"[91]

They then proceeded to experience a full levitation of the table where it was at least a foot off the floor. For the finale of the night, Playfair got the idea that to be sure none of them were pulling any tricks, they should all climb onto the table while it was moving around. Playfair climbed on first and the others followed one at a time. When they were all on Playfair could clearly feel one back against his own and the backs of the other two against his elbows. He mused that if the table continued to move with all four of them sitting on top of it then he would finally have his proof that this was legit. After all, they later worked out that the total weight with all four of them on top plus the weight of the table would have been around 760 pounds. Anything that could move that kind of weight would have to be a very powerful force. Playfair describes what happened with all of them sitting on the table:

> "It moved. It very definitely moved. It did not leave the

ground, as I had hoped it would, but it twisted and slid as
before, in a series of brief but powerful motions that ended
only when this unbelievable PK-driven passenger vehicle
crashed into my chair, forcing it against the sofa, which had its
back to the wall. Before it had come to rest, I managed to bang
my feet together and call out for the others to do the same,
and I then slid forward until my feet touched the floor and tried
to get the table to move normally, by grasping the edge with
both hands and forcing my feet against the floor. No harm in a
little artifact-induction at this stage, I reckoned. The table
would not move an inch."[92]

Playfair got the impression on this night that there was definitely an
intelligence at work guiding the movements of the table, and it wasn't
governed by their conscious minds. So what mind was guiding the
movements of the table? Was it their subconscious minds? Their
superconscious minds? A disembodied "spirit" mind? We may never know.
However, it may turn out to be a cooperation of multiple levels of mind.
Consciously they may desire the experience and through some subtle
movements of the table may become convinced in the reality of PK,
thereby overcoming any conscious or subconscious doubts. Their
intentions, then, might be used by the superconscious mind, which
manifests and controls the information of the physical world, to give
them the experience with the superconscious filling in the details about
the specifics of how the table moves. One thing is for sure, the
intelligence that is responsible for the psychokinetic phenomena is
operating at a higher level of mind, in a higher dimension. This was
evident in the days of mediums, who used to go into trance in order to
produce the effects. From the trance state they were able to manifest all
kinds of psychokinetic influences, from tables and other objects levitating
to objects dematerializing from one location and reappearing in another.
Whether their own inner selves were responsible or other conscious
forces, what is evident is that these phenomena were produced and
effected by higher dimensional conscious forces.

For now there's one more curiously similar phenomenon to table
tilting, which is spoon bending. It was made famous by psychic Uri Geller.
He claimed to have psychokinetic ability and demonstrated this on
numerous occasions. On his website he lists a substantial number of
quotes by respected scientists attesting to his mind-bending feats.[93]

Parapsychologist Jeffrey Mishlove, for one, claims to have seen Geller perform "on the stage of the Zellerbach Auditorium at UC-Berkeley." He successfully bent a ring using only the power of his mind, "while the ring was held tightly inside the palm of its owner, Jean Barish." Mishlove knew Jean and can vouch for the fact that she was definitely not a "confederate with Geller." She told Mishlove afterwards "that she could feel the ring bend inside her hand, as Geller cupped his hands over hers." Mishlove also witnessed first-hand as Geller performed for others, including two physicists. In one instance while visiting the Berkeley physics department, Mishlove was standing two feet from Geller when he bent, using only psychokinesis, "the gold ring of physics professor Forrest Mozer." Mozer was astonished and said that he wouldn't have believed anyone who told them about what he just saw happen right in front of his eyes. Another time Mishlove was present when he bent the key of physicist Edwin May. Mishlove describes, "This key was bent so much that May had to hire a locksmith to fix the key in order to drive his Audi back home." Interestingly, the two physicists ended up trying to explain away Gellers feats. One insisted that he must have used hidden pliers, and the other claimed that it proved nothing because it was not done under controlled laboratory conditions.[94] As we learned in the last chapter, it's much easier to explain away anomalous data than it is to change your entire belief system in accordance with that data.

However, it doesn't matter if Geller was using trickery or not, he successfully convinced a number of children watching him on TV that he, and they too, could perform such psychokinetic feats. Investigative author Guy Lyon Playfair reports that numerous children who watched Geller perform on TV and believed he was doing it using only the power of his mind have found themselves able to replicate the phenomenon. Children don't have the fully developed rational/skeptical qualities of adults which makes them ever more able to obtain that instant faith necessary to perform such feats. Playfair explains, "When he tells them they can bend spoons like him, they do. Quite a few of these mini-Gellars have found that once they have done this, they learn that it is supposed to be impossible and then find that they cannot do it again."[95] Not surprising since we've already seen that it takes a certain level of belief for the mind to exercise its powers and change the way reality behaves. If we can become more conscious of these processes through which we co-create reality, then no doubt we can exercise this power to alter our reality both individually and collectively.

When ideas become real

The ability to alter reality through thought is a most intriguing idea. J. Newton Rayzor Chair in Philosophy and Religious Thought at Rice University, Jeffrey Kripal, has brought up a number of accounts of where fiction crosses over into reality in his outstanding recent books *Authors of the Impossible* and *Mystics and Mutants*. I wish to explore this a little bit because the implications are tremendous. For instance, he draws the parallel between the opening of the Esalen institute in Big Sur California in 1962 and the X-Men series comic book which debuted in 1963. Esalen institute co-founder Michael Murphy suggested "that the human potential includes all sorts of extraordinary powers that are 'supernormal,' from psychical abilities like clairvoyance and telepathy, to [. . .] apparent levitation or flight." Esalen was founded "as a kind of alternative private academy for this evolving future body."[96] It was a place where human potentials could be fostered, nurtured, and developed further. This is just a little too similar to the X-men mythology and Professor Xavier's school for mutants. Here we have a real life event followed by a work of fiction which draws on the same theme. But sometimes the time order is reversed.

I'm going to quote now from Kripal's masterwork, *Mutants and Mystics,* as he gives a number of successive accounts of when fiction crosses over into reality. The first two examples deal with comic book writer Jack Kirby and the last one with the sinking of the Titanic. I think you'll agree that these parallels are striking:

> "[. . .] Kirby drew, in 1959, a story about a face on Mars seventeen years before the NASA *Viking* probe took a photograph in 1976 of what many took to be a face on Mars. [. . .] In his *OMAC: One Man Army Corps* series [1974-75], Kirby drew and named a nonexistent technology called 'smart bombs,' drew an evil dictator named Kafka who looks remarkably like Saddam Hussein, and even had the dictator arrested in a ground bunker and put on trial for a series of crimes that replicate those of the Iraqi leader.
>   [. . .] One wonders what Morgan Robertson thought when the

Titanic, the largest ship on the planet and considered unsinkable at 880 feet long, crashed into an iceberg in the north Atlantic on April 14, 1912, just before midnight with far too few lifeboats. Robertson, after all, had published a novel in 1898 entitled *Futility*, about the *Titan,* the largest ship on the planet and considered unsinkable at 800 feet long, which crashed into an iceberg in the North Atlantic on an April night carrying far too few lifeboats. In both cases, the disaster happened because the ship captain, pressured by his company, was trying to break a speed record in clear violation of the safety regulations."[97]

These kinds of correlations just seem too uncanny to pass off as coincidence. And wait, there's more! Kripal also examines the work of French Sociologist Bertrand Méheust, who started out his career writing about UFOs. He found correlations involving fictional literature about UFO encounters that predated the actual encounters that were reported as fact. Kripal states:

"The focus of the work is a series of elaborate demonstrations of the historical coincidences that appear to exist between the narrative and visual frames of the UFO experiences of the second half of the twentieth century (1947 to the present) and the science-fiction stories of the first half of the twentieth century (1880-1945). Flying discs accompanied by buzzing noises, harmful or healing beams of light zapping people, abductions via levitation or teleportation, large-headed dwarves or humanoids, physical examinations on board a spaceship in a lighted room--point by point, detail by detail, Méheust demonstrates with texts and glossy pulp-fiction art how later encounters 'realized' or reenacted the earlier sci-fi scenes, and this down to astonishing details. Rhetorically, Méheust is mischievous here. So, for example, he will present three encounter stories without telling the reader which ones are 'fictional' and which ones are 'real' until a few pages later. Through techniques like this, he shows, over and over, that it is simply impossible to tell the difference between fiction and lived reality within the two sets of stories."[98]

What are we to make of this? Well, one way to interpret it is that the authors of these stories somehow had precognitive abilities which allowed them to channel future information into their stories. But a more *fantastic* way to interpret this is that these writers, through their thoughts, were contributing to the creation of reality; the hypothesis that the things we imagine and give creative expression to can become real through some mysterious co-creative process with the divine Source.

This all leads to the astonishing conclusion contemplated by physicists Bruce Rosenblum and Fred Kuttner at the end of their book *Quantum Enigma*. They state:

> "It has been wildly speculated that postulating a theory that is not in conflict with any previous observation actually creates a new reality. For example, Hendrick Casimir, motivated by the discovery of the positron after its seemingly unlikely prediction, mused: 'Sometimes it almost appears that the theories are not a description of a nearly inaccessible reality, but that so-called reality is a result of the theory.' [. . .] If there's anything to Casimir's speculation, might Einstein's original suggestion of a cosmological constant have caused the acceleration of the universe?"[99]

What they are getting at in no uncertain terms is that our theory of reality may actual instantiate that reality. It becomes real because we believe it. Might a belief be a request to the universe? Might the Source Consciousness, Super-Conscious, Mind at Large, whatever you want to call it, be listening to us? Co-creation of reality, our minds and God's mind working together--united--in the creation of reality. What immense power!

Mental beliefs and our experience of reality

We can also see this co-creative aspect of reality when we look at evidence suggesting that the things that are brought into our experience are influenced by our emotional and thought patterns. One aspect of this is in peoples psychological makeup and their life experiences. Many people, myself included, seem to encounter repeating patterns in their lives whether in relationships, work, or responses to situations. The psychiatrist Stanislav Grof considers these themes that reoccur in our lives "COEX Systems."[100] These are collections of experiences revolving around a specific theme in an individual's life, usually one charged with emotion. These themes can go back as far as birth and structure a person's responses to situations in life, as well as draw similar types of experiences to oneself. Grof gives one extreme example of a man who was locked in a dark cellar by his mother as a form of punishment. Later in life, he was forced at gunpoint by two Nazi soldiers during World War II to perform homosexual practices. He also vividly remembered the entire atmosphere of Nazi tyranny. These experiences combined to lead to a compulsive desire on his part to seek out partners who would lock him up in cellars and perform sadomasochistic acts.[101] So, our underlying emotional complexes, shaped by experiences that we've had, do influence our actions and thoughts, and may serve to draw us into certain life situations.

Another aspect of things being drawn into our experience can be seen in people's research and their findings. For example, former Harvard Psychiatrist John Mack, who famously worked with UFO abductees and wrote two comprehensive books on the subject, said in an interview:

> "And there's another dimension to this, which Budd Hopkins and Dave Jacobs and I argue about all the time which is I'm struck by the fact that there seems to be a kind of matching of the investigator with the experiencer. So what may be the archetypal structure of an abduction to Dave Jacobs may not be the uniform experience of, say, Joe Nyman or John Mack or someone else. And the experiencers seem to pick out the investigator who will fit their experience."[102]

What he's bringing up in the above quote is that different researchers have different ideas about the abduction phenomenon. They have different theories and interpret it in different ways. And it struck John as quite interesting that different investigators into the phenomenon of abduction received validation for their theories via a kind of matching of abductee to researcher. It's as if the universe drew the two together based on their congruent perspectives. Of course, it could just be that the different researchers are pulling out of the experiencers what they want to see. But an interesting finding by Grandmaster of Ufology, John Keel, seems to suggest otherwise. That is, reality really does work with our belief systems to give us the evidence we're looking for. Noting this strange correspondence of theory with observation, he states:

"Somehow the phenomenon reflects back material that supports whatever beliefs or theories motivate the investigators. Once, just for the hell of it, I doodled with the notion that some of our parahumans [aliens] might be aquatic. They were often seen wearing turtleneck sweaters and I wondered, not very seriously, if their turtlenecks might be concealing something like gills. Naturally, I didn't discuss this preposterous theory with anyone, but -- and this was utterly amazing to me -- the week I played with this idea I suddenly received a letter from a young man in Florida who described a remarkable encounter. He had been hitchhiking and was picked up by a very strange man who had gill-like flaps on his throat. I've never received any other reports of this type. It is a one-of-a-kind."[103]

Reality in this case truly was conforming to his beliefs. And you wonder if this is not more often the case than not. Take for instance the beliefs of a certain psychiatrist who thinks that demons sent by Satan can cause someone's emotional and physical problems.[104] She literally talks to these demons while her patients are under hypnosis.[105] Is this not simply a case of reality conforming to her preexisting beliefs, as well as the patients that were drawn to her, in the reality of Satan and demons?

However, it may not be the case that she had a prior belief in Satan and demons, but was presented with anomalous data regarding demonic possession, and then chose to believe and enter into the belief system. Then, as her belief grew, she was presented with more and more data to support it. This seems to be the case with others whose courses in life have been steered far from where they started due to an encounter with data that they could not deny, nor find a conventional explanation for.

Brain Weiss, author of many books on past-life regression, finds his patients complaints related to past lives they've had, but not once does he mention demonic possession. Weiss, having been trained at Columbia and Yale Medical School, at first didn't believe in such things as past lives. However, he was presented with anomalous data. His first case involved a woman who drowned in a past life and was deftly afraid of water in this life due to the past life influence. He had used hypnosis on her to alleviate her phobia only as a last resort. But upon making a simple suggestion to her subconscious mind to "Go back to the time from which your symptoms arise," he was bewildered when she started describing herself living in a valley in the year 1863 B.C.[106] She ended up reliving a flood or tidal wave that swept through the area and killed her by drowning. Weiss was perplexed but he could tell that his patient was sincere and not making this up; she was really experiencing this in her mind; it was an authentic reliving. Weiss proceeded over the next week to consult books on reincarnation, but was still skeptical. When his patient came back to his office one week later she said her lifelong fear of drowning had disappeared.[107] She still had some other symptoms though, so Weiss, with his interest in the matter peaked, decided to continue the hypnotic regressions. Eventually, after she was able to channel Weiss's father and son from the other side--spontaneously at that; he did not prompt her to contact them--and relay specific accurate information, including his father's Hebrew name, the fact that his daughter is named after his father, and that his son's death was due to a rare condition where his heart was backwards, he was convinced that this was for real.[108] He started seeing more and more patients using his hypnotic regression technique to take people back to past lives and relive traumatic events that were the apparent source of present life problems. He went on to write a number of books about the subject and become one of the leading voices in the field of past-life regression.

Harvard psychiatrist John Mack, too, didn't believe in the reality of UFO abductions before he started his work with abductees. Originally, a psychologist asked Mack if he wanted to meet Budd Hopkins, one of the pioneers of exploring alien abductions. Mack did not know anything about Hopkins and when his psychologist colleague told him that he explored alien abductions, Mack thought that this kind of thing "was absolutely crazy." But, the psychologist assured him that it was very real and he should check it out. So he decided to pay a visit to Budd Hopkins and take a look himself at some of these so-called "abductees." This turned out to be a life-changing experience for Mack. In his meeting with Hopkins and a number of abductees Hopkins had worked with, Mack describes, "I was struck by the fact that they were very regular people, ordinary people, except that they had extraordinary experiences. And that was mind blowing for me."[109]

Mack went on to work extensively with people who thought they'd been abducted and wrote his first book on the subject, aptly titled *Abduction,* in which he argues that their experiences cannot be ascribed to any kind of mental pathology.[110] They are real experiences that challenge the reigning materialist paradigm of modern science.[111] This belief was not well received in the academic world, however, which resulted in an investigation committee led by the dean of Harvard Medical School being formed to look into his activities. Mack didn't exactly know what led the elites at Harvard to perform this exhaustive:

> "15-month ordeal involving lawyers, appearances before the group by myself and my patients, faculty witnesses, the submission of massive briefs, reports from the committee and my response, documents concerned with standards and ethics, letters of support, and sworn affidavits by 30 patients with whom I had worked."[112]

This was, in fact, unprecedented for a tenured faculty member to be subjected to such treatment over his work. But Mack did have clue as to what might be going on when Adelstein, then executive dean for academic programs of the Harvard Medical School faculty, said, in Mack's words: "I would not have gotten into trouble, he said, if I had not said in my book that my findings required us to look at reality differently. Instead, I should have written that I had come upon a new psychiatric syndrome of unknown etiology."[113] This clued Mack in that this whole fiasco was not about his work with abductees, per say, but about challenging a deeply entrenched scientific ideology. Instead of trying to explain abductions away with some nifty sounding pathological label, he was implying that these people were really experiencing contact with Alien beings and that we needed to expand our definition of reality to be able to include such beings and experiences. Luckily, Mack put up a good defense and in the end he was kept on the faculty at Harvard and allowed to continue his research.

A similar story of initial skepticism followed by belief in the extraordinary is told by Dr. Michael Newton who wrote bestselling books on the topic of past lives and life between life. However, he started out as a traditional therapist working in behavior modification with people who had problems with sleeping, depression, or similar kinds of problems. He worked with hypnosis in this work, but didn't believe in past lives. If one of his patients asked him to take them into a past life he declined and said he was very traditional and didn't do those kinds of things. Finally, though, he had a patient that complained of a very sharp pain in his side. He had been to many doctors and had x-rays, and was told that it was psychosomatic, meaning the pain was all in his mind. He asked Newton to explore his childhood for a possible cause. Under hypnosis, Newton was unable to find anything related to his pain in his childhood, and then, very reminiscent to what happened to Weiss, Newton asked his subconscious mind to "go to the source of your pain." Suddenly, he was in a battle in France during World War 1 being bayoneted. Newton, being skeptical and an amateur historian himself, started questioning him about the battle and specifics such as what his division patch on his arm looked like, what battle it was, where he was, and who he was fighting. Having described all of these details accurately, Newton realized that past life regression was real. He was still a little skeptical, but now had an inclination to believe. Eventually he had another patient who was suffering from loneliness and being isolated from society. Again, he started by trying to find causes for her symptoms in early childhood but didn't come up with any reason she should be feeling the way she was. So, again he put her under hypnosis and told her to go to the source of her problems. She described being in front of a group of "spiritual soul mates." In this case, he discovered to his shock that he had touched upon a life *between* life; the afterlife. He went on to transform his practice into one dedicated to helping people learn about their immortality and explore the in-between-life state and past lives.[114]

These new age belief systems were not perpetrated by crazy people who were ready to believe in anything paranormal. Far from it, Mack, Weiss, and Newton were all traditionally trained and couldn't care less about these matters before they were presented with the data. Once they were convinced of the authenticity of the reported experiences, they were willing to explore and alter their initial preconceptions. After exploring and accepting the data, they then entered into a belief system, a mythology, that arose directly from their investigations and allowed them to understand the data they were getting. You almost wonder if they were not guided on some higher level into their respective areas of research. In any case, their cases show that anomalous data present us with a challenge and, if one is open-minded enough, can lead to the acceptance of a whole new belief system.

Summing up: The mind and the shaping of reality

In this chapter we've seen evidence for the impossible. That is, impossible according to the ideas about reality propagated by the current intellectual elite. But the ideas we live by, that sometimes we take as absolute truth, are really myths. We live by myths based on ideas. Ideas that somehow get turned into a reality based on our belief in them. Somehow we are shaping reality through thought. This prescient point was brought up by Jeffrey Kripal when reviewing the work of Sociologist Bertrand Méheust. Kripal calls it "the striking notion that human intellectual and social practices, particularly in their naming and institution-creating functions, somehow circumscribe reality, somehow create the real for a particular place and time."[115] This is a great mystery-- one that needs to be carefully examined.

It's certainly not always the case that one's experiences conform to their beliefs. Quite the contrary, we are often presented with data that doesn't support our belief system. (In science this is referred to as anomalous data and, as we've seen, it's often ignored.) For instance, other people who have different belief systems than us can present us with anomalous data, such as the Kahunas who walk on barely hardened molten lava. It could also be the case that a higher level of mind influences us in a new direction or compels us to expand our system of beliefs by presenting us with new information.

I propose that reality is the creation of a Source Mind, what Aldous Huxley would call Mind at Large. This Source Consciousness has unlimited energy resources and potential to create any reality. Astrophysicist Bernard Haisch compares the creation of reality to movie projection:

> "The esoteric traditions tell us that creation by subtraction is one of the fundamental truths underlying reality. [. . .] these traditions teach that creation of the real (the manifest) involves subtraction from infinite potential.
> Return for a minute to the slide projector. Turn it on without any slide inserted and project the pure white light onto the screen. That white light contains the potential to create every image you can imagine—your Thanksgiving family gathering, your trip to the Rockies, your high school graduation. Every one of these images, and an infinite number of others, are contained in potentia in the formless white light flowing from the bulb to the screen. All you have to do to project the picture you want is put in the slide that subtracts the proper colors in the proper places. The white light is thus the source of infinite

possibility, and you create the desired image by intelligent subtraction, causing the real to emerge from the possible. By limiting the infinitely possible, you create the finitely real.

Let's take this optical metaphor one step further. The white light of a projector can convey more than just a static image. Project a series of images in rapid succession and you create motion. Although, on one level, that motion consists of a series of still shots, when those still shots are projected rapidly enough, the sum becomes greater than its parts. The resulting "motion picture" is more than just the sum of the images created out of the white light. People and actions and even emotions are made manifest by acting upon the formless white light in just the proper way, in just the right sequence. A replica of our real world can thus be created out of the unlimited potential of the white light through a process of intelligent subtraction carried out in space and time. A virtual reality is thus created out of formless possibility. In fact, motion pictures are a concrete example of how a filter, the film, by selectively subtracting from a formless potential, can generate a virtual reality."[116]

We consider physical reality to be composed of energy. Well, the Source consciousness has infinite energy which can be filtered to create all of the various atoms and molecules that make up our universe. Literally anything can be created from this vast storehouse of cosmic energy by subtracting from the Source's pure energy. The physical dimension, in the final analysis, is just one of many dimensions being projected by this Source consciousness all the time. It is an actualization of potential.

As we've been exploring, we seem to play a part in this creation of reality from infinite potential. Our minds are part of the Source. We are like children of the Source who have come here to experience this reality. So, reality is a co-creative process between us and the Source. We inform the Source through our beliefs of that which we want to experience. Our beliefs and thoughts, in this sense, inform the Source about that which we want to experience.

This creation of reality from infinite potential goes on on an individual and collective level. An individual, for instance, may have a belief in the existence of fairies. So, they would look for evidence of fairies and read books about fairies. And the universe, being co-creative, would bring this sort of evidence into their experience. Then they might convince others who are primed to believe in such things to believe in fairies. They would then form a group and share stories and go over accounts of people who have seen fairies. Beliefs about the fairies would be formed and a thriving fairy community would spring up. Chances are, as the community of fairy believers grew, fairies would indeed become more common in reality due to our co-creative action with the Source. This increase in the number of fairies seen would then create a feedback loop with the beliefs of the fairy community. The fairy sightings and/or their interactions with people would affect people's beliefs about them, which would feed back into how the phenomenon presents itself.

If reality is subjective, and we play a role in its creation, then reality can be anything we want it to be. Before we can take an active participation in this co-creation with the Source, we need to be conscious and aware of this process. Most likely, it involves not just the conscious mind, but also those subconscious beliefs and "programs" which have been fed to us by society through our education, advertising, etc... This may be a barrier to creating the reality that we want for ourselves in this physical dimension. Developing a higher level of consciousness, a higher level of conscious awareness, may be a prerequisite before we can really take control of our reality. We need to advance beyond our childish notions of reality that limit the mind to the brain or the universe to random unconscious processes. It's time to wake up and see reality for what it is--unbounded, unlimited potential fueled by conscious, intelligent processes. We have advanced far in the realm of technology. It's time to step things up in the way of conscious development.

3

WELCOME TO MULTI-DIMENSIONAL REALITY

From the physical to the other-dimensional

I've already introduced you to the fantastic nature of physical reality. When we get into the experiences people have in other dimensions, it gets even more fantastic. We're going to take a trip through the larger reality and explore many nooks and crannies along the way. Strap yourself in because this trip won't finish for a whole lot of pages. I hope you're as excited as I am. We're going to zip through people's real experiences in other dimensions and, it's gonna be quite the ride.

One of the first things you learn when investigating the paranormal is that there must be other dimensions to reality besides the physical. We are never going to explain reality based entirely on this one physical dimension. Source Consciousness is not limited to manifesting one dimension and we're not limited to experiencing just one. There are lots of dimensions, planes, levels (pick your preferred term) to explore.

The first thing that really impresses one about experience in another dimension is how magical it is. That is, there are much fewer limitations than we usually experience in our lives here. It's literally like the world of Harry Potter. Harry Potter could even be said to be a fictionalized account of higher dimensional experience. It's telling that the children in Harry Potter board the train to Hogwarts by running through a brick wall, literally, by going into another dimension. This is a dimension hidden from the masses of everyday normal people. They are kept in the dark for the most part and only find out about this other world through some anomalous phenomenon perpetrated by beings from this other world.

Sound familiar?

Well, we've all heard of poltergeists and ghosts, mothman and springheel jack, aliens and angels coming here to scare, interact with, and sometimes help people. The more interesting thing is that not only can these denizens of other realms come over here and mess around with us, but we can visit their realms too. We don't get there by running through brick walls and vanishing like the children of Harry Potter, but there are some definite commonalities in the crossover between this world and another. Some kind of energetic phenomenon is involved. We know this because of the buzzing and humming sounds, as well as the vibration people often feel in their bodies preceding other dimensional encounters.

We can muse that the filter of the brain needs to be bypassed to allow one's consciousness to perceive information of another realm. The energetic phenomenon may also be involved in the separation of consciousness from the body. However, out-of-body explorer Rosalind McKnight contends that, "Even though the self experiences itself to be in movement or out-of-body, it is actually functioning in higher-vibratory levels within the physical body. I say 'within,' because in reality there is only within. In fact, life is not spatial, but dimensional."[1] I tend to agree with this statement. The physical is one dimension of Mind, whilst there are many others existing on different planes, levels of vibration, or frequency.

Energetic phenomena during the transition to another dimension

Let's take a look at some crossover phenomena that occur in the movement between this physical and other dimensions. A typical out-of-body experience (OBE), for example, will be preceded by a vibratory state. Out-of-body experiencer (OBEr) Steve describes, "I would go to bed and before I could go to sleep a buzzing sort of vibration would start in my head. The vibration would become so intense that I would start thinking that I couldn't stand it anymore and then with a soft sort of click, I would feel myself sliding or gliding out of my body."[2]

Sometimes even the air in the room can be tinged with electricity. As Katherine was laying down trying to sleep one night, she

"[. . .] noticed some type of static electric type charge in my
covers sort of repelling my sheet blanket with my upper heavy

one away from each other. The heavy blanket lifted and started to slide down off of me then I didn't feel any heavy cover on me at all but the sheet was still on me. I opened my eyes and found my heavy blanket now completely off of me and pulled it back on me again. As I laid there I thought, boy I hope that doesn't happen again!

Well the same electric type feeling came back and this time it was on my body too. At that point is where something weird happened. All of a sudden I was lifting from the bed and then in a different place altogether and it was real in every way. I felt everything and the background noise during the latter part of it was like a radio that had about three stations crossing over each other with static and garbled noises. I went all over the place sometimes walking and sometimes floating. In buildings and by streams and outdoor things. I went to a place with a tree and there were two dogs there. One ran up to me and it was BB the dog I used to have here that died violently by a neighbor boy shooting him multiple times with his .22 rifle. This was about five years ago that he died. I petted him and his fur was smooth. I thought to myself, boy I had forgotten how smooth and soft BB's fur was. He seemed fit and happy to see me and was playful."[3]

Here, the electrical sensation is clearly not just in her body, but somehow penetrates the physical atmosphere before she is whooshed off to "a different place altogether and it was real in every way." This electrical feeling is also frequently reported in connection to UFO Abduction experiences. For example, abductee Kim Carlsberg reports one experience preceding an Alien encounter thusly:

"I slipped under the covers and it hit me. A wave of energy rushed through my body, lifted my left hand to my forehead and glued it there. [. . .] The familiar sharpening of my senses began and everything in the room, including me, took on an electrical charge. Then I went to the other extreme and passed out."[4]

Upon becoming conscious again, she realized that she was in another realm, just like Katherine. However, she doesn't meet her deceased dog, but instead some humanoid beings. Sometimes there's even a visualization which accompanies the electrical and vibrating sensations. Robert Monroe, who is a Grandmaster of out-of-body travel, describes one instance where he could see "a ring of sparks" passing over his body when he closed his eyes. He says, "As the ring passed over each section of my body, I could feel the vibrations like a band cutting through that section. When the ring passed over my head, a great roaring surged with it, and I felt the vibrations in my brain."[5]

Monroe even once felt a beam of light initiating the vibrations. Laying on the couch for a quick nap one day, he describes how "a beam or ray seemed to come out of the sky to the north [. . .] It was like being struck by a warm light. Only this was daylight and no beam was visible, if there truly was one. [. . .] The effect when the beam struck my entire body was to cause it to shake violently or 'vibrate.'"[6] The commonality between this experience and UFO encounters is, of course, easy to see.

An abductee named Carlos was looking out over a bay from a field above it when he saw "a great, long, peach-colored shaft of light descending from the thick clouds to the surface of the water."[7] After taking a picture of this shaft of light he reports that the beam came over him,

> "which he regards as connected to sexual energy; as, for example, the frenzied orgasm he relived during hypnosis--his body seemed to go 'in layers . . . expanding and contracting in the mist.' He felt a vibratory tingling sensation in his body and then the sense that 'my body is dissolved or diffused into its transparency . . . The body just dissolves and goes up.'"[8]

Subsequently Carlos has a typical encounter with aliens aboard the well known UFO. Once, I myself experienced these vibrations, but unfortunately fear caused me to abort the process. I had prayed for a spiritual experience before going to bed. As I was falling asleep I saw in my mind's eye a monk-like figure smiling. He proceeded to use something like a sewing needle to touch what looked like cells or something in my body. What I visualized then was like water waves rippling out from the center. At the same time there was a loud noise like a humming inside of my head. I recognized that this sound was not external, but internal, meaning only I could hear it. Not that there was anyone else in the room with me to hear it. But anyway, the monk seemed to be working up my body touching different areas with his magic needle and me continuing to visualize the rippling waves as he did. The buzzing in my head got louder and my breathing also changed. It was kind of like I was breathing faster or heavier in shorter breaths. About the time the Monk worked his way up to my head, I saw a light, just like a yellowish orange light that was occupying my visual field. But by that point I was no longer in a sleepy passive state. The great buzzing and shift in breathing patterns as well as the light brought me to full conscious awareness of what was happening. The part I regret is that once I became conscious of what was happening I didn't just go with it and see what happened. Probably I would have had an out-of-body experience and shifted into another dimension. But instead, I experienced great fear and tried to pull out of the experience, to come back to normal reality. The fear worked, it aborted the experience and to this day I have not been lucky enough to have a repeat of the experience despite repeated prayers.

Visual phenomena during the transition

Other times, the transition from one dimension to another will not be accompanied by electrical or vibratory sensations, but visual displays. Dr. Raymond Moody performed experiments with mirror gazing, an ancient technique once used in ancient Greece for the contacting of the departed. They didn't use mirrors, but highly polished cauldrons filled with water.[9] The object is to stare into a reflecting surface and hold a certain intention, such as to contact your deceased mother. If you're lucky, your deceased mother will show up in the mirrored surface and talk to you.

Moody tested this method by placing a mirror three feet in front of a comfortable reclining chair. He inclined the chair slightly backward in order to create "a clear depth view of the mirror" where the person would not see their reflection in the mirror but only the darkness behind them. From the ceiling, he draped a black velvet curtain all the way around the chair and mirror. Finally, behind the chair he placed a lamp containing a dim 15-watt light bulb which provided the only illumination in the room.[10]

People interested in contacting deceased loved ones would go into this chamber and focus on the person while gazing into the mirror. The results were interesting and many people made contact, but I want to focus on the effects preceding an encounter. People often reported a mist clouding up the mirror or colors appearing. For example, one person said, "After a while it seemed that the mirror was clouding up with mist, like swirls of fine dust. And that just vanished and I saw forms like geometrical designs floating around momentarily."[11] He then felt like he entered the mirror and went to a platform where he met his deceased cousins. Another participant remarked, "I saw various images and forms and colors in the mirror, patterns mostly. Then, after a while, I was surprised to hear my grandmother suddenly start talking to me."[12] Another described, "I saw many clouds and lights and movement from one side of the mirror to the other. There were lights in the clouds that were changing colors also."[13]

Seeing colors, geometrical patterns and mists or clouds is not uncommon in the crossover to another dimension and occurs in many contexts. Abductee William Konkolesky reports an experience when he was playing in the backyard with a friend. He was "surprised by a thick white fog rolling in from the side of the house [. . .] I realized it was an odorless and very fine mist."[14] This strange mist just rolled on by him, but after it passed he noticed a fresh scar across his upper arm and, as we'll get to later, this is a classic sign of an abduction.[15]

Grandmaster of UFO research, Jacques Vallee reports an incident involving a Buenos Aires couple who were driving and suddenly found themselves "surrounded by a thick cloud of mist and fell asleep."[16] When they woke up, they were on a dirt road in Mexico with the paint completely removed from their car! Try explaining that one to the police. But it did happened and was reported in the press. They had to go to the Argentine Consulate in Mexico to make plans for their return, while their car was sent to the United States for testing.

Dr. Rick Strassman undertook a study of the effects of the chemical DMT, which is found in the shamanic brew ayahuasca and is known to produce altered states of consciousness. The study participants commonly reported colors and various geometric designs. One said, "There were visuals at the peak, soft and geometric."[17] Another referred to what she saw as "aggressive spinning colors."[18] Behind these kaleidoscopic colors seem to lie other dimensions. We just have to break through to the other side, such as in this experience:

"I realized what Rick said was true, that the most intense part of each trip was spent tangled up in these colors. This time, I quickly blasted through to the 'other side.' I was in a void of darkness. Suddenly, beings appeared. They were cloaked, like silhouettes. They were glad to see me. They indicated that they had had contact with me as an individual before. They seemed pleased that we had discovered this technology. [. . .] They wanted to learn more about our physical bodies. They told me humans exist on many levels [. . .] They told me to 'embrace peace.' I could feel myself begin to slip away from them as the drug wore off. As I started to come down, I saw these things from their world that I really can't describe. [. . .]"[19]

Transition Assistance

Sometimes, the denizens of another realm will even help you cross over into their dimension. Such is the case with not only OBEs, but many UFO abductions as well. First, let's look at an account of an OBE initiated with some help. In an interesting parallel to Kim Carlsberg's experience of her left hand gluing to her forehead, long time out-of-body experiencer in Brazil, Dr. Waldo Vieira describes how he was assisted in leaving his body by "extraphysical consciousnesses," his word for conscious beings in a non-physical dimension. He says that these extraphysicals helped induce the energetic state in his body and transmitted ideas to him about how to go about leaving the body.[20] At one point, he describes seeing "an invisible right hand [which] appeared resting on the center of my forehead, pressing the area between the eyebrows with the palm. I felt the energetic manifestations of the frontal chakra."[21] He then says that the vibrational state increased, he mentally concentrated on projecting, and left the body floating above it.

An abductee named Abby reports that during a camping trip with her husband-to-be in Mexico "their tent and surroundings were bathed in light, and she saw four luminous beings with large heads and thick necks and arms 'float through the side of the tent.'"[22] Grandmaster of UFO abduction research, John Mack reports that,

> "One of the beings, a female, calmed Abby by touching her on the forehead. Her body shook as she recalled the 'energy flow.' Then she remembered being lifted from the bed, floated 'sideways,' and taken 'through the side of the tent.' 'Wow,' she

said with wonder, as she felt a tingling as if all her cells were 'coming apart.' 'It was so quick and subtle,' she said, gasping, 'and then you're on the other side. Then you're whole.' [. . .] Her body seemed to remember 'how it's done,' she said, 'becoming separated molecularly' and then 'the coming together.' 'I unbecome and then I become.'"[23]

This is reminiscent of Carlos, who felt as if his body dissolved and went up into the UFO. It's as if these alien beings can change matter into pure energy and then back into matter again. But whether or not they are somehow disintegrating and reintegrating her physical body, or if they are just energetically inducing an out-of-body experience is an open question. Instead of it being a purely physical thing, it may be a process of shifting one's conscious awareness into a higher-dimensional body; a disintegration from the physical into a higher energy body useful for interacting in another dimension.

Aliens also like to help us cross over in a very Harry Potter like way, you know, by using a wand of course. Oh, I just love this one. John Mack had this to say about how one of his abductees abductions started:

> "She experienced unusual light streaming through her window ("as if someone had a big spotlight outside the room"), and had the impression of beings in the room--'one of them coming towards me with a big wand thing with a light on the end of it and pointing it towards me, and that was a half-dream remembrance.' She found that her right leg and then her entire body was becoming numb."[24]

Sometimes it's not described as a wand but as a flashlight:

> "The smaller being was holding an instrument that looked like 'the flashlights policemen hold with a head on it and it's pulsing.' [. . .] The smaller being lifted up the light, 'holds it there and hits me in the head with it.' After that Peter felt cold, shaking and shivering on the couch in terror as control of 'my functions' was 'shut down.' A shift occurred then--both at the time of the incident and in the session--and he felt more peaceful. [. . .] Then 'the little guy walks beside the couch. He does something with that thing again, like waves it over me, under me. How can he get it under me?' The light lifted Peter

off the couch and he 'felt really light.'"[25]

One time abductee Jim Sparks was experiencing the familiar whirling sound and paralyzation that he knew meant an abduction was upon him. Struggling, he managed to open his eyes and was surprised to see a being dressed in a hooded black robe that looked human, with blond hair, a light blond beard, and a moustache. He was standing over his bed "holding a thin, silver metallic rod or wand, about eighteen inches long." Sparks relates that,

> "When he saw that my eyes had opened, he leaned forward and started waving the wand around my face in a circle. As he did so, I started to lose control of my eyes. It was as if they were being forced shut by some invisible energy that apparently was coming from the wand. I was also losing consciousness. I yelled mentally 'No! No!' and struggled to open my eyes again. When my eyes opened, he looked even more surprised. He leaned in closer to my face with his wand, and waved it even faster until I could no longer fight it and finally blacked out."[26]

Lost time and the magic wand

This kind of thing is not confined to abduction experiences. Grandmaster of out-of-body exploration, Robert Monroe, describes an OBE where he found himself in a house in a rural countryside setting. He saw "a device," get ready for this, "*about eighteen inches long*, on the floor." Remember the wand Sparks saw and described as "eighteen inches long." Well, Monroe picked up the "rodlike" device and was then shown how to use it by a man standing outside on the patio. He relates how he was shown "how to 'focus' the device by moving the tube or cylinder back and forth, away for a narrow beam, and toward you for a wide, evidently more gentle, beam or ray."[27] He then was asked to try it out by pointing it at a man outside who was having a conversation with someone else. Monroe relates:

> "He said to push the cylinder forward for a narrow beam. I did, and pointed the device at the man outside just as you would use a rifle. I saw nothing, no beam or ray, emitted from the

device. However, the man beyond the window opening instantly slumped in his chair as if he were dead. I turned to my host, frightened and worried that I had unintentionally killed the person outside. He smiled, and told me to point the device again at the unconscious (?) man outside, this time pulling back on the focusing device to produce a wide beam. I did, and the unconscious man sat up and resumed his conversation as if nothing had happened."[28]

Monroe then proceeded outside whereupon he asked the man he had pointed the wand at if he had felt anything unusual or noticed any lapse of time. The man just looked at him confused and reported that he had noticed nothing unusual. One minute the man was rendered unconscious and the next minute he just returned to normal consciousness and continued his conversation as if nothing had happened. This lapse of time with no memory of what happened is not uncommon in abduction reports. One experiencer, Amy, heard a funny "beep" from her phone at 11:17p.m. She continued to study at her desk but felt funny and a little anxious. The next thing that happened was her daughter coming into her study at 12:07 a.m. She yelled at her for not being in bed, then a few minutes later she heard what sounded like the doorknob of the front door turning. She thought it must be her daughter looking for her thinking that she took the dog outside. So, Amy got up, turned on the porch light and looked outside, but saw no one there. She thought that was strange but went back to her study, whereupon she looked at the clock and saw that it was 1:27 a.m. She had lost an hour and twenty minutes. The time gap was seamless with her having "no memory of any disruption."[29] Another experiencer, Leah Haley, remembers driving home one night in the rain. As she got close to her neighborhood she saw "a bright white light shining" in her car. Shortly thereafter, she suddenly found herself standing outside of her car "wondering when it had quit raining and noticing an eerie quietness." She no longer saw the bright light, but did see "an object shoot through the sky and vanish, and a helicopter circling the area." She then drove home and looked at the clock to realize that it had taken her a lot longer to get home than it should have, but she could not remember what happened during the missing time.[30] The rodlike device used by Monroe to incapacitate the man has strong parallels to another of John Mack's clients who reported losing control of his body after the alien beings "touched him with a rod behind his ear."[31] Again, another experiencer reported a blunt instrument that "sent 'a shot, like a burst of energy' into his head [. . .] and left him feeling 'foggy' and disoriented."[32] Kim Carlsberg also reports waking up to the familiar buzzing sound and then going back to sleep again only to wake up later, "standing in the corner of the room as I observed two Greys pointing a sharp metal object at the tailbone of someone lying in the bed where I had been. Oddly enough, that person looked suspiciously like me."[33]

Who are these wizards with wands that can control our bodies and induce out-of-body experiences? And what is the nature of these magic wands? Well, we've already seen that they are some kind of energetic devices that can be used to paralyze people, produce numbness, energetic sensations, loss of consciousness and lead to OBEs. They also seem to be devices that can concentrate thought energy and amplify it in order to manipulate the external environment. For example, after making the unsuspecting man on the porch unconscious and waking him up with a wand, Monroe aimed it at a fire which caused it to go out.[34]

Sometimes abductees, too, are given one of these devices to try out. One of John Mack's clients reported being given "a metallic rod, about a foot long, or maybe a little bit longer [like eighteen inches?]. It's about an inch in diameter, and there's a thick, short antenna coming out of the top. It's silver/gray, and smooth."[35] He describes pointing the rod at a floating metallic ball and being able to control its movements through concentrated efforts (focused thought). Another abductee, Bonnie Jean Hamilton, reports an experience she had involving a golden ball that floated in the air and "emitted an intensely compacted energy."[36] She experiments with this ball by focusing her thought energy, which is then amplified by the ball, to make a plant grow, turn on a radio, and adjust the volume--all done through mental intent, thought energy amplified by the device.[37] It's starting to sound a little too much like the wands used in Harry Potter, whereby a wand is used in conjunction with a spoken command, or voiced thought, to do magic. It's almost like Harry Potter is a fictionalized account of other dimensional experiences.

For our final "wand" encounter, let's take a look at abductee Betty Andreasson Luca. She experienced being aboard a craft (UFO) and entering a "huge vivarium" where plants, and possibly animals, were raised indoors. She describes it as clean and beautiful with fresh air that is "so nice to breathe." She sees a pond teaming with fish and many trees, like some type of artificial nature reserve.[38] While she's there she sees the pond being drained and replenished with fresh water. This is an interesting observation due to the fact that people have often seen UFOs hovering over water with a hose going into the water. For example, former directors of the Ariel Phenomenon Research Organization, Carol and Jim Lorenzen, reported the experience of "a senior executive of the Steep Rock Iron Mines and his wife" who were on an outing at a lake in Ontario. After beaching their boat, they were sitting on the shore enjoying some food when, "Suddenly a shock wave was felt--the air seemed to vibrate." They looked out onto the water and saw "a large shiny apparently metallic object resting on the water about a quarter of a mile down the shoreline." The object was "like two huge saucers stuck together, lip to lip." Where the saucers joined there were some kind of "round black-edged portholes" arranged around the circumference. They then saw "little men" exit the object who they described as moving "like automations, [they] did not turn as normal beings do, but changed direction laboriously as though it was a difficult task, and turned their feet before turning their bodies." The beings were between three and four feet tall and wearing dark clothing with what looked like shiny metal on their chests. They witnessed "two bright green hoses" that went into the water from the object and could hear a humming sound. Their impression was "that water was being taken into the ship with one hose and that it was being discharged back into the lake through the other."[39]

Back to Betty's experience, after witnessing the refilling of the on board pond, she was prompted to sit down. Then some tiny little alien "babies" came in and stood next to her. She describes them as "perfectly proportioned" and "able to walk like adults," but only "twelve or sixteen or eighteen inches tall." These little babies just looked at her with curious expressions.[40] Next, a full-grown alien came over and opened a box with a "wandlike" instrument in it and asked her to hold it. She was prompted to direct the wand toward some shimmering lights in the trees that seemed alive, like living lights. She directed these lights with the wand and they landed on the little babies' heads right between their eyes. When Betty asked what the lights were for she was not told but felt that "It's something to do with the spirit of man."[41]

Dimensional travel continued

When examining these kinds of experiences, mostly we're dealing with a dimensional thing. After the energetic phenomenon ceases, or they pass out, experiencers either find themselves outside of their bodies accompanied by alien beings who float them out of their house into a waiting craft, or they find themselves already in another realm. For instance, abductee Jim Sparks woke up late one night to a strange sensation creeping up his body and a whirling sound that got louder and faster.

> "Then I felt a tremendous rushing feeling. I was accelerating as if I were going down the steepest grade of a roller coaster, without any kind of safety harness. [. . .] Then it all stopped -- the sensation of acceleration, the sound in my head, and the feeling of imminent death. My heart had calmed, and I was breathing normally. There was one big difference here, though -- I was sitting now on some sort of hard bench. 'Where the hell am I?'"[42]

The way sparks describes this sounds quite a bit like Near-death Experiencers (NDErs) who rush through a tunnel. One woman who feared for her life as her car was spinning out of control and about to be hit by another car reports, "I was in a black tunnel, or funnel, shooting through it incredibly fast [. . .] head first, spinning round the edges--like water going down a plug, or like a coil. There was a loud roaring--it was very noisy. . ."[43] One time, Jim Sparks struggled to retain awareness while he experienced the familiar whirling sound and sense of acceleration common at the beginning of his abduction encounters. He was sitting on the couch at the time and reports:

> "[. . .] the first thing I noticed was a crackling sense of static electricity all around my body. [. . .] Then the sights and sounds of acceleration hit me. [. . .] The living room furniture started turning transparent. My television, chairs, sofa, then the walls themselves started to fade away. [. . .] The whirling sound became so loud I almost blacked out. I could feel the soft fibers of my carpet against my bare feet. I could also feel my rear end sinking into the foam rubber sofa cushion. Slowly my feet began to feel cold as though they were dangling in the air. At

the same time I could feel cold hard metal under my butt. I looked down. My feet were dangling in the air as if propped on a hospital table. Yet at the same time I could see my feet firmly planted on my living room carpet. [. . .] 'Damn!' I said. 'I'm half here -- and half there....' But where was there? I certainly didn't seem to be on the alien craft. All about me were my furniture, my walls, my television, lamps, and pictures of my living room, yet they were almost invisible."[44]

Eventually, his familiar room at home completely faded out and he found himself surrounded by military personnel in some large facility that looked human in construction. He saw others wearing white lab coats and one of them, an Asian man of medium build, congratulated him by handing him "what looked like a high-school graduation cap" and explaining, "you graduated." Although he recognized the man, he did not have any memory of how he knew him and was equally perplexed at what he had graduated from. They didn't answer his inquiries, only came up to the table where he was sitting to congratulate him one by one. One of them then waved good-bye and he felt the "familiar low-pitched whirling sound" spring up again, heart pounding, and acceleration as the "rooms and lab equipment slowly faded, and my living room started fading back into place around me."[45] Spark's experience clearly shows the shift in dimension, as his conscious awareness fades from this reality and tunes into another, like changing radio or TV stations. This is accompanied by the familiar phenomena of a loud whirling noise, a sense of acceleration, and sometimes an electric-like energy in and around his body.

Many times it seems that the aliens, or extra-physical entities, actually work from another dimension to induce the person to sleep so they can be brought into another dimension. Consider in this regard the following experience:

"I was working in my shop. All of the sudden, I became very sleepy and extremely tired. I was so tired that I could not walk back to my house, [. . .] As soon as I placed my head down on the saw table, the alien that has always come for me in the past appeared. He seemed to appear through the wall. [. . .] He told me that I must go with him. The next thing I knew we passed through the wall and I was in a dome-shaped room."[46]

The best explanation is that the alien itself caused this unexpected and sudden sleepiness to fall over the abductee. Kim Carlsberg remarked that, "I usually become inordinately exhausted hours before an abduction. It is one of the little tricks they use to get me into bed to relax or sleep so they can do their dirty deeds."[47] These alien beings from another dimension seem to have some kind of subconscious control over our minds, being able to induce sleepiness and also, as our next case will show, prompting us to act in unusual ways.

Astonishing dimensional excursions

Sequoyah Trueblood

Native American Sequoyah Trueblood is no stranger to being prompted by other dimensional beings to lay down so his consciousness can be freed up for a joy ride in another dimension. While sitting by his pool one sunny afternoon watching his children swim with his wife sitting next to him, he felt a strange compulsion to go inside. Without knowing why, he packed a bag, changed clothes, and drove to the airport. From there he boarded a plane to Oklahoma City and, after arriving, called a friend to drive him to another friend's house in Norman. Once he arrived at the friend's house he felt strange and asked to lie down to take a rest. After laying down and taking some deep breaths to relax, "he saw a kind of vortex of swirling lights 'like a rainbow,' into which he was sucked." Next,

> "Sequoyah then found himself standing in a beautiful garden surrounded by hedges. He was now wide awake, 'no different than me sitting right here with you now.' In front of him was a silvery saucer-shaped craft and a shimmering small silver-looking being standing on steps that were coming down from the bottom of the craft. The being looked grayish and had a large bald head with large eyes, and Sequoyah sensed it was 'androgynous,' neither male nor female. The being communicated telepathically that it was from 'another place' and had been sent to take him there because 'they' wanted to talk with him. [. . .] Once inside the craft, Sequoyah heard no sound, but through a small round window he saw the moon, the sun, and 'millions of stars' instantly go by. Then they were hovering over a beautiful white city in what he felt was another

planet in another realm or universe. [. . .] Getting down to the
ground occurred in an instant and seemed like
'dematerialization and then rematerialization,' Sequoyah
recalled."[48]

He then gets taken on a little tour of the city where the people, male
and female, live in harmony, have fair skin, wear white robes, and have
"hair that was glowing like the color of sunlight." They don't need food
because they get all their nourishment from the air they breathe.
Beautiful white buildings no more than three stories tall lined the streets.
He was taken to a park where he saw a marriage ceremony and was
taught that in this place "people just decided to spend their time
together," and there was no effort to control or manipulate one's spouse
as there was on Earth. He was told by a leader figure to go back and teach
others "about the great peace and love that fills all creation." He was
taken there "to be shown the potential of the human race on Earth." He
was also instructed about past experiences he had that were preparing
him for this task. He was told that some of his more difficult experiences
in life had been "to help him overcome fear" and to gain the awareness
and strength necessary to serve humanity in his teaching role. After being
told he could stay for awhile, Sequoyah began to panic thinking about
leaving behind his "family, car, home, [and] possessions." He says, "I
almost went into a psychosis, for this was my first lesson in realizing how
attached I was to the material world." He was told that this attachment to
material things was a major impediment for people on Earth, and he
needed to realize that, "You're only here temporarily. These bodies of
yours are just tools that you've been given to learn with." He then went
inside the craft and was transported back to the garden where his journey
began and returned to his physical body again through the vortex.[49]

Neale Donald Walsch

This kind of dimensional undertaking prompted by the "other side" is
not restricted to abduction experiences. Neale Donald Walsch, who wrote
the immensely popular series *Conversations With God,* went into his
bedroom one night after fighting with his then wife. It was early in the
evening and he wasn't ready to go to sleep, but he had nothing to do so
he decided to try to go to sleep anyway. He laid down and started
questioning why it was so hard for people to just get along. "What does it

take just to simply get along?" he asked. Lying there pondering this question he said he just sunk back into hopelessness, and then he describes falling asleep "as all the energy drained from me." As he fell asleep he says, "I had the very clear experience, the very clear knowing, that I was about to have the deepest sleep of my life. And instantly I experienced myself being sucked off the bed. [. . .] I felt literally sucked up off the bed." He describes this as like a fly getting sucked through a vacuum cleaner hose. "Suddenly, I looked down and there I was on the bed. And I looked strange, I looked very strange. And I knew instantly that that was not me. And I thought, 'Oh, my! I thought all this while that I was that.'"

This classic out-of-body experience was followed by him flying out of the room like lightning into a tunnel racing toward a light at the end. Coming out of the tunnel, he found himself in the presence of "expansive Light that existed everywhere, but it seemed to be brighter and hotter in the direct center, although it was everywhere." He felt "enormous emotional warmth and incredible peace" coming from this Light. He then was telepathically communicated to by the Light, which said, "You are perfect just as you are, and I am so pleased with you. You must be told that you are incapable of doing anything bad or wrong." After mulling this over and thinking that couldn't be right as he had experienced doing lots of bad things in his life, he was told, "This is a process by which you simply become grander than you were before. You call this evolution. It is a process. It is simple and it is utterly acceptable, and no one has ever been damaged by you nor could anyone ever be."

His perspective then switched over to a different environment with millions and zillions of particles resembling pulsating lights, all interconnected units of energy, that blinked on and off changing shape and color. When one unit changed shape the one next to it changed shape, which continued in a Domino fashion. It was, "A vibrating pulsating overall mass created by these individual particles that never lost connection with itself, but at the same moment maintained the individuality of each individual, each separate element." He describes it as "jewelry of the universe," with the most amazing colors he's ever seen (and he's colorblind in physical life). He wanted to get closer to this "unspeakably beautiful energy." But he found that as he tried to move toward it, it moved away. He then realized that it was all around him and it was simply impossible to move closer to it. He was told that, "You can no sooner get closer to that than you can move your eyes closer to your nose. As you move it moves for the very simple fact that you and it are one." He experienced himself as part of this swirling mass of pulsating lights and was told, "You are already where you are trying to be, submerged in the Oneness. Simply experience it."

He then shifted into another location where he saw in front of him a huge book that held all knowledge. He was told that his soul had yearned to know, and that this yearning had been pure, not for ego reasons or to make himself better than others. He had just wanted to know and was now being given the answer to everything. The pages flipped by and he absorbed all the knowledge in this humongous book. Afterwards he just thought, "how elegantly, unbelievably simple it all is, the whole system, Life, Everything." Finally, he was back in his body.[50]

That is an incredible, fantastic experience. And we see that he was intentionally taken to this other realm to experience a different side of reality. This Presence, this Light, had induced his deep state of sleep, even though he wasn't particularly tired at the time, in order to give him this experience that he had been yearning for. And this is not the only experience like this.

Barry Smith

Another fascinating experience of this sort which gives one the same sense of depth and profundity is that of Barry Smith, as told by Grandmaster of Religious and Paranormal Studies (a title I have bestowed upon him) Jeffrey Kripal in his book *Mutants and Mystics*:

> "Suddenly, he became really, really tired, 'as if the force of gravity had multiplied itself a hundred-fold.' He fell into his couch unable to move, unable to resist whatever force was overtaking him, unable to open his eyelids. He fell into a deep sleep.
> Now Smith found himself lost in an utter and infinite blackness. There was no linear time in this 'perfect nothingness.' But there was 'a supernatural calm' and 'the completeness of forever.' He eventually recognized all of this as a Presence, as an 'embodiment of all Time and all Place.' Once he accepted it as such, this Presence shifted dramatically and took a new form, that of Dimension. Smith is careful to explain at this point that our three dimensions of space cannot capture

the sense of what he knew then, namely, that 'a fourth and possibly a fifth or even more elements existed that all the words and grammatical tools in the English language could not describe.' [. . .] 'I had no heart, no lungs, no electrochemical systems pulsing in a red meat factory of materiality. My consciousness was my sole, prevailing existence.' Pure transcendent Consciousness. Nor was there any clock time, no linear 'before' and 'after.' That sense had been replaced by another kind of dimension, the dimension of 'meaningfulness.'

As the meaning grew, another form or movement appeared-- Energy. This Energy appeared as an immense, black wave moving from a point of origin impossibly far away and expanding exponentially as it approached his sense of self. He understood that 'in perceiving this movement, I had perceived light.' As this black light 'broke upon my shore of perception, just in front of me, perhaps a million miles away, I realized that the wave was actually blacker than the ultimate black of the surrounding infinity!' And then, to his utter confusion, came a second wave, blacker than the first. And then a third, and then a fourth, each blacker than the previous, each bringing 'uncountable experiences transmigrating Time and multi-dimensional space; the histories of trillions of otherwise unknowable events since this universe spawned consciousness. Each wave contained all the experiences of the previous waves, vested in the depths of all the knowing that exists everywhere, but is as yet unrecognized by the human race.'

Barry Smith--if we can speak of such a person in such a state-- could not long bear such a cosmic perspective, where endless waves of time flooded him with trillions of bits of experience and linear time was replaced by meaningfulness in an Everything All at Once. He certainly understood that his humanity 'was immaterial to the cosmic everything that has always been, and shall always continue to be so.' But he just wanted to be back in the city, preferably with his girlfriend in the bed he knew that she was curled up in at the moment.

[. . .] And so Smith panicked. In a kind of phantom body, he began to scream and throw himself about in a desperate rage. He wanted back to his goddamned three dimensions. [. . .] The omnipotent intelligence that was the Presence responded by trying to correct his 'disorder,' but then sadly acknowledged what the frightened little earth creature willed: 'I have never before or since experienced such a deeply palpable sense of regret as that which pervaded the Presence that had journeyed so determinedly to my door of self. First it was a momentary confusion about my actions, then an adjustment of sorts, then a profoundly pained retreat that accepted my free will to return to my existence as a flesh-bound being.' And then it was over. Smith came back into this world and looked at his watch. It was 3:45, Monday morning. He had been in infinity for sixteen hours, earth-time."[51]

I'm struck by the deep similarities of their respective experiences, and also by the profound differences. They both experienced being unexpectedly pulled into a deep sleep. Walsch experienced seeing an ocean of pulsating lights of beautiful colors and shapes, while Smith experienced an ocean of infinite blackness. Walsch experienced receiving vast amounts of information from a book, while Smith reports immense waves of light energy, which ironically were perceived as "blacker than the ultimate black of the surrounding infinity," containing the information of trillions upon trillions of experiences. And finally, they differ in the way they handled the experience. Walsch accepted the experience and was happy to absorb the knowledge he'd always wanted to know, but Smith was frightened and didn't know how to handle all of this information he was being given by the Presence. He couldn't handle it and just wanted to be back in his comfortable safe bed in physical reality.

The mistake people make when looking at other dimensional experiences is to assume they aren't real. It's kind of like our dreams; most people assume that dreams are just hallucinations, that there's no real substance to them. But even dreams can be experiences your mind is having in an alternate dimension. The energetic phenomena described in the beginning of this chapter, as well as the fact that most of the encounters happen while asleep seems to indicate that one's consciousness needs to be disconnected from the physical in order to cross over. When you enter another dimension, you're usually entering a higher plane, a higher level of energy, a higher mental dimension-- whatever you want to call it. The reason it seems unreal is that, for one, the experiences had in these other dimensions are so unlike the experiences you have in physical life. Abilities such as floating around, travelling by thought, communicating telepathically, and using your concentrated intent to alter the environment are mostly alien in our physical world. Second, we are not taught to acknowledge these higher realms and sometimes don't remember much of what happened in them.

Remembering other-dimensional experiences

Concerning memory, Grandmaster of out-of-body exploration Waldo Vieira reports that the longer and more distant his excursions out-of-body are, the harder they are to remember.[52] He says, "At times, it seems that a thick veil falls over my recollections."[53] Intriguingly, others, such as Lucid Dreamer Robert Waggoner, report that their memory of a long OBE is clear and detailed, but memory of a long lucid dream--one in which you become consciously aware while in the dream state--is more difficult to recall in detail.[54] Then again, near-death experiencers (NDErs) often report that their NDE memory is crystal clear even many years later.[55] So, the ability to remember the experience may just depend on the person.

The situation gets more complicated when looking at abduction experiences because the aliens often deliberately inhibit memory of these events. Even while under hypnosis to recover abduction memories, the memory can be blocked. In a hypnotic regression session, Grandmaster of Ufology and abductee himself, Raymod Fowler reported that he was "programmed to forget" certain incidents regarding an abduction he had.[56] In another memorable event, abductee Betty Luca reports under hypnosis, "And he's [an alien being] telling me, I must, I must not, I must not remember this for a long time. Until they decide when it should come forth. I must not, I must not remember this, [sniff] until they decide."[57] Following this abduction encounter her telephone rang and, getting up to answer it, she heard a high pitched woman's voice on the other end asking, "Ees Jimmy they-a?" When, after exploring another unrelated abduction, this same thing happens again it leads to the healthy speculation that this call is there to reinforce the posthypnotic suggestion to forget about the abduction experience.[58]

Abduction memories may surface years later or be triggered by an external event that poses some similarity to the original experience. An abductee named Pat had an encounter in 1954 involving "scenes of a brilliant orange ball of light, little gray entities both inside and outside the farmhouse, and, most disturbing of all, military personnel on the property." However, she didn't remember these events until more than thirty years later in 1986 when "it all came flooding back into her consciousness." At first she thought she must be crazy to be having these bizarre memories come back to her after such a long period of time. But, she verified with her sister and brother that these events did take place. Specifically, her sister recalled the aliens and military personnel and her brother remembered his interactions with the military personnel.[59] This makes you wonder about the cryptic statements made by aliens to many abductees about how, "you'll remember when the time is right."[60] Well, maybe the time was right for Pat to know about her abductions and be a part of UFO researcher Karla Turner's book on abductions called *Taken*. This wouldn't be surprising as some other abductees in her book either contacted her because they had a compulsion to do so or they were specifically told to do so by the alien beings.[61]

Learning from other-dimensional experiences

Chris meets Peco: A lesson in dimensionality

When there is memory of the event, the experiences people have in these other realms can be quite fantastic and exhilarating. They can also teach us a lot about reality. A man named Chris had an interesting experience after doing drugs and taking a good sized hit from a massive balloon filled with nitrous oxide. After having an out-of-body experience and watching from above as his friends had a good ole time drawing on his face with a permanent marker, he felt an acceleration and reports:

> "I felt as if I was falling into it at amazing speed, but the tunnel appeared to be falling with me as I never seemed to close in on it. There was an ever increasing sound enveloping below me. It was a strange, metallic, "Shirp shirp!"..like when swords meet in battle. As odd as that description sounds...then again, "Shirp shirp, PING!". That ping scared the hell out of me as it was so loud and direct it shook me to the core, if I still had one. I realized that maybe I was on my way to hell, and this was the sound of Satan's bullwhip. It doesn't make sense now, but that's the thought that occurred to me.
> There was a loud, SHHHHHHHIP. Like air being blown out of a balloon...suddenly. A white all encompassing light...white and bright as anything I could describe, though not painful to the eyes. This faded, oddly, to a white sand beach...I thought maybe this would be heaven. I scanned my horizon, it was the

most beautiful beach imaginable...literally. I believe that everyone's version of the afterlife is custom fitted to that person. This was my construct. I suddenly was aware of another presence.

There was a man, in his late forties with a three day beard growth. I felt normal now. I felt as I had before, with my body intact. I asked him, "are you God"? He said in broken English, "No, me llama Es' Peco". I don't speak Spanish, so I may have spelled that wrong. I was struck with a feeling of absurdity. I have died and gone on to spend eternity with an immigrant named Peco'? Who can't even speak English? I did a gut check to try and ascertain if I was in fact dead. Either I'm dead, or this is one hell of a buzz, I thought. Not laughing, but just registering it to myself. Suddenly Peco began to talk to me, not in words, but in pictures and concepts that he relayed to me via mind speak, or telepathy..but I think telepathy supposedly worked the way verbal communication did...regardless.

I asked in my head if there is reincarnation, and he answered to the positive by showing me some of my former lives, I could see different aspects of these lives and they were not familiar, but they were strangely comforting. Like looking at a younger brother or something...too odd to describe.

I asked Peco where we were and he showed me a mental picture of a planet more green than blue. He minded me the word, "Midus 22". I asked him if this was another world and he answered back that it not only was another planet, but another dimension parallel to my own. I asked if this planet was inhabited and he just nodded, as to say 'over there'. I turned around and seen a family interacting much as they would on Earth. They were throwing giant green stones that were shaped in spheres. I marveled at their strength and Peco minded to me that it was the way gravity affected certain objects, not the strength of the children. I was astounded.

I asked Peco how long it took me to get to Midus, high school physics taught me that you could not travel faster than the speed of light. Peco looked at the watch on his arm, shook it, held it to his ear, and then shrugged in a totally annoying way. Even in the afterlife, I thought. He minded me that I had not traveled distances, but through dimensions. He gave me a brief lesson using rudimentary examples. In my mind I seen a bed sheet. Objects roll around, traveling to different places on the sheet. Large objects make an indent in the sheet, this is an objects gravity. Large objects, making a large indent, have other small objects rolling into it. Apparently in an orbit; of sorts. Then he took a dagger, in my mind, and stabbed the sheet. Sticking his finger through the sheet, he then pointed at me. So I had not traveled a distance to get to Midus, I had traveled through the fabric of space/time. So this is death I thought. Coool. Odd, I know. But that was an appropriate response at the time. This was all done without speaking.

To make a long story shorter. Peco and I spent time walking around, he explained different aspects of the alien environment. It was nice. It was a very pleasant planet. Like Montana in the spring time. I began to feel a burning sensation in my chest; the most intense pain of my life/afterlife. Peco sent me a message. He told me that it was not my time yet; He relayed that though we had spent over an hour together, time was not proportionate between this universe and my own, so only a short time had passed on earth. I thought to him a thanks before I had a sense of falling. Not the sudden and intense acceleration as before, just like falling a great distance.

I woke up on earth to my friend's mother, who was a nurse at the local hospital, performing CPR on my body."[62]

That is still, without a doubt, one of the coolest NDEs I have ever read (and I've read hundreds, maybe even a thousand). And it's very insightful. I especially like the lesson on dimensionality. Also we even get an in depth look into telepathy, which is the standard form of communication in other dimensions. Peco communicates by relaying pictures and concepts directly to his mind.

Duane's NDE – telepathic communication

Another fascinating NDE where telepathy is used concerns a man out on a rafting trip with his daughters and some neighborhood kids. He has the unfortunate accident of falling in the river and drowning. After struggling to free himself from the treacherous waters, he finally gives up and:

"Then as if I was a toddler and my father had grabbed me by my Osh-Kosh overalls and lifted me over his head I was standing several feet above the water. I could feel the sun shining down warming my face but no longer was it too bright to look at. The gentle breeze was comforting. My thoughts turned to the sound it made rustling through the vibrant green leaves of a large tree to my left. My focus on the tree left me actually feeling the breeze blowing through the leaves as if the leaves were my fingers and the tree was a part of me. All of my senses were heightened color brighter sight crisper and better defined the smells and slight mist of water on my skin were wonderful. A bird began to sing behind me and as the melody gained my attention it was as if the trees and brush hiding it parted and I had full view of this tiny creature. Not only could it be seen and heard but I could feel that the bird was happy even joyous just to exist and this feeling became a part of me. Although much of what was going on around me was to my left, right or behind me I did not have to turn to witness it for I could see a full three-hundred and sixty degrees around me comprehending many things going on in the immediate vicinity at once.

As I stood in awe of what was going on a voice came, clear as the voice of one very near you, asking me 'What do you want to do?' Turning my attention to the sight before me I began to take a survey as it were checking to see what could be done. My youngest daughter was just climbing out of the water some seventy-five yards downstream near the raft. The oldest had already walked some thirty or forty yards along the rocky bank upstream of the raft. I on the other hand was here and my lifeless body there which was no problem for me as my old life was as much of a dream to me at the moment as the afterlife is to most of us now. No feelings of pain or sorrow only such peace and love as few have ever known. After gathering this information it was like I simply bundled it up in a neat little package added a bit of no comprehend and handed it to the entity that had asked the question. The response was immediate 'What do you want to do?' and the answer much the same as the survey was taken again. As I looked at my eldest daughter, whom I found out later was trying to guide the older boys to what then was my lifeless body, it was as if someone took me and threw me inside of her. I saw from her eyes heard with her ears and understood all that she knew and felt at that moment but was only a bystander in her world. This twelve-year-old faced with this terrible situation was about as calm and logical as anyone could possibly be. My sister is ok now, she had also fallen from the raft and been caught in the same undertow but had a life jacket on so was safe, the other girls are ok too. Now I have to save of my dad. These were her immediate thoughts. Then as fast as I had been introduced into my daughters world I was returned to my own and stood above the water in the same spot as before. The voice came again, 'What do you want to do?' It asked. Finally I understood I needed to choose between the icon before me of raising my daughters and the life I had so recently left. Or this new existence and a life I knew was with my heavenly father for I could feel his love emanating from a point up and to my left just behind me. A love that reminded me of the peace and contentment one feels as a small child being rocked gently in the arms of their mother after a perfect day. So strong was this feeling of love, peace and well being that I was torn as to what should be done. There was no coercion for me to choose this or that nor was I led to believe that one choice would be better than the other. The matter was entirely up to me. Knowing that my daughters really did need me, and how much I truly loved them, I almost reluctantly made the choice to return and do all in my power to raise them the best I could. To communicate this decision I simply took all the information and feelings gathered and handed it as a whole to my friend whom was never seen. Saying that 'I wanted this,' that is the icon before me and all that it represented."[63]

Here's a great example of telepathy, defined by Duane as a bundling up of all of his thoughts and handing this bundle of thoughts over to the entity who asked the question about what he wanted to do. Similarly, another near-death experiencer (NDEr) telepathically communicated "a transfer of information in the form of an inexplicably complex matrix," which included layers and layers of information about "events, thoughts, incidents, and groups in all their relationship complexities."[64] Yet another describes it as "a definite communication, but not like words being exchanged. Rather ideas, thoughts, emotions directly exchanged."[65] Robert Monroe reports receiving out-of-body communication in the form of *rotes*, which he defines as "packages of total experiential information to be absorbed instantly and stored thought balls."[66]

More on telepathy

Telepathy is a direct mind-to-mind communication method that allows us to communicate faster and with fewer limitations. Think about someone else who is listening to their favorite music with headphones on and feeling happy. If they communicate this experience to you through spoken word, then you can imagine what they are experiencing and relate it to your past experiences to get an idea of what it's like. But what if they could directly transfer the sensations of happiness and even the sound of the music to your mind? It would be like recreating the energy patterns going on in their body in your body. That's what we're dealing with when it comes to telepathy. Ideas, concepts, complex associations, feelings, sounds….any experience can be directly transferred from one mind to another. Of course, you may interpret that experience based on your own past knowledge and experiences, but the experience itself is intuitively known, directly felt.

Telepathy seems to be a universal communication method of consciousness. You think thoughts in your head, whatever language you think in, and those thoughts are received by the other consciousness. But the words you may have thought won't be received. Instead, the underlying meaning of your communication will be picked up and then translated back into the familiar words and concepts of the recipient. So, even if you meet someone who speaks in a different language, telepathic communication won't be a problem.[67] Monroe says, "you have received the message (thought) and your mind has translated it into understandable words."[68] Again, you're picking up the meaning of what the other person (mind) is trying to communicate and translating it back into words and concepts familiar to you. Also, during telepathy, you can pick up the thoughts of another instantly. There seems to be no need to transfer information through some medium. It's more like an idea pops into my head which I wish to communicate and you instantly pick up that thought. On this point, one of famed NDE researcher Dr. Raymond Moody's participants, in a mirror gazing technique designed to allow contact with deceased loved ones, noted that when speaking to his deceased mother through the mirror, "At first I verbalized my questions, just said them right out loud. But before I got a few of the questions out, the answer would come back to me in a mental form. There was no sound of her speaking, I just knew what she was saying. I asked more questions, just by thinking them."[69] Similarly, an abductee remarked to John Mack that, "He's answering the questions before I even think of them."[70] Finally, Kim Carlsberg spoke telepathically to a shape-shifting liquid energy form and referred to the communication as "instant knowings."[71]

Discussing the work of famed psychic Ingo Swann, Jeffrey Kripal says that, "he suggests that telepathy does not happen *between* minds or brains but *within* a shared universal consciousness."[72] This "shared universal consciousness" may exist in what quantum mechanics refers to as "non-local space." This is an invisible space (not directly observable) where the elementary particles and forces that make up our universe "have all become one and as such do not exist."[73] It is a space of infinite possibility where the wave functions, or information, of the physical universe are stored and, "all information is always and everywhere immediately available."[74] Cardiologist Pim Van Lommel speculates that this non-local space is the origin of "complete and endless consciousness."[75] Telepathy occurring between two beings may just be an exchange of information in this shared consciousness, where time and space do not exist. That way, the communication could literally be "instant."

Telepathy, however, is not always such a perfect communication method. It should be noted that in physical life, and possibly out-of-body, there can be what's called analytical overlay. This is when the mind takes the telepathically received information and then interprets it based on the recipients repertoire of ideas, concepts, and associations. In other words, the mind tries to make meaning out of the received information and form it into a construct understandable to the recipient. This leads to the recipient experiencing something in their mind that slightly differs from the original telepathic signal. Investigative journalist and author Guy Lyon Playfair gives one example where the experimenter drew a pair of scissors and tried to mentally send the image to a recipient. The recipient drew dumb-bells which, like the scissors, looks like two circles joined together. The experimenter said try again, whereupon the recipient drew a pair of spectacles. Finally, on the third try he drew scissors.[76] In each case, he had the right idea but his mind formed slightly different images based on his associations with the telepathic information coming through.

Grandmaster of Lucid Dreaming, Robert Waggoner, tried out some dream telepathy experiments in which one person tried to send the image of a picture to another person who intended to dream about the image. On one such occasion, Waggoner was the recipient and dreamt of "a round, bald head with a funny, triangular eye area, looking out over a valley." It turns out the image his sender was trying to send "was of a hot air balloon hanging over a valley." Furthermore, Waggoner says, "The balloon had an interesting triangular eye shape on it, much like the triangular eye shape that I saw in the lucid dream."[77] Trying to make sense of the data he was receiving, his mind had reconstructed the balloon image with a triangular eye shape into a face with a bald head and triangular eye. We can receive telepathic data, but it seems that our minds need to make sense of that data and ascribe meaning to it. In order to do so, our mind uses past experiences and associations to construct a meaningful picture.

Experiencing the mind of another

Duane's NDE is also remarkable in that he was able to experience the consciousness of a tree, bird, and even his own daughter. I have coined a term in this regard called *conscious entanglement*. This is how telepathy works and also the experience of being aware of other forms of consciousness. Duane says, "My focus on the tree left me actually feeling the breeze blowing through the leaves as if the leaves were my fingers and the tree was a part of me." Again, in regards to the bird he remarks, "Not only could it be seen and heard but I could feel that the bird was happy even joyous just to exist and this feeling became a part of me." Finally, in regards to his daughter he relates, "it was as if someone took me and threw me inside of her. I saw from her eyes heard with her ears and understood all that she knew and felt at that moment but was only a bystander in her world."[78] It's as if he entered into and experienced what it's like to be the leaves in the tree, the singing bird filled with happiness, and his poor daughter trying to figure out what to do.

Entanglement is a term used in quantum physics to refer to the instantaneous connection between two particles from the same source that were split apart and went their merry separate ways. If we measure one particle, the other particle will automatically and instantaneously show a complementary measurement.[79] So if one particle is measured spin up, the other will be measured spin down. Even though separated by great distances, the two particles act as though they are both complementary aspects of one single particle. In conscious entanglement there is an identification of some other consciousness with one's own so that whatever the other experiences is experienced by you. You retain your individual perspective with your own memories, knowledge, and thinking processes, while at the same time being aware of the thoughts, feelings, and sensations of another. One example from the literature will help show this process of conscious entanglement. This involves a participant in Holotropic Breathwork, an exercise in inducing altered states of consciousness pioneered by transpersonal psychiatrist and Grandmaster of consciousness research Stanislav Grof. Describing what she experienced in an altered state, one woman said:

> "After a powerful sequence of being born with triumphant emergence into light, things started to quiet down. I was feeling more and more peaceful and calm, and my experience seemed to acquire incredible depth and breadth. I had an increasing sense that my consciousness had a distinctly oceanic quality until I felt that I actually became what can best be described as the consciousness of the ocean. I became aware of the presence of several large bodies and realized that it was a pod of whales. At one point, I felt cold air streaming through my head and had a taste of salty water in my mouth. A variety of sensations and feelings that were alien and definitely not human imperceptibly took over my consciousness. A new, gigantic body image started to form out of the primordial connection to the other large bodies around me and I realized I had become one of them. Inside my belly I sensed another life form and knew it was my baby. There was no doubt in my mind that I was a pregnant whale cow. And then came another wave of the birth process. However, this time it had a different quality than the previous episodes. It had gargantuan proportions, as if the ocean were stirred from its very depth; at the same time it was surprisingly easy and natural. I experienced my genitals in the most intimate way, with all the nuances of these birthing activities associated with profound visceral understanding of how whales give birth. What I found most amazing was how they use water to expel the baby by sucking it into their genitals and working with hydraulic pressure. It seemed significant that the baby was born with its tail first."[80]

Literally, her consciousness became entangled with that of a whale's, so that she could feel and sense all that the whale felt and sensed. She accurately describes the birth process, similar to Graham Farrant in the last chapter who accurately experienced the processes concerning the sperms race to the ovum. She was able to accurately describe it based on her direct experience of being a whale. That is the type of knowledge afforded by conscious entanglement, direct experiential *knowing*.

In the end, all is consciousness. Any subject can become the object of their study through conscious entanglement. Even the consciousness of inanimate objects such as rocks have been reported during altered states.[81] As we explored in the last chapter, consciousness has no boundaries. Consciousness exists at every level and within everything. Consciousness is All. Next, let's turn our attention to the thought directed nature of other dimensions.

Shaping the experience

Believe!

Just as our beliefs have a profound effect on our physical lives, they have an even more noticeable effect in altered states of consciousness. Robert Waggoner refers to something called the expectation effect, which means that your expectations about what should happen in the lucid dream or out-of-body state usually do happen. Waggoner gives an example while out-of-body, "if I decided to fly through a house, I might find a window to fly through where no window exists in waking reality."[82] His intention of flying into or out of the house creates the window for him to fly through. Similarly, talking about the lucid dream state he says, "pinching myself in the lucid state, for example—actually hurt. But if I pinched myself while telling myself it would not hurt, it didn't hurt. [. . .] My experience would normally follow what I lucidly expected to feel."[83] Waggoner describes how once he was flying through a wall in the lucid dream state and then had just a twinge of doubt about his ability to fly through it. Lo and behold he got stuck halfway through the wall. Fortunately, he quickly realized that he was lucid dreaming and actually could fly through the wall, so he "expected" his way through it. Commenting on this he notes that, "Just that little bit of doubt tinged my expectation, and my situation symbolically reflected my mental state."[84]

Co-creating with the deeper Self

One of the most interesting examples given by Waggoner of creation based on expectation and belief in the lucid dream state is when he was apparently feeling a little horny:

> "I am in school with friends and acquaintances. I head off to my school room and open the door. In opening the door, I realize that I no longer attend college. 'This is a lucid dream,' I happily say to myself.
> Lucidly aware and feeling energized, I look around the classroom of young people and desks, wondering what to do in this setting. An idea comes to me. Since I don't see enough desirable women in the class, I intend to change that! I shout out to the class, 'I want to see more attractive women in here when I open this door again!' I step outside the room and shut the door behind me.
> In the hallway, I wonder, 'How long do I have to wait out here for more women to appear? Five seconds? A minute?' I feel like a kid on Christmas morning, not sure what to anticipate but hoping for the best. I wait a few seconds longer in the hallway and decide, 'That's enough time.'
> I open the door into the schoolroom and find a U-shaped line of perhaps fifteen attractive young women, completely naked. Amazing! It worked! I walk along and briefly touch each one, awestruck by the ability to create all of this."[85]

Keep your dick in your pants Waggoner! Oh, I kid. Too bad for Waggoner, the dream didn't continue any longer. Essentially though, Waggoner is creating an intent in the dream which he fully expects to manifest. But as he himself comments later on, he doesn't supply any of the particulars. He simply asks for more attractive women. Who's the mastermind behind the scenes who can manifest this intention in his reality? Who brings the women to him and determines their characteristics? Certainly he is not consciously supplying this information. Waggoner knew that something hid behind the dreams, some inner tinkerer behind the scenes that threw together the dream scenes and manifested his intents.[86] It was like he was communicating with a Higher Self that worked with his desires and expectations to construct reality. As we discussed in the last chapter, this may not be so different from the way things work in physical reality.

To experience something in the lucid dream state, as Waggoner did with manifesting the ladies, all one has to do is shout out an intention to the Higher Self of what you want to experience. In one instance, Waggoner made the announcement in a lucid dream that "All thought-forms must now disappear." One group of people in his dream disappeared, but another group didn't. He said the group that stayed in the dream gave him a disdainful look implying that he should be able to tell the difference between a thought form and a real conscious being.[87] Another example is mentally or verbally announcing an intent to project your consciousness into another life form, like a bird, and experience what it's like to be a bird flying through the air.[88] That, or you could just verbalize an intent to see a bird and one would appear in your environment. Again, the Higher Self would fill in the details left out of your intent such as what kind of bird it is that appears. But you have to be careful because the exact wording of the intent matters. For instance, if you requested to look for art in a lucid dream, you would find yourself "doing just that—literally looking for art—trying to find art somewhere in" the lucid dream. But if you requested to look at art you would instead find yourself in a room looking at works of art.[89]

Not this time: When the deeper Self throws you a curve ball

However, just as physical reality doesn't always jive with our intents and expectations, so too does higher dimensional reality sometimes throw us curveballs. Once when Ed Kellogg was lucid dreaming, he asked for a superstring to manifest so he could see one. However, moments later he heard a voice that instructed him, "it does not seem a good idea to do an experiment of this type, at this time, as you still seem too unfocused and distracted."[90] It seems that some higher level of mind blocked his intention.

Sometimes unexpected events occur in the dream. In one lucid dream, Waggoner was flying around knocking off people's hats in the crowd below. However, on the third attempt a hand reached up from the crowd and stopped him in mid-flight leaving him struggling to get free. He had not expected this result at all and it got him wondering if the dream figures had a mind of their own, or perhaps the tinkerer behind the scenes had decided to teach him a lesson.[91] Sometimes the characters in the dream even argue with the lucid dreamer about their ontological status! When the lucid dreamer tells them they are merely dream characters, they get angry and assert that they are real or that the dream is real. This kind of backtalk can be very surprising to the lucid dreamer.[92]

Waggoner found that to be able to consciously direct the dream state required a constant focus on one's intent. When not focused on exactly what you want to do, the hidden Self behind the dream takes over and introduces new elements that were not intended by the lucid dreamer. So, when you're not actively taking part in the dream creation, some Higher Self, or hidden bricoleur as Waggoner puts it, takes over and leads the dream for you.[93] In other words, we can either take an active participation in creating the reality that we want, or sit back and let reality happen.

Things are much similar when it comes to out-of-body experiences. Astral Projector John Magnus has lots of practice exploring extra-physical reality. Just as Waggoner found asking the dream useful to have a certain experience, Magnus too found that it was useful to shout out commands while astral projecting. For instance, if he was in a blank void space, he would shout out "Clarity Now!" and an environment would "spring into existence out of nothingness."[94] However, he experimented with many other commands while out-of-body, including "Go to X Now!"[95] Just fill in the X with a place or person you want to visit in the projected state. Again, while out-of-body it is easier to manifest your expectations, but sometimes it doesn't work.

Once John Magnus went to a park while out-of-body that was filled with people picnicking, camping, and having a good time. He had an inner knowing that he shouldn't fly in this area, as that might be alarming to some of the campers who weren't accustomed to such feats and may not even realize they're not living a physical existence. Magnus meanders around and asks one of the female picnic goers if she'd like to have sex with him. (What better to do really) She, however, declines for the moment saying she has to change and listen to the band. Maybe afterwards they can get it on. About this time it's getting dark outside and everyone meanders on over to the nearby club where the band is playing. Horny ole Magnus, thinking he's about to get laid when this is over, floats to the front of the line eager to get in. However, he's abruptly stopped by the doorman who demands to see his club stamp. He tries to create a stamp with his mind, but his creation doesn't look anything like the actual club stamp. It isn't really a problem though because, remembering he's not in his physical form, he just decides to float right through the wall and into the club. Unfortunately a little while later the doorman and some other bouncers come in and head towards his direction to throw him out. He quickly leaves through the wall and serendipitously meets the woman who he had seen earlier standing outside, now wearing a short skirt and looking oh so fine! They go off to a secluded area of the park where there's a pool, and quite conveniently a bed next to it.[96] Well, you know what happens next.

We can muse here that his only real limitation was not having enough knowledge about the stamp to create a replica using his mental intention. Another time Magnus decided to go snooping around his neighbor's room while out-of-body. However, he floated to her door and found that he couldn't pass through it. Passing through doors had never been a problem for Magnus. He thought maybe his own conscious was stopping him because his intentions weren't the best. He gave up quickly and then tried to think of his girlfriend with the intention of visiting her. However, nothing happened and he soon found himself in the street outside his parent's house where he continued to explore.[97] Robert Monroe didn't always go where he wanted to while out-of-body either and speculated that this had to do with conflicting desires between the conscious and superconscious minds.[98]

A further source of limitation: When two minds conflict

Sometimes the thoughts and intentions of others will affect your out-of-body state. Once OBEr Waldo Vlelra was walking around what he calls an "extraphysical colony" while out-of-body. This is a place, of which there are many, where conscious beings who are not physically embodied reside. You can think of it like an after-life realm. He found that everyone was walking in this city. When he tried to fly it took an immense amount of effort, and even then he was only able to fly at low altitude. He thought maybe it had something to do with the denseness of the atmosphere, as it was a particularly gloomy place.[99] Could it also have been due to the collective thought patterns of the colony's citizens who didn't accept flight?

Once Waggoner intended to visit a friend in the lucid dream state and proceeded to fly in his friend's direction. However, as he continued on he saw "a strange black zone" that he understood was impenetrable, and which effectively blocked his way. The next day he found out the reason why he couldn't visit his friend. The friend told him via telephone "that he had intentionally determined not to be bothered by others in his dreaming that night."[100] His friend's intent not to be bothered had prevented Waggoner from visiting him.

An energetic barrier can be used for this purpose as well. Abductee Bonnie Jean Hamilton had the feeling that aliens, or "star people" as she calls them, were coming for a visit that night. So, before bed she went around the room visualizing a protective white light circling her room. Her intention was to create a barrier so the aliens couldn't enter her bedroom (in the higher dimension which they visit her in). After going to sleep and entering an alternate dimension, she looked out the window to see two star people on the roof outside her bedroom window. They were unable to break through the energetic barrier she had visualized and enter her room.[101]

What we've learned

So, limitations while in higher reality may be due to many factors. One may be the competing intentions of others. Another factor may be conflicting desires between your conscious mind and a higher level of mind. Finally, your own doubt or habitual thought patterns may prevent you from actualizing what you want. We examined before the expectation effect, which says what you expect to happen often does in higher dimensional realities. Waggoner gives one example of flying. If you try to fly using physical effort, like flapping your arms, it will be extremely difficult and require more effort than if you expect to be able to fly easily just by willing yourself in the air with no physical effort.[102] Vieira, similarly, says that our habitual patterns of thought determine how we react to events and situations in higher dimensional reality.[103] So, if we think in a certain way our mind will structure our reality and actions in accord. Now let's take a look at some more interesting higher dimensional experiences.

Experiencing higher consciousness

Once while out-of-body Magnus had an itch to check out higher dimensions, so he commanded "My frequency is increasing." He then spins and goes upwards. After stopping his rotation he says, "Everything around me is blindingly bright. There are white and turquoise lights, arranged in vertical layers. I can't make out anything except bright lights."[104] He then quickly goes back to his body as he starts thinking about how changing his frequency like this usually pulls him back to his body. However, he did get a glimpse of very high dimensions which are filled with light and very fine energy.

Waldo Vieira is no stranger to the upper dimensions as he describes in his book, *Projections of the Consciousness*, going to a higher dimension where he "saw only lights and vivid colors of indefinite shapes." He describes how beings in this dimension had no form, "only centers of energy radiation constituting familiar consciousnesses." He says, "it was a free consciousness. A lucid vortex of vibrant energetic emanation; free from matter, form and space..." He describes "an unimaginable level of mental elevation, unapproachable with Earthly descriptions, and indefinable in known terms." He also experienced "A constant 'nirvanic orgasm.'" Finally, he sensed a "Higher Consciousness" which manifested itself through everyone present and even spoke to him in the form of a silent inner voice. He says the influx of information "emanated from an invisible, impersonal, superhuman consciousness with a serene knowledge, and no emotionalism."[105]

This impersonal, superhuman, emotionless consciousness is spookily reminiscent of Robert Monroe's encounter with an impersonal beam of light. He was lying down one night when he felt bathed in a powerful beam of light "that seemed to come from the north, about 30° above the horizon." He describes it as "a very strong force" with an intelligence beyond his comprehension. This intelligent force:

> "came directly (down the beam?) into my head, and seemed to be searching every memory in my mind. [. . .] This intelligence force entered my head just above the forehead, and offered no calming thoughts or words. It didn't seem to be aware of any of my feelings or emotions. It was looking impersonally, hurriedly, and definitely for something specific in my mind."[106]

He has another encounter with this same intelligent light force and realizes that he is "inextricably bound by loyalty to this intelligence force, always had been, and that I had a job to perform here on earth."[107] Another time the beam searches his mind to find out what controls his breathing, giving Monroe the impression that this intelligence "was looking for some substance that might permit breathing in earth atmosphere." He was shown that currently they use a pouch hung on a belt at the waist to breathe on earth. Reminiscent of a UFO, after the intelligence, via the beam, was finished searching his mind for this information, "They seemed to soar up into the sky." Monroe relates that, "It is an impersonal, cold intelligence, with none of the emotions of love or compassion which we respect so much, yet this may be the omnipotence we call God."[108]

Are we being used?

From reading Monroe's second book, *Far Journeys*, one gets the impression that our emotions are a type of energetic fuel used by higher level beings. He refers to our emotions as "Loosh," the purest form of which is Love. Love was shown to him to be a pure white light, while other emotions, such as greed, envy, anger, etc... were different colors on the electromagnetic spectrum.[109] However, when you combine the colors/frequencies of these other baser emotions, the combined total will produce pure "Loosh," or Love.[110] He was told that "Someone, Somewhere....requires, likes, needs, values, collects, drinks, eats, or uses as a drug a substance ident Loosh."[111] In fact, this "Someone" cultivated Earth as a garden of sorts for producing Loosh, to be collected and used "Somewhere." "Someone" cultivated the environment of Earth to be supportive of life, and then set about creating first simple life forms and later working his way up to plants, animals, and eventually humans. "Someone" organized a group of "Collectors" to supervise the loosh production and periodically harvest it. All life forms supposedly produce loosh, but humans are the crowning achievement of Loosh production with the ability to produce large amounts of it, and even sometimes produce the purest distilled form of it when we are engaged in a loving act.[112] This Genesis type narrative is certainly interesting and leaves you wondering if higher intelligences don't feed off of our emotions as we feed on the meat and plant matter of lower life forms. Certainly abductions do point to this possibility.

One of Mack's abductees communicated from the perspective of the aliens that, "it's like candy to a child your emotions to us. It is like a drug that we enjoy very much."[113] Kim Carlsberg reports an encounter with a mantis insect type creature that she feels has a high level of authority in the alien hierarchy, like the queen bee. And apparently it's thirsty for her mind as she describes how, "It hungers for my mind--it must devour my every thought, my every emotion as if these are its sustenance." She tries to resist but it's futile and in the end, "Its eyes thrust forward--a papery, wrinkled forehead presses against mine. Its skeletal frame shivers in victory while it 'swallows' my mind whole!"[114] Finally, one of the volunteers in Dr. Rick Strassman's experiments with the psychedelic molecule DMT reports:

> "When I was first going under [the influence of the drug] there were these insect creatures all around me. They were clearly trying to break through. I was fighting letting go of who I am or was. The more I fought, the more demonic they became, probing into my psyche and being. I finally started letting go of parts of myself, as I could no longer keep so much of me together. As I did, I still clung to the idea that all was God, and that God was love, and I was giving myself up to God and God's love because I was certain I was dying. As I accepted my death and dissolution into God's love, the insectoids began to feed on my heart, devouring the feelings of love and surrender. [. . .] They were interested in emotion. [. . .] They feasted as they made love to me [. . .] it was extremely alien, though not necessarily unpleasant. [. . .]"[115]

Insect type creatures who emotionally rape us! That's wicked sick. Aliens interested in our emotions, feeding off of our "Loosh"? Well, maybe Monroe wasn't so far off the mark after all. The aliens may just be the collectors of the Loosh. Abductee Betty Luca says the aliens, "are the caretakers of nature and natural forms--The Watchers. [. . .] They are curious about the emotions of mankind."[116] She goes on to say that they collect the seed of man and woman and also that of every species of plant. It is their responsibility to take care of the Earth. I ask, caretakers of natural forms, or Collectors for "Someone's" garden? You be the judge.

The thought-directed nature of experience

I want to get back for a second, before we stray too far into the hinterlands of "What the fuck!?," to creation while projected in an out-of-body state. Robert Monroe states that, "'Mere' thought is the force that supplies any need or desire, and what you think is the matrix of your action, situation, and position in this greater reality." Thought "is the vital creative force that produces energy, assembles 'matter' into form, and provides channels of perception and communication."[117] Where you go in this "astral" world is "grounded completely within the framework of your innermost constant motivations, emotions, and desires."[118] However, these desires may be subconsciously rooted and not necessarily things that we consciously think we want to experience.[119] Furthermore, like attracts like, so "when you leave your body, you end up in surroundings that match your thoughts, among people who think like you do."[120] You can either be in your own mentally created astral world, or you can join with others in the multitudes of consensus realities created by the thoughts of multiple consciousnesses.

John Magnus speculates that changing reality is much harder in consensus worlds, like the physical, because of the multitude of beings with thoughts about that reality.[121] It's very evident that Magnus sees reality as a mental creation based on our collective perceptions and beliefs. We, as a group of beings, create reality and share perceptions through what Magnus calls "mind transference." He says, "Your perception is picked up by people around you and used to reinvent what you see into their own perception." But it's not as if there is an external world that we are all perceiving. "Your perception is a self-invented picture" according to Magnus. "Everything around you is your perception. There is nothing underlying it. You are creating your perception, and people who see the same are creating the same perception, influenced by your perception [via mind transference]."[122] He has a great point here and that is: our minds create the reality that we see. A perfect example is Tom from the last chapter, who was hypnotized to believe his daughter was invisible. Literally, by going into the deep structures of his mind and inputting a belief he was able to change his subjective perception of reality. Ultimately, reality in and of itself may be a vast void of nothingness, a nothingness that is also a plentitude because it contains every possibility in unmanifest form. We create reality through thought, thought that manifests energy into being.

In higher dimensions, we easily see this molding of reality through thought. Robert Monroe was fighting with an entity while out-of-body who wouldn't leave him alone, so he "visualized two pieces of highly charged wire" and "mentally stuck them into the side of" the enemy. Then the entity deflated and seemed to die.[123] Abductee and astral traveler Bonnie Jean Hamilton also has practice using focused thought energy to manifest a needed object. She woke up in an alternate reality where her husband was yelling excitedly about a UFO that landed in the yard right outside the house. Bonnie, afraid that they might be negative entities, took precaution by focusing her thoughts and using subtle energy to create knives for each of her family members. After three dark grey star people disembark from the craft and float into her home she realizes that they are friendly. She goes to greet them but they jump back in fright. She looks behind her to see what's so scary and then realizes that she still has a knife in her hand. At that point, she says "I opened my hand and willed the knife to disappear."[124] And that's really the secret to creating and shaping your environment in a higher dimension. You just have to use focused thought. Bonnie describes it as focusing her thoughts and "drawing energy from around me, pulling it into a new form."[125] Similarly, if you want to fly around or go somewhere, you just have to think of going there or will yourself up in the air. Belief and expectation play a big role here. If you don't believe that you can do something, then trying to do it won't help you much. You have to believe.

Going to a cemetery in the out-of-body state Waldo Vieira saw bright and pretty objects in the graves, such as "a small reclining angel that glowed like a light bulb." He intuitively understood that these objects were thought creations generated by the loved ones of the person buried there.[126] So, whenever you think of something, that object of thought is actually created on a higher plane of energy, in a higher dimension. It is also important to note that emotion gives power to one's thought in order to materialize it faster. Waggoner says, "Emotions energize the area of focus."[127] Vieira says, "The essence of everything in life is thought, emotion, and energy. What we think with passion, we materialize and impregnate with life by emitting energy."[128] Emotion fuels our thoughts giving them much greater power than if not accompanied by emotion. Therefore, the focus of our thoughts can manifest in higher dimensions much easier when fueled by emotion. I started this paragraph with an example of how human thought actually creates that reality on a higher plane. I wish to explore further now how our thoughts and fictional creations here on Earth actually create that reality in higher dimensions.

Giving shape to the unseen world

One night Robert Waggoner had the following lucid dream:

> "I seem to be at a college like Michigan State, where I seem to be taking two courses, one on 'forms' and one on 'philosophy.' After talking with others about the classes, I say, 'It's not like I actually have to weld anything together, like a rhombus and an octahedron . . .' Then they all pipe up, telling me that the test involves exactly that--welding things together!"[129]

What Waggoner didn't know is that another fellow lucid dreamer named Ed Kellogg had awoken about the time he had his dream to read a book "about a boy named Robert who in a lucid dream learns about mathematics and shapes by cutting out and pasting together figures, including an 'octahedron.'" It seems that Waggoner had actually lived the scene in the book. The scene in the book had come to life in his lucid dream.

Experienced out-of-body traveler Robert Bruce writes about a time when he floated through the wall of his house while out-of-body and then found himself "in a strange new world." He describes the scene in detail. There was a rail fence in front of a dilapidated building and a nearby lake. The atmosphere was gloomy, misty and damp. He saw a huge man about eight feet tall come out of the shadows accompanied by a black dog. The man didn't reply to his calls, just climbed the fence and proceeded toward the lake. Bruce checked out the building and didn't see anything inside. Then it hit him. He recognized the scene as that of a painting he had hanging on his wall, and realized he was now inside the scene in the painting. He had crossed through the wall at the exact spot where his painting hung. He was literally inside of his painting which had come to life in the astral world.[130]

Kim Carlsberg reports speaking to a shape-shifting entity one night. She woke up in the middle of the night and decided to meditate. After beginning her meditation, she then felt vibrations moving upward through her body and in an instant she "was standing in the entry hall of an empty house."[131] Going outside, she saw that it was "an ordinary suburban environment." The only problem was that "a dark, ominous form that resembled a spacecraft" was approaching. She observed as this craft changed shape, shifting "from square to oblong to oval in constant motion like an organic, breathing life-form."[132] She said, "It moved through the air, further transforming into a tide of pure energy, and rushed toward me." Then, this pure energy form took the shape of "a dozen perfect bodies" resembling trendy young adults like you might see on Melrose Avenue in Los Angeles. They wore hip clothes and sported "unconventional hair styles." Since Kim regularly interacted with such types in her line of work as a commercial photographer in L.A., she realized these must be "images to facilitate communication." Now I will quote picking it up as she begins conversing with the entity:

"Patterns of nonverbal communication danced between us. My questions were answered before I could finish the thoughts, but I needed to hear my own voice to verify my experience. 'I know what you are, you're a shapeshifter,' I announced, directing my words to the young man on the end. 'That's correct,' he said sweetly. I was so excited I couldn't contain myself. 'So will I ever evolve to be like you?' I directed my question to one of the females and realized, no matter which face I spoke to, I was addressing one being, one consciousness. 'You will never be like me, we are not the same.' Of course, I was disappointed by the answer but another question immediately jumped from my lips. 'What is your natural form?' The same male responded, 'You would recognize it as something similar to your liquids.'

Then it was my turn to answer the questions. A female, with her head tilted to one side and looking very confused, asked, 'Why do the females of your species love more?' Every word and expression was infused with total, unconditional love. The innocence and sincere interest in her query brought me to tears. My voice quivered as I explained, 'It's not that we love more, it is simply a condition in our society that men do not express affection as easily as women.' Her eyes lit up and twinkled. 'I see,' she responded joyfully, and I knew she fully comprehended.

We stood in silence briefly, then I received an idea that there weren't very many of its kind in the universe. Another thought caressed my mind, and I realized it was time for the being to go. The communications were not verbal; they weren't even words inside my mind, which is the way telepathy occurs when I'm with the Greys. They were instant 'knowings.' It was the most efficient mode of exchanging information I've experienced thus far.

   We shared mutual admiration and appreciation for the interaction, and I felt the most tender, pure love I think I have ever known. [. . .] [After hugging each of the figures goodbye] They formed a straight line at the door and, as the first male stepped over the threshold, his physical body became fluid. He then pulled the other bodies into the river of light he had just become. Once again in the form of pure energy, the being flowed to the street, regained the shape of a craft, and zipped away.

   I was suddenly aware of my body sitting on my bed vibrating like a guitar string that had just been plucked."[133]

If the encounter itself wasn't amazing enough, she then called a friend to tell him about the experience and found out some startling information. It seems that the shape-shifting entity she met corresponds very well to a character named 'Odo' on the TV program *Deep Space Nine*. The character on the show is a shape-shifter whose natural state is liquid, and claims that "there aren't many of his kind in the universe."[134] These details all match up exactly with the being encountered during her other-dimensional excursion. You wonder what came first? Did the TV character inspire the creation of its astral counterpart or did the already existing astral 'Odo' inspire the writers of the TV character? We may never know, but taking the three preceding accounts all together we get a pretty clear picture that our works of fiction can actually be experienced as reality in higher dimensions.

We can think of our thoughts, then, as energetic templates that take on existence in the higher dimension of the astral. While writing a novel and thinking deeply about the subject, werewolves, Michael Talbot actually had the experience of seeing a ghostly image of a werewolf form around his body. He didn't feel like he'd actually become a werewolf. It was more like a holographic, translucent image of one just cocooned his body. It looked very real and he could see the individual hairs in the fur and the protrusion of canine nails from his hands. To top it all off, he had a houseguest staying with him at the time. When she came into the room, she reacted immediately and said, "Oh my, you must be thinking about your werewolf novel because you've become a werewolf."[135]

Giving life to your fictional creations is no new game in town. Author Walter Gibson wrote many novels centered around a character named *The Shadow*. This shady character in the novels was "fond of lurking in dark alleys dressed in a cape and broad-brimmed slouch hat." What's interesting is that after Gibson vacated the home where he had written many of these novels, people started reporting a strange ghost "dressed in a long black cape and wears a wide-brimmed slouch hat pulled down over its eyes as it slinks from room to room."[136] If this isn't an exact copy of his fictional novel character, I don't know what is. By giving so much thought and energy to this character, he had actually created an independent ghostly entity, effectively giving life to his novel character.

In another interesting story of this type, explorer and mystic Alexandra David-Neel made many visits to Tibet and became fascinated with the Yogic concept of a tulpa. In the tradition of Yoga, during meditation the Yogi would focus his thoughts intently on a specific deity he wished to manifest and provide instruction. The tulpa itself is defined as "a physical manifestation of the entity [deity] which would appear to instruct the Yogi in the completion of his training." Alexandra was intrigued with this concept after she saw a "cloud-like apparition" of a Tibetan god following behind a painter who had been obsessed with this particular god and had painted the deity profusely over the years. Alexandra tried this technique of intense meditations and focused thought, not to manifest a deity, but to create her own thoughtform which "took on the appearance of a jovial monk resembling 'Friar Tuck.'" As time went by she was able to concentrate on the monk and he would appear "as though projected into her surroundings from within her mind." Eventually this creation began to take on a life of its own appearing "regularly, as though the result of some will other than hers, and to her astonishment Alexandra soon began to hear others in the encampment discussing 'the strange little lama' that was frequently seen moving about." It even changed its appearance and appeared to lose weight and take on "a sly expression."[137]

After being taught by "the star people" that people can be controlled by their fears, Bonnie Jean Hamilton decided to take action against a "government psychic" that had been harassing her in her higher dimensional experiences. These psychics apparently wanted to know information from her about the star people. Sometimes they would come up to her and directly ask questions and other times they would try to scare her into telling them what they wanted to know.[138] This is not uncommon with abductees. They often report so called "military abductions," or MILAB for short, in which military figures are seen during an abduction or other-dimensional experience. Usually the abductee is taken to some place resembling a military base or hangar. Sometimes they give the abductee a kind of drug, like a truth serum to extract information.[139] Other times they use fear to get the information, like implying that the abductees life is on the line.[140] Abductees may also be told to stop talking to investigators about their abductions.[141]

Bonnie herself decided to get revenge. She spent an entire day concentrating her thoughts on becoming a snake because she knew that this government psychic was afraid of snakes. All day long, she thought intensely about what is feels like to be a snake. That night when she entered her fourth dream she found herself in a room which the government psychic entered. She focused her energies inwardly and then when he was just a few inches from her she let loose, shape-shifting "into a 10-foot snake poised on its tail end in a striking position, looming over the psychic's head."[142] She was surprised at how well her concentration during the day had worked to allow her to so easily become this snake in the alternate reality. She had all that energy already stored up and ready to burst out. The psychic was scared shitless. "He stood motionless, eyes bulging and mouth hanging open..." She never saw him again.[143]

The unseen world shaping this world

Just as we can influence the realities in higher dimensions by way of thought, it works the other way too. We are also influenced in our daily lives by the energetic templates created on these higher levels. Consider the thoughts of medium James Van Praagh who writes that, "The greatest works of humankind are created first on the upper astral level. Many ghostly scientists work together in this realm focusing their energies so that new ideas filter down into human minds."[144] Or then again, consider the thoughts of lucid dreamer Harvey Grady. He had a mutual lucid dream with another lucid dreamer. During the dream they were in the desert searching for ancient artifacts with a team of others. He states:

"In the dream, I felt that we were going through the motions of the search in the astral plane in order to establish energetic templates for the persons who would conduct the search on the physical plane. The energetic templates created from our experiences would guide the search of some physical explorers. Therefore, we went through the motions of the search like actors playing out roles, in order to generate thoughts, emotions, and desires for the template.

In the role of explorers, we acted as though we were ignorant and blindly searching for something we had only slight reason to expect might be there. On a higher level, as actors outside of the role, we knew what would eventually be found. We were well aware of the ancient civilizations and their contributions to history and had accepted tasks in helping reveal them to the physical plane. This double level of awareness made the dream more interesting to me."[145]

This dual level of awareness speaks to the fact that he was aware that the explorers on the physical plane were searching in a state of perceived ignorance, but were in fact being guided the entire time by their subconscious minds. Their "astral" selves/unconscious minds were already ripe with thoughts, emotions and desires to guide their expedition.

On a personal note, sometimes I wonder why I'm driven in the direction that I am. I truly do feel compelled to gain knowledge about consciousness and reality. One instance in college really shines through in this regard. I used to work at the desk of the dormitory on the graveyard shift, either from midnight to 4am or from 4am to 8am. Suffice it to say, there wasn't much work to be done. If a student happened to come in during these hours, I was to check their ID and make sure they actually lived there. So, it was an easy job. I did a lot of studying during this time and occasionally flipped on the radio. When the radio was on, it was invariably tuned into an fm station playing the latest top 40 hits. But one night on a whim I decided to check the am talk radio stations, something very unusual for me. As soon as I scanned the am stations, a program called *Coast to Coast AM* began broadcasting over the speakers.

On the program they were discussing UFOs. My mind just locked on to this program and it's like something just clicked inside of me. I instantly knew that this is what I needed to be studying. My life from that point on took a definite turn, and I haven't looked back. Ever since then I've been researching UFO encounters, life after death, altered states of consciousness, physics, you name it. I'm interested in understanding reality, the mind and consciousness. I had been interested in mysterious things like UFOs when I was a young teenager, maybe 14 or 15, but I lost interest in these things for quite awhile -- until that radio program triggered some awakening in me. It was like I was being guided by a higher level of my mind in the right direction.

My experience relates very well to what psychologist Michael Newton discovered when analyzing people's subconscious memories of what happened before they incarnated into their current Earth life. Some of his clients described being given "signs" before incarnating on Earth that would trigger their subconscious minds into remembrance and action in physical life.[146] These "signs" are not things we consciously are aware of. They are buried within the deep structures of our subconscious. In any event, they trigger us into action when they appear. For example, one of his clients reported being given the sign of "a silver pendant ... I will see it when I am seven years old ... around the neck of a woman on my street ... she always wore it. It shines in the sun ... to catch my attention ... I must remember ..."[147] In physical life she had indeed seen the pendant shining in the sun and asked about it. She subsequently became friends with this woman, who read to her, talked to her about life, and taught her to respect people. In other words, they were predestined to meet for a specific purpose.

This brings up the idea of soul mates and others who come into our lives at specific times in order to help us or guide us in a certain direction. It all relates back to the idea of purpose and a plan for each individual's life. And we must accept that there is more than one layer to the mind. Consciously we may reflect on certain experiences and learn from them. We may gain new information which causes us to rethink old ideas and sometimes adopt new ones. But we must all the while be aware that below the threshold of this conscious awareness lies deeper levels of mind with vast influence over our present selves.

Mental Influence

There is even ample evidence that our subconscious minds can be influenced by others. Now, this gets a little strange but stick with me. A Dr.

Konstantin D. Kotkov carried out experiments in Russia with thought transmission at a distance. His subject in these experiments was a teenage girl. At the time of the experiments she was not present in Kotkov's laboratory and she had no knowledge of any experiments being carried out with her. Author Guy Lyon Playfair describes how Kotkov performed the procedure:

> "First, he had to get comfortable, relax in silence, and 'mentally murmur' his instructions. Then he had to visualize his subject doing what he wanted 'with the most vivid hallucinatory or hypnagogic intensity.' Finally, and most important of all, came 'the factor of wishing.' He would 'strongly wish' the subject to obey."[148]

In some experiments she was given orders, through the method described above, to come to the laboratory at a specified time. She inevitably did and, "when asked why she had come, she generally answered, looking embarrassed: 'I don't know ... I just did ... I wanted to come.'"[149] In other words, she perceived this idea to come to the doc's laboratory bubbling up from her subconscious as a thought of her own, when in fact it had been the doctor working in an altered state of consciousness inputting this thought into her subconscious. This caused her to "feel" like going there for no apparent reason.

Another similar case involved a subject being put in an altered state of consciousness similar to hypnosis, called mesmerism. While in this state, the mesmerist would give instructions to the subject, such as to come to his house at a certain hour of day. After returning to a normal conscious state, she would not remember the suggestion consciously. However, even if it was an inconvenience for her to carry out the suggestion, she would inevitably do it. Once, after being instructed earlier in a trance to come to his house at a certain time, "she felt compelled to leave a dinner party, though she could give no explanation for her action except that she just could not help herself."[150] Again, we have an inexplicable urge to follow orders given to our subconscious minds.

Entities in higher dimensions routinely use this kind of subconscious control over us. Specifically in alien abduction accounts, I wish I got a dollar for every time an abductee says something like, "suddenly, I just had an urge to..." Take for instance one of Harvard Psychiatrist John Mack's clients who reported that "she had driven, as if under some sort of compulsion, to a wooded area in the town of Saugus, north of Boston."[151] She says, "I go out on roads I've never gone out before. Just for the hell of it." She ends up driving through a wooded area where she recalls an abduction experience.[152] Reflecting on the experience she "realized that in some way her trip north was forced upon her and 'they made me think I was doing it for other reasons.'"[153] One abductee even made the comment "that even before he built his house he made a large clearing about 150 feet from it, perhaps unconsciously inviting a UFO to land there."[154]

In another interesting case of this kind, Betty Andreasson Luca reported an out-of-body abduction while an alien stayed stationed in her trailer "as a guard against any kind of intrusion," like someone unexpectedly stopping by for a visit during her abduction. Betty wrote a letter to Ray Fowler, the investigator of her multiple abductions, explaining that she was told that "If any outsider was to approach the trailer [. . .] the guard would activate the power to change the thought in the intruder's mind, to turn away. An intruder would have thought it was his natural decision and will, as not to disturb me."[155]

Working through deeper layers of mind these beings are able to manipulate our thoughts, desires, and actions. At least, that is what it seems like. This is perhaps one of the scarier aspects, that we may be guided for good or evil in certain directions by unseen entities in higher dimensions.

This brings up the idea of archetypal forces which manifest through our psyche and guide our actions. Astrology is all about figuring out which driving forces are present in an individual person. As we are guided though, we can also take an active part in our destiny. We can dream ourselves into being with clear focus of our goals and where we want to be in life, or we can allow ourselves to be dreamed by the higher levels of the psyche and play out passive roles as we enact the desires of higher levels of mind.

The little creatures within

Regarding alien beings who have a hand in guiding reality, John Magnus had an interesting out-of-body experience in which he saw a bunch of little people that looked like gnomes. They were dressed in green and brown and may have even had greenish skin. He says they were busy running around and working hard to arrange his experience. He relates, "They control every event by some invisible machinery."[156] This brings up Waggoner's idea that there must be some tinkerer behind the scenes arranging the lucid dream experience, populating the dreamscapes and manifesting his intentions. Dr. Rick Strassman, who did a study on the chemical DMT which is found in the shamanic brew ayahuasca and is known for inducing visionary experiences, reports this kind of machinery being seen by his subjects as well. One of his subjects said,

> "There were creatures and machinery. It looked like it was in a field of black space. There were brilliant psychedelic colors outlining the creatures and machinery. [. . .] There was a female [with an elongated head]. I felt like I was dying, then she appeared and reassured me. She accompanied me during the viewing of the machinery and the creatures. [. . .] They seemed like guardians, gatekeepers. They kept pouring communication into me but it was just so intense. I couldn't bear it. There were rays of psychedelic yellow light coming out of the face of the reassuring entity. She was trying to communicate with me. She seemed very concerned for me, and the effects I was experiencing due to her attempts at communicating.
>
> There was something outlined in green, right in front of me and above me here. It was rotating and doing things. She was showing me, it seemed like, how to use this thing. It resembled a computer terminal. I believe she wanted me to try to communicate with her through that device. But I couldn't figure it out."[157]

Creatures and machinery, computer terminals, pouring information into him... This is intriguing. Let's take a look at another of his subjects memories from their DMT session:

> "[. . .] I watched a low-lying city on a flat plane on the far horizon mutate through a variety of colors and hues, with many ill-defined 'things' floating in the 'air' above the city. Then I noticed a middle-aged female, with a pointed nose and light greenish skin, sitting off to my right, watching this changing city with me. She had her right hand on a dial that seemed to control the panorama we were watching. She turned slightly toward me and asked, 'What else would you like?' I answered

telepathically, 'Well, what else have you got? I have no idea what you can do. [. . .]'"[158]

Wow, ok. Here we have a creature that looks exactly like a gnome right down to the green skin and pointed nose. There's definitely a machine involved as she controls the scene they are watching with a dial. I wonder if the rotating "something outlined in green" from the first experience isn't such a dial? From the tone of the dialogue at the end, it seems like she could create any scene he wished to see if he asked for it. However, no new scene was created. At the end she just does something to his head to release some pressure and make him feel better. Another of Strassman's DMT participants said,

> "[. . .] There were a lot of elves. They were prankish, ornery, maybe four of them appeared at the side of a stretch of interstate highway I travel regularly. They commanded the scene, it was their terrain! They were about my height. They held up placards, showing me these incredibly beautiful, complex, swirling geometric scenes in them.[. . .]"[159]

Elf-like creatures commanding visual scenes of exquisite geometry and beauty is certainly a facet of extra-dimensional reality that deserves to be studied more. These gnomes working busily at machines to create an experience for us deserve our attention! And I want to know more, don't you?

Life after death

Now, let's switch gears to the afterlife realms experienced by Near-Death Experiencers (NDErs). This is a favorite topic of mine. What do people do after they die? Some people prefer to rest and integrate their previous life experiences, or recover from the trauma of a physical life and might go to a hospital-like setting to do so. Ed Kellogg visited a friend in the afterlife during a lucid dream. He was led "into a sort of dingy gym-hospital like basement." After awhile his old friend comes out to greet him. At first looking about 50 years old Ed teases his old friend and says, "You know in this place you can choose your body--and you can do better than that!" He makes a comment to the effect that it doesn't matter, but complies and changes his appearance to look around 35 years old. They talk for awhile and he tells him that "he has the task of recording all of his memories." The aide that was there at the "gym-hospital" was happy that Ed stimulated his old friend because he had been obsessed with recording his memories, dictating them into a suitcase sized machine.[160]

Robert Monroe visited his father in the afterlife. He was in a "hospital or convalescent home." There were many rooms in this place and he found his father in a small room with a window on the wall. His father was surprised to see him and said that he felt much better now and, "The pain is gone."[161] Similarly, Waldo Vieira went to a place of recuperation, this one a little more extravagant:

> "The area was similar to a resort on Earth, made up of neat houses scattered throughout a forest that was permeated by soft light. The area was divided by inviting trails and clearings richly carpeted with soft grass. Sublime music penetrated the pleasant environment, affecting all the senses. [. . .] Carnot [a friend and resident of the colony] explained that the delicious sound waves, which could be felt but not heard, constituted music therapy taken to the extreme. It is capable of restoring the memory, the imagination and the judgment of extraphysical consciousnesses still traumatized by human experiences. It dissolves conflicts, apprehensions, doubts, regrets, fixed ideas and opinions. He informed me that there was an extensive number of inhabitants in the colony and that the majority were convalescing from their biological condition at the time of death, as they had arrived in the extraphysical dimension at an advanced earth age, suffering from senility."[162]

So, if you've had a hard life or just need some time to run through your memories, there's a place for you in the afterlife. There are many realms in the afterlife, literally probably as many as you can think of. But let's take a look at one of my favorite descriptions of where one ends up in the afterlife. It's from a man named Bill and this is what he experienced:

> "When I died on the operating table for the first time, I didn't realize I was dead. There was no out of body experience, no tunnels, no light at the end of the tunnel, no spirits, nothing. I was out of my body and just popped into the most beautiful place I have ever seen. Light is not visual there. The senses are all-encompassing impressions flooded into my being all at once.

The experience is so intense, that it is hard to explain because it doesn't follow a logical sequence and it is totally wrapped up in emotion. Words are far too limited to explain, but I'm doing my best to try to say what happened.

The senses are extremely heightened and don't really work like they do here. Words are completely inadequate, because all the senses are wrapped up in each other. We have the largest vocabulary on earth based on describing events in terms of what we see. Although I felt the experience, I can best describe it in terms of vision.

The grass was so green it hurt to look at it, and it felt so good! I could even taste the grass by feeling it, it tasted like watermelon. Walking on the grass was wonderful – it was an incredible feeling. The best way I can describe it was, "OH MY GOD! WOW!!!" The sense of smell was not with the nose. It was more like it permeated through my cheekbones under my eye, like smelling through the sinuses.

[. . .] Then three yellow lights came forth. They came from the left side of an unbelievably intensely colored green pine tree (color of maple leaf in summer time with light coming through it). I got the feeling of yellow and the taste of lemonade. Not yellow like a banana, but it was more the emotion and feeling of yellow. Sort of like a flame dancing on top of a candle during an emotional dinner and also like the feeling of warm yellow sunshine. I didn't really see them, but I knew they were there. I can't really call them entities, angels, or devils. They were more like presences. These presences were more like potential battery power, they were energy, that was just there.

I didn't hear with my ears. Rather I heard in the middle of my head, close to the back of the frontal lobe. The presence on my right, communicated telepathically to me. Communication is not with words as we know it. This being communicated a feeling with the gist of the meaning, "You can stay if you want, or you can go back. But if you go back, you have to do something." I knew that I had to go back for a reason. The reason was more like I was not done yet, not because I have to do something. This is hard to explain, but it is like if you are the boss, something has to be done, but who's going to do it? I elected to come back and finish a few tasks."[163]

I just love how he describes everything. He says the senses are all wrapped up in each other. So, when you encounter something, you don't see it or smell it or hear it: you *experience* it! Everything is energy. What Bill is experiencing is the "essence" of the grass, complete with all the sensory information of sight, smell, taste, sound, etc... It is like a complete package of energy, where you at once experience all aspects of it. The energy just radiates out to you and comes into your being. Everything in this dimension is also much purer and possessed of much more clarity than on Earth.

Next let's meander our way into an afterlife city by following David Oakford, who was taken to a spirit city located just above the Earth, in another dimension of course. In this city he saw "beautiful white-colored buildings" which "were made of wooden frames with plants merging into them." Trees, plants, and water were present, but purer in essence than their Earthly counterparts. The people there were spirits, each with "a unique vibration, but no real physical body presence like I was accustomed to on the surface of Gaia [another name for Earth]." Spirits in this city worked and played like on Earth. They didn't need transportation though, as floating worked just fine. However, there was something peculiar missing from this place. Negativity was conspicuously absent. There were no people trying to manipulate others or harm one another. No gangsters hitting people up for money. Nope. They were just easy going and positive, although he did see someone who looked sad and described others coming back here from Earth who were sad or scared. But for the most part, this was a place of positive vibes.

David took a little tour and saw people engaged in artistic work with paint and paper, and also others who were "learning all about earth, its purpose and operation" in classrooms. I guess you need to train up before coming to live on Earth; it makes sense doesn't it. This rough and tumble environment--you damn better get some training first.

Finally, he was taken to a very special building with green foliage growing on it. Inside it "was decorated with this glowing wood paneling that Bob [his guide] said was from the trees that grow in this wonderful city." He then sat "on a bench made of this 'living wood.'" Afterwards he was directed into a room where there was a council of high level spiritual beings. He was given a life review and talked over his decision with the council about staying in the spirit city or going back to his earth body.[164] Well, we know what he decided.

He's not the only lucky one to visit a spirit city during a NDE though. Another NDEr experienced going at tremendous speed towards an immense city. She saw a street which had "a look of gold, but it was clear, it was transparent." She describes how everything had such a purity and clarity and also a smoothness and softness to it. She says:

> "Everything was very defined, on the one hand, but it also had a blending with everything else. The flowers and the flower buds by that street--the intensity, the vibrant colors, like pebbles that have been polished in a running stream, but they were all like precious stones, rubies and diamonds and sapphires. One that I remember in particular had a yellow color to it and yet I would relate it to a diamond . . . all these things were just around flowers. [What did the flowers look like?] They looked like . . . tulips . . . and yet they had the fragrance of roses. Strong fragrance of roses."[165]

Unfortunately she was not allowed to explore further than this. But we get the idea that this is a place of great beauty unimaginable by earthly standards. Another NDEr, Nancy, was thirteen when she got whacked across the temple with a baseball bat. She describes seeing,

> "a bridge that led over to a magical, colorful, loving land. It was filled with everything a 13 year old kid would LOVE! It seemed to have colors I'd never seen before, flowers, fun animals, puppies, an amusement park with a Ferris wheel made of candy!...absolutely indescribable. I wanted to cross that bridge and get here until this loving presence floated down and gently redirected me."[166]

NDEr Jean was also shown a city during her NDE. She describes, "The buildings in the city looked like milk glass to some degree with veins of gold going through it. But there seemed to be a great deal of flexibility to its construction as well. Seats seemed to be able to mold to your shape." She visited a library with gold covered books that contained the life plans of people on earth including key experiences and what they hoped to achieve through those experiences. Then she was shown around some more:

> "I was shown other parts of the city as well...where souls were working with people on earth...scientists, the arts, and more. There is always a push there to "inspire" those on earth to create beneficial things for mankind in every area [. . .] This

city had many different places...all geared to a different need. There was a place of rest...where souls could recover from traumatic lives on earth. There were working places where souls could help mankind and others grow and be more. There were libraries and theaters and schools. And there was also the Temple of God...

[. . .] I was taken into this large hall and before me were beings of pure light. One was sitting directly in front of me on a chair or throne. These beings did not have human shape but were more like pure energy of light. I found myself prostrating before them in awe. The love that emanated from them...particularly the one in the center...was overwhelming. I definitely did not feel their equal, but did feel this great, great honor to be there. I was embraced by this entity in the center and told, "You have done well, My Child, and I am pleased." The love that came flowing through me and the approval made me weep."[167]

But not everyone wants to live in a city. Some prefer the country. NDEr Cynthia got a tour of such a place with a friendly guide. She relates:

"The second time we were walking in a beautiful mountain with so many gorgeous flowers, plants and animals. He told me that I didn't have to be afraid of the animals because He had made them as well as me. So many of them were funny, and others just talked. When we had walked down the path quite a bit we were walking by a farm. A woman walked out and gave us a loaf of 12 grain bread that was fresh out of her oven. We thanked her and began eating the bread. He [her guide] said that it was His favorite type of bread. We walked further and we began going a little lower again. We went inside a small cabin to talk with a woman who was sweeping her floor. We sat down and she brought each of us a glass of apple juice. She said her son was down by the creek fishing, and her husband and his friends were hunting. As we were walking down further I mentioned that I had not thought anyone would have a gun, let alone kill anything in heaven. He laughed and said Cindy's Heaven is made of whatever makes her soul happy and comfortable."[168]

So, it's starting to look like life just continues on in the afterlife. Our consciousness enters a higher dimension where we can work, play, and act out our desires just like on Earth. The only difference is that there are fewer limitations and we exist at a higher energy level. And that's just it, you can create or enter whatever reality suits you best in the afterlife. You can join a community of likeminded individuals. If you're a kid and want to play in an amusement park, you can. If you like hunting, that's cool too. Robert Monroe visited a friend in the afterlife who lived in cabin by the ocean with a forest in the back. Monroe explains, "He likes to be reminded of his favorite physical place, so he made a copy."[169] In the afterlife, we can use our thought energy combined with that of others, and also higher beings, to create whatever environment suits us. We can live in a collective world with people who have the same interest or we can create our own individual world where others can come and visit us. Construction workers, don't sweat. There's a place for you in the afterlife too.

NDEr Glenda found herself in an unfinished house, which she took to be her future spiritual home, that was under construction. She did come early didn't she! She describes:

> "I had walked right into what appeared to be a house under construction, with workmen carrying panels or wallboards. They spoke telepathically to each other in a different language, I remember thinking it was Italian. One of the men had a cigar in his mouth, even though he never seemed to actually 'smoke' the cigar. In fact, the cigar was the only indication to me that there was actually a mouth on the man's face.
> There was a foreman with a clipboard who looked up and with a surprised face, and told me telepathically, 'It's not finished!' He picked up immediately that I was confused as to where I was, and gestured with his arms still holding the clipboard that there was no problem. 'It's okay', he said. 'You may stay here if you want, and we can just finish it around you'."[170]

Once again, you get the idea that you can do whatever makes you comfortable in the afterlife. We all have passions and things we like to do, and being in the afterlife doesn't stop us from pursuing those things. Afterlife realms can be more ethereal or more physical depending on your taste, but generally there are always fewer limitations in the afterlife.

Just as what you do and where you go is determined by your thoughts and desires in the afterlife, so too is your appearance. When you die at a ripe old age of 90, by no means do you have to look that age in the afterlife. Shit no! You can be any age you want to be, and most people pick an age when they were in their prime. NDEr Garth saw a beautiful Earth-like world with lots of flowers and a tree. His wife was there picking flowers. Describing her, he said "The body was not the one we buried, but the form and face of the young woman on the day we married. She was so beautiful."[171] NDEr Glenn got to talk to his father who had died at the ripe old age of 76. However, now "he was young and healthy. I remember he had his legs again! (he lost both legs to Diabetes before passing.)"[172] Disabilities, see you later in the afterlife. No more bodily restrictions. Only if it's a strong thought form and you continue to believe in the disability will you take it with you after you die.

Some, however, may like a little negativity in the afterlife. Waldo Vieira visited a place in an out-of-body excursion that was gloomy. He saw a city next to a deep canyon that had filthy looking sewage-like water running through it. He was told by some beings there that he should "Beware of robbers." Well good damn thing he got the memo because moments later a being lunged at him and tried to drain his life-force like some vampire. However, Waldo "emitted energy of peace" and the being backed away. He then had to tango with "a horrid-looking elderly female extraphysical consciousness with sensual intentions." Luckily he got rid of her too. Things did improve though. He proceeded across the canyon into the city. He entered a park area and that seemed a little better. People were hanging out in groups there and he spoke to a few people. Then going further into the city he saw that they had paved streets and sidewalks like on Earth. Then he reached an open square where everyone was "satisfying one another with hugs and kisses [. . .] It gave the impression of an orgy." He saw houses in this city and buildings which "appeared to be as solid as physical ones." Everyone walked around in this place and Waldo found that he could only fly at low altitude "in spite of mustering every bit of willpower." It definitely seems like this is a more Earth-like environment with denser forms of energy and beings with a mix of positive and negative attributes, probably more on the negative side.[173]

You have to be careful about your thoughts and any unresolved emotional issues in the afterlife because they will determine your course.

One prime example comes from Medium James Van Praagh, who reports going to a haunted house where a woman who has died is stuck. It's not that she's evil or anything. She just wants to find her cats. You see, she loved cats and had seventeen of them when she was alive. However, now that she's dead and in a higher-dimensional space, she can't find them and continues to obsessively look for them. Even though her husband comes around from time to time to try to bring her over to the other side, she doesn't even notice him because she's so focused on finding her cats.[174] There's so much more to reality that she's missing, all because she can't stop thinking about her cats.

Out-of-body explorer Rosalind Mcknight also had an encounter with an earthbound spirit who was stuck in an obsessive thought-form. His name was Patrick and he had died after an explosion on the ship he was working on. When Rosalind contacted him he was stuck floating on a log waiting to be rescued, unwilling to accept that he is actually dead. He explains that that's all he ever had in life--his boat and his family. He says, "I can just barely lift my head out of the water. If I could just see them [his shipmates]. I think I have been out of my head, because I've been seeing faces around me. I just know that I am still alive. I am clinging to my log . . . ." The faces around him may be deceased loved ones ready to bring him to the other side, to another place in the astral world. Rosalind tries to convince him that he died during the explosion and can let go of his log. His consciousness is now free and no longer bound by materiality. Once he realizes this, he lets go of the log and floats above the water. He then sees his mother and father reaching for him to move on to the other side. He is happy and says, "It's so good to get out of the water . . . out of the darkness. Thank you. . . ."[175] Later it was explained to Rosalind that, "When a soul is programmed to believe that certain things will happen upon death, the soul will experience that strong thought-form once out of the physical body."[176]

Medium and Psychic James Van Praagh communicated with yet another spirit who was locked into a strong thought-form. This spirit, named Peter, was from a loving family but nonetheless got mixed up with the wrong people, started doing heroin and estranged himself from his loving parents. Blaming his mother for his actions, he told her that it was her fault that he ended up being a junkie because she never loved him as he was. As before he was an honor student and a leader, he was under the misguided idea that she only loved him for his achievements and for being "perfect." After dying from a heroin overdose, he was under an immense amount of regret for his actions. Describing his situation in the afterlife, he communicated to Praagh that it "felt like he was in a nightmare." He said, "It's very dark here, and people are crying . . . I feel imprisoned by my own thoughts, and it's hell. I feel so guilty for blaming my mother for my own problems." He refused to go to the Light because he felt that he didn't deserve happiness. He desperately needed his mother to know the depth of his sorrow for what he had done with his life and for not loving her in the way she deserved. After receiving his mother's forgiveness, he was finally able to move out of the dark place he was in.[177]

Locked into his guilt and depressive thoughts, he found himself in a realm of darkness where others too were crying over past mistakes. Like attracts like in the afterlife. We have to let go of past mistakes and look towards a brighter future.

The beliefs of a soul determining their place in the afterlife might help explain the many realms seen by NDEr Sarah. She went through a tunnel and saw a number of doorways in the sides of the tunnel leading to different realms, some hellish some beautiful. She describes:

"I floated along and up observing that some "door-ways" were open while others seemed to have been shut. The first doorway I peered into resembled a classic Hell. There was the sound of shrieking and agonizing screams. Naked human beings were strewn about a blasted landscape with pools of bubbling excrement and jagged boulders. Devils and other animals were torturing people in all imaginable ways; and people were also torturing each other. As I neared the doorway to this sinister scene, I felt a sucking sensation drawing me in like a whirlpool, and I found myself "flying" above the miserable landscape. The smell was putrid and the heat was almost unbearable but a part of me was fascinated by the seemingly infinite varieties of pain and anguish that was being inflicted on the inhabitants of this realm. Most of me wanted to leave so I had no difficulty and my feeling was that anyone could leave if they wished. I felt that no one or nothing had put those people in captivity except their belief in the agony they continued to suffer. I "flew" back to the doorway which was clearly visible from everywhere in the "Hell" I left with nothing but joy, but I still had a sense of myself as apart from that joy. The next doorway in the tunnel wasn't much better. As far as the eye could see people walked on barren yellow ground with their heads down, completely engrossed in their own depressed self- pitying thoughts, unaware that anyone else was around them. A great feeling of loneliness and isolation emanated from the scene, and I shied away from getting too close, although no sucking sensation was felt near this opening in the cloud tunnel. I flew along further up the tunnel and glanced in other doorways but the next one that made a lasting impression on me was a world of almost indescribable beauty. I looked upon a beautiful wooded garden with fountains and waterfalls and streams and bridges that glowed and sparkled with iridescent colors."[178]

She had the feeling that the souls in these realms were not there because they had to be, but because of their continued belief in the agony, or the beauty, that they were experiencing. If you are depressed and feel guilt about something which you can't let go of, then you can enter an afterlife realm filled with likeminded souls who are "engrossed in their own depressed self-pitying thoughts." If you think you deserve torture and or have been condemned to such a fate, well, there's a place for that too. But ultimately there's freedom. Your soul after death is like a bird being freed from its cage. You choose where to go and what to experience.

You can imagine that if you're an atheist in this life, finding yourself alive after death must be quite the shocker. That's what happened to Howard Storm, who had a NDE while in great pain laying in a Paris hospital awaiting a surgical operation for a large hole in his duodenum.[179] This condition caused hydrochloric acid from his stomach to leak out and spread throughout his abdominal cavity, and literally eat him up from the inside.[180] Unfortunately for him, it was the weekend and there was only one surgeon in the entire hospital.[181] Finally, after waiting for nine hours for the surgeon to perform the operation, he was told that the surgeon decided to go home and he wouldn't have his operation until the next day. In serious pain, this confirmed atheist decided to just let go and die, knowing "for certain that there was no such thing as life after death. Only simpleminded people believed in that sort of thing. I didn't believe in God, or heaven, or hell, or any other fairy tales."[182]

After drifting off into darkness and expecting annihilation, he suddenly found himself standing up between two hospital beds feeling more alive than he ever had in his entire life. He describes how all of his senses were working and heightened. He could hear sounds of his breathing and the blood rushing through his veins. He could smell "odors of stale urine, sweat, residue of bleach from the sheets, and enamel paint." He could feel the air move across the surface of his skin. He could taste a staleness and dryness in his mouth. He squeezed his fist and said, "I could feel the bones in my hands, the muscles expand and contract, skin pressed against skin."[183] For all intents and purposes, he felt totally alive like he was still in his physical body. Of course, he wasn't. His mind was creating all of these sensations.

After yelling at his unresponsive wife and trying to figure out what the hell was going on, he heard some voices out in the hallway calling his name. He describes the voices as pleasant and they were calling him to follow them. However, they got irritated when he asked questions and he was afraid of them. He decided though, that following them was better than staying where he was with his wife and hospital mate ignoring him. He describes the people as male and female with gray clothes and pale skin. As he followed them deeper and deeper into a thick, dark atmosphere, he kept questioning them about who they were and what they wanted, but they would not answer him and demanded that he keep up. After awhile, "They became increasingly angry and sarcastic. 'If you'd quit moaning and groaning, we'd get there,' they said."[184] They became authoritarian and started whispering about how pathetic he was. He got the idea that they were liars and were deceiving him. But it was too late, he had already been led too far into the dark abyss. After telling them he wouldn't continue with them and they should leave him alone, he relates:

> "I could feel their breath on me as they shouted and snarled insults. Then they began to push and shove me about. I began to fight back. A wild frenzy of taunting, screaming, and hitting ensued. I fought like a wild man. As I swung and kicked at them, they bit and tore back at me. All the while it was obvious that they were having great fun. Even though I couldn't see anything in the darkness, I was aware that there were dozens or hundreds of them all around and over me. My attempts to fight back only provoked greater merriment. As I continued to defend myself, I was aware that they weren't in any hurry to annihilate me. They were playing with me just as a cat plays with a mouse. Every new assault brought howls of

cacophonous laughter. They began to tear off pieces of my flesh. To my horror, I realized that I was being taken apart and eaten alive, methodically, slowly, so that their entertainment would last as long as possible."[185]

Damn, sounds like a place Jeffrey Dahmer might like. As they continued to torment him and relish in his suffering, a voice seemed to bubble up from inside of him that said, "Pray to God." Of course, Howard thought that was the stupidest idea ever because there is no God. Only stupid people believe in that fairy tale bullshit. But the voice grew stronger and, seeming that he didn't have any other options, he searched his mind for a prayer that he might have remembered from his childhood Sunday school experiences. He ended up mixing up a jumble of different phrases "from the Twenty-third Psalm, 'The Star-Spangled Banner,' the Lord's Prayer, the Pledge of Allegiance, and 'God Bless America,' and whatever other churchly sounding phrases came to mind." After murmuring what he remembered from these prayers and songs, he was amazed to see that the beings who were tormenting him absolutely hated this. It was like he had thrown boiling water on them. They screamed at him telling him there is no God and spoke in the most obscene language. However, he saw that they were backing away, so he kept singing, this time a little more forcefully. They continued to retreat becoming "more rabid, cursing and screaming against God. They claimed that what I was praying was worthless and that I was a coward, a nothing."[186] Apparently they wanted nothing to do with goodness and love. They fully retreated into the darkness leaving Howard alone. Finally with all the energy he could muster, he "yelled out into the darkness, 'Jesus, save me.'"[187] Then a light appeared off in the distance moving toward him. It was Jesus who took him to a great Light that he knew to be God.[188]

Notice how, although he was coerced into going by these negative entities, no one forced him to go or stay in the hospital. In fact, they couldn't have forced him. But Howard, oblivious to any notion of life after death, was totally helpless to go his own way. He simply didn't know what else to do but follow them. His ignorance allowed him to be manipulated as easily as he was. That's why it's so important to understand that there is an afterlife and you have the freedom to go where you want. First, though, you have to realize that you do have this power. Any place you want to be is literally a thought away in the afterlife. If you want to be with a deceased loved one, it's as simple as thinking of them and calling out to them. By focusing on love and positive feelings, you will go to someplace beautiful. If you're trapped in obsessive thoughts about material things, worries, or guilt you will go to a gloomy place or stay on Earth in spirit form.

It's also important to know that negative beings feed on negative feelings. They try to degrade and make you feel worthless. The trick is not to believe them, but instead know that you are of God. You are a spiritual being with great power. If you express love to these beings they will surely run away or be transformed by your love. However, if you are overcome with fright or believe what they say then they will get the upper hand.

The reality of other-dimensional experiences

There is a tendency to discount other dimensional experiences as not real, or only in the person's mind. They are, after all, subjective experiences. However, as we've seen, there are many similarities across reports which is suggestive of a real underlying phenomenon. We need to stop thinking in terms of the physical being real and anything else not real. The physical is just one dimension of the larger Consciousness multiverse that's out there. And we can access these realms through our consciousness. Sure, we can poke and prod the physical with the instruments we make. We can see deeper and deeper into the microscopic and macroscopic worlds of physical reality. But we have to use our minds to penetrate other dimensions.

Yes there are heavens, yes there are hells, yes there are alien consciousnesses, yes there are unicorns. You see, whatever we imagine can and does exist, maybe not in the physical but somewhere out there in the conscious multiverse. Consciousness is a great ocean of infinite potential waiting to be expressed. Thought is the power that takes from that infinite energetic potential to create the manifestly real. When we think a thought, we give it existence in a higher plane of mind. And if we focus hard and long enough, it may even come into physical expression here in this dimension.

Physical effects of other-dimensional experiences

This transition from higher-dimensional reality into the physical means there isn't a nice clean separation between the dimensions. There's what you might call "crossover" between the various dimensions. We see this clearly with UFOs and alien abductions, but it is evident in other kinds of experiences as well. For instance, Jeremy Taylor tells the story of a lucid dreamer who told a woman in his dream, "This is a dream and none of it is real." The woman got annoyed and said, "You mean you think I'm not real?" After he replied in the affirmative she said, "I'll show you who's real or not!" and crushed a lit cigarette on the back of his hand. He woke up instantly in pain and turned on the light to see "a round burn the size of a cigarette on the back of his right hand."[189]

The preceding case, although purely anecdotal, indicates that other dimensional reality is very real and can affect us here in the physical. Michael Murphy reports a case of a patient who, while sleeping, relived "an episode during which he had been tied in bed to inhibit his sleepwalking." His psychiatrist wrote:

> "On the night of April 9, 1944, the patient was observed by the nurse on duty to be tossing and turning violently on his bed. He was holding his hands behind his back and appeared to be trying to free them from some imaginary constriction. [Afterward] the nurse noticed deep weals like rope marks on each arm, the patient being apparently unaware of their presence. Next day the marks were still visible and were observed by myself and others. The patient had only a vague recollection of what had happened the previous night. By the evening of April 11 the marks had disappeared, except for some residual subcutaneous haemorrhagic staining.
>
> On the night of April 11 the incident was abreacted under narcosis. I watched him writhing violently for at least three-quarters of an hour. After a few minutes weals appeared on both forearms; gradually these became indented; and finally some fresh haemorrhages appeared along their course.
>
> [Later] he gave a clear account of everything that had happened and related the incident to his experiences in hospital in India. Next morning the marks were still clearly visible and were photographed.[190]

Clearly while he was having the experience he was experiencing it in another dimension, but it had real effects on his physical body. The wounds from the ropes tied to his wrists, that he was struggling to free himself from, literally crossed over from the other dimensional experience to his physical body. This is reminiscent of the scars and scoop marks commonly reported after alien abductions. Remember William Konkolesky who saw the misty fog roll into his backyard while playing with a friend. After it passed he had a fresh scar. Well, later he finds out through hypnosis that an Alien did appear in the fog and speak with him, but that's not when he got the scar. He got the scar the night before when he was abducted. Under hypnosis, he remembered interacting with a tall gray being with dark, liquid eyes. He felt a sudden sharp pain and looked down to see "a thin clean slice across my upper arm."[191] After waking up the next day he didn't immediately notice the scar until later, after the mysterious cloud floated past him in his backyard.

Abductee Kay Wilson experienced in an alternate reality being injected in the jaw multiple times with a blue liquid by a young female. She thought she was in a laboratory and saw several human scientists. A doctor checked her face after receiving the injections and was waiting for her to pass out. She feels she was injected with some type of drug, but she had received the drug in an alternate reality before and built up a resistance to it. She kept running her mouth, determined not to relinquish control or pass out. This worked and she stayed conscious during her time in the other reality, but the next morning after she woke up she said her jaw hurt and she had a bad headache.[192]

Another abductee shared the following story with investigator Karla Turner:

"When I was almost six months into the pregnancy [of her second child], I was very worried because the baby wasn't moving. One night I remember that I suddenly felt so sleepy that I got in bed, and I had a dream. I saw myself on a doctor's table. A strange doctor put a needle into my navel. When he did this, I felt something like an electric shock, and the baby started moving. I also felt that something was put up my nose. And then I woke up, [. . .] and when I awoke, I was having a very heavy nosebleed and the baby was moving."[193]

169

These cases seem to be real physical effects stemming from other dimensional encounters. Bruises, cuts, scoop marks, and signs of pregnancy followed by removal of the fetus during a subsequent abduction are commonly reported by abductees.[194] Some abductees even report waking up in the morning with their clothes on backward.[195] Sometimes after encounters, they will report strange configurations of red dots on their body, such as four red dots arranged in a diamond pattern, a circle with a seventh dot in the center, or dots arranged in a triangular pattern.[196] Some of the more interesting crossover phenomena include a high lymphocyte count like that seen in astronauts after experiencing periods of weightlessness.[197] Also, a powdery substance on the body occasionally appears after an abduction. Abductee Kim Carlsberg woke up after one encounter and notes, "My belly was bloated and smeared with a white powdery substance, and a long red 'cat scratch' ran up my right inner thigh."[198]

Zulu Shaman Vusumazulu Credo Mutwa had a strange encounter one day. He was outdoors alone when a strange silence came about. This just lasted a moment and then a blue smoke surrounded him and obscured the landscape. The next thing he knew he was in "a place made of iron." He had been stripped of his clothes and was lying on a table. He said there was "a horrible smell" in the place. He tried to get off the table but found that he was paralyzed and couldn't move except for his eyes. He then saw "six or more small doll-like beings, about three feet tall, with huge black eyes." Typical of modern day aliens they had slits for mouths and just two small nostril holes. "They had very small jaws, and their faces were like white clay with a pinkish tinge." A female creature a little bigger than the others seemed to be in charge. She had a wrinkled face, lacked breasts, and had "only the slightest swell of hips." Concerning what was done to him, John Mack reports that "One of them stabbed some sort of pipe into his thigh, and something was stuck in his nose that seemed to cause a kind of explosion in his head." Then a doll-like woman who was more human looking, but with limbs too short for her body and polished skin, climbed over him and made love to him. However, it wasn't good sex. He referred to it "as cold as if you were making love to a dead body, sir, as cold as if you were making love to a machine." He said, "Her large eyes did not blink, and she felt as if she had no bones." He even felt like she attached "something to his penis [after the sex?] that caused him to ejaculate 'too much.'" After the sex was over and he ejaculated, "His penis 'was burning as if I had put it in scalding water.'" He was then shown a creature swimming like a frog inside of a "big round bottle" filled with a "pinkish liquid." He felt certain that this was an unborn baby.[199]

The next instant, he was back in the bush again, but not as he was before. Something had definitely happened and there were clear physical signs to show for it. John Mack reports:

> "His trousers and shirt were torn, and his mining boots (with heavy nails 'good for kicking crocodiles if a crocodile catches you by the neck') were gone. His body was covered with gray dust, and he smelled 'awful, like in that stinking place.' Credo followed a track that led to a village, and when he finally made contact, he asked for Mrs. Zamoya. He was shocked when he was told that he had been missing for three days. [. . .] He showed me a nearly half-inch scoop mark in his thigh, which he attributed to this experience. [. . .] Villagers found his boots in the bush, but curiously they were still laced, 'as if somebody or something had pulled me out of my boots without unlacing them.' [. . .] Most horrifying of all to him, skin started to peel off his penis, which developed sores and became 'an ugly pink.'"[200]

Here we have drastic physical effects following an encounter that seems clearly dimensional with the strange smoke that seemed to surround him preceding the encounter. In a case like this, we may have to postulate that these extra-dimensional creatures are able to cross over from their dimension entirely into ours and back again. Pulling him out of his still laced boots seems like quite the trick even if they did fully manifest in the physical and perform their work here. Maybe they dematerialized his body and pulled him into their dimension where they did the work and then returned him. But then why would his shirt and trousers be torn? You see how a case like this is wide open for interpretation. But one thing's for sure, no ordinary explanation will do. This kind of extraordinary case calls for an extraordinary explanation.

Sometimes there are even healings following an encounter. Ufologist Jacques Vallee reports about a doctor in France who had been "wounded by a mine explosion in Algeria, where he was serving in the French army." This disability affected his right side and made it painful for him to support his weight on his right foot or stand for long periods of time. Furthermore, while cutting wood the doctor had wounded his leg with an ax, cutting a vein which resulted in a hemorrhage and the area becoming inflamed. This was three days before he had a UFO sighting which took care of his injuries. Getting up in the middle of the night to attend to his crying fourteen-month-old son, he noticed some bright flashes outside the window. His son was "standing in his crib, pointing toward the window: behind the shutters a bright light was moving." The doctor wasn't really interested in whatever this light was, and after giving his son a bottle he went back to sleep. But those damn lights were still flashing outside, so he went out on the balcony to see what the hell was going on. He saw two large silvery white discs. Each had a tall vertical antenna on top and shorter horizontal antennas on each side. There was a white beam of light emanating from the bottom of the disks.

The objects "got closer to one another, emitted small sparks between their horizontal antennas, and eventually merged into a single object that changed course and came toward him." Finally, the object turned to a vertical position and cast a beam of light right on the doctor. Right afterwards, "He heard a bang and the object vanished, leaving only a whitish form like cotton candy, which drifted away with the wind." After going back inside to wake his wife, he noticed that there was no longer any pain in his leg. "Not only had the hematoma disappeared, but all traces of his war wound had vanished as well." A couple of weeks later he noticed a red triangular discoloration around his navel. This same shape was seen around the navel of his child.[201] Commenting on the physical effects of this case Vallee states:

> "Not only did the earlier condition disappear completely (although it had been tested and established without any doubt by military physicians), but Dr. X also had a subsequent spontaneous healing of an open fracture. In this case, he was so embarrassed by the rapid disappearance of the injury that he left town for a few days so that one of his medical colleagues (who had tended the fracture) would not ask questions as he saw him walking normally. Dr. X also told me that a dermatology specialist had been consulted about the triangular skin patch. He stated that the desquamation (dry skin) consisted of dead cells, but that he could not speculate on their probable origin."[202]

You see why it's pointless to dismiss these kinds of encounters as just imagination or hallucination. These are real experiences. They feel real, seem real, and have real physical effects. In one of the strangest cases of this crossover from alternate reality to physical reality, abductee Jim Sparks reports having dreams in which:

> "I feel something beside my bed. I am pulled up by strange entities and guided out of my bedroom, down the hallway, and into the guest room of our house on the ground floor. It had a large double-paned window with blue drapes and white mini-blinds. I walk to this window, then walk right through it, without stopping. My escort and I go across the front lawn, over the street and into the woods adjacent to the house.
>
> In our front lawn we had honeysuckle bushes. I don't think there's anything sweeter than the smell of honeysuckle. In my dream, I could smell that honeysuckle quite vividly. When in bloom, the tiny flowers that had fallen to the grass would stick to my feet. I remember looking down and seeing the blossoms on my feet just as I entered the woods.
>
> I have no memory of what happened in those woods during those dreams. However, I always emerge out of that blankness and cross the street again, walking through that solid window into my home. Down the hallways I march and end up back in bed. Upon waking, I would have vague, incomplete memories of my 'dreams' and would be unable to move for a while."[203]

These dreams occurred about two or three times a week over the course of a few months. He didn't make much of them until early December, when he woke up with paralysis after one of these "dreams." When he regained control of his body he went to look in the guest room and was shocked to see that, "Honeysuckle flowers were strewn across the carpet. They clung to imprints in the pile carpeting. *The heel of one imprint was in the yard and the toes were on the carpet.*" Since there was a few inches of wall below the window, it was as if he had walked right through the window and wall. "There was a right footprint on the lawn outside, and a left footprint on the pile carpeting. Also, there was that footprint, half on the grass and half on the carpet."[204] Apparently he walked right through the window and wall, just as so many other abductees report being floated through windows or solid walls. But this time there was real physical evidence of the honeysuckle flowers that were stuck to his feet during his reentry. Was he in a semi-physical out-of-body state, dense enough for honeysuckle flowers to stick to his feet but subtle enough to be able to pass through a wall and window? It's another-dimensional experience, yet physical. It's fact-fiction. This is another case that is wide open for interpretation, but one thing's for sure, it's going to require an extraordinary one.

Signs of crossing over

There are many typical signs of the crossover of an extraphysical entity into this dimension. Sometimes these may also be signs of our entry into their world as well. The crossover works both ways. Investigator John Keel notes that apparitions are usually accompanied by tell-tale signs, such as "sulfuric odors, bright flashes of light, or actual changes or distortions of the landscape where they appear."[205] We've already seen the nasty odor Credo smelled in the "place made of iron." The other signs are also worth a look and before we finish, we'll add to this list tears in the sky and loud explosive noises.

We can find distortions of the landscape in John Mack's classic book on abduction, *Abduction*. Dave liked to explore the woody mountain by his home as a young boy. Once when he was twelve, he came upon "a path that led to an intersection with two other paths where there was mossy ground and a tree overhead." He remembers thinking how beautiful that spot was but then doesn't remember what happened after that. His next memory is of "walking onto the patio below our house." A time gap had occurred. Even more strange, Dave continued to go back to the area over the following week or two but could not locate the trails he had seen during his encounter.[206] In another instance, he and a friend located a cave at "the end of the mountain where it drops off to the river." Too frightened to go in and explore, they left. Again though, Dave went back to look for the cave explaining, "It's not that big of an area." Still, he never was able to find that cave again.[207] If we assume that his sense of direction and knowledge of the woods is half decent then there is no reason after extensive searching that he shouldn't have been able to locate these areas again. Adding to that, under hypnosis he recalled being back on the mountain and suddenly found himself lying below the tree he had seen feeling a tingling sensation in his body. Then he saw, "Several beings 'come floating up around the bend' of a trail that was not ordinarily there, created now on a steep slope in the side of the mountain."[208] These sorts of distortions in the landscape may be an indication that these encounters are not happening in physical reality but in an altered state of consciousness.

A flash of light is also common when crossing over to other dimensions. One abductee remembers sitting up in bed after awakening one night and seeing a short flash in the room. After another flash, "this being is there and she's motioning me to come to her."[209] Jim Sparks describes seeing a UFO disappear in a flash.[210] Bonnie Hamilton describes how she navigates through alternate realities by "vanishing and reappearing in flashes of white light."[211] Betty Luca was with an "Elder" during an abduction. Elders are described as "tall beings in white, with white hair" that look more like people than aliens.[212] At one time, the Elder told Betty that they had to go to another place and, placing his hand on Betty's shoulder, she "experienced a brilliant flash of light and found herself in what appeared to be a hospital room." He touches her shoulder again and she experiences the same effect, "Just bright, white light. [*pause*] Oh, we're in another place."[213] They are just moving from place to place in flashes of bright light. Medium James Van Praagh says he notices blinking white lights behind a person, which signifies "that a spirit is beginning to materialize behind an individual."[214]

Jacque Vallee reports that on May 13th, 1917 in Fatima, three children saw a bright flash which startled them. Walking toward the area where the flash occurred, called Cova da Iria, the children saw a little woman inside of a glowing light. The woman spoke to them and asked them to return monthly. The children returned each month as crowds began to gather and watch the young children as they communicated with this little woman, who said she was from heaven.

She came back on cue every month on the thirteenth and spoke with the children. The tone of the messages was very much religious in nature, giving prophecies about what would happen "if people do not stop offending God." Soon large crowds began to gather to watch the spectacle. The people in the crowd could not see the lady, but did notice some strange happenings. On the June 13th encounter, "witnesses heard an explosion and saw a small cloud rise from the vicinity of a tree [where the children were seen speaking with the apparition]." One witness even reported a faint buzzing noise during the time the children spoke to the unseen entity. On July 13th an even bigger crowd gathered to watch and also noticed a buzzing in the air, a white cloud around the tree and a loud noise when the lady left. On August 13th the crowd gathered once again, but the children were absent due to being jailed by an official who didn't want this fiasco to carry on any longer. However, even with the children absent, the crowd heard a clap of thunder followed by a bright flash. "A small whitish cloud was forming around the tree. It hovered for a few minutes, then rose and melted away."

The finale was on October 13th, when a real spectacle occurred. A whopping seventy thousand people showed up for this one. Again, there was the same flash of light that brought the entity into this world. The children looked as if enraptured by the vision and were seen talking, but the crowd saw no lady nor did they hear the conversation. This time though, as the lady left a brilliant silvery disk was seen in the sky spinning and throwing off magnificent colors. The spinning disk "plunged downwards in zigzag fashion toward the Earth and the horrified spectators." Then it once again went back up "and disappeared into the sun." The crowd wasn't hurt, but their clothes were miraculously dry. It had been pouring rain before the disk appeared, but as the lady left the clouds had parted. After the spinning disk left, everyone's clothes that had been soaked were completely dry. Even the ground and the trees were perfectly dry.[215]

In the last account we had classic signs of a dimensional crossover, including flashes of light, loud bangs or explosions, and a cloud-like formation. In the next account we add to that a tear in the sky. A retired police officer living in Holland, Michigan was watching TV on the couch one night when he suddenly found himself standing outside in the yard of his house. An eerie silence permeated the dark night. He said, "Ahead, in the near distance, I saw a pin-size light and then a very bright wave-like flash that seemed to move through and pass me. It almost knocked me back a step." Sensing a presence behind him he turned around and saw three classic, gray, science-fiction-like aliens standing shoulder to shoulder. Telepathically they asked for his assistance and he willingly agreed to help. He doesn't remember what happened after that, and next found himself back on the ground semi-paralyzed, extremely tired and breathing heavily as if he'd just done a lot of work. Out of the corner of his eye he noticed other humans nearby looking equally as paralyzed and out of breath as him. They were all looking up at this huge craft in the sky.[216]

"The next thing I remember was looking up at the craft in the night sky. There was a thunderous sound and an opening two- to three-hundred-feet wide appeared in the sky. It was amazing! I could see blue sky and clouds through the opening— but it was still night time where I stood. Clouds were 'turning into themselves' around the opening [which was round]. Then, in the blink of an eye, the first [and largest] craft flew into the opening, followed instantly by the second ship. Then, the sky closed up."[217]

After hearing another clap of thunder he found himself back inside of his house wondering, "What the hell just happened to me?" It was about 5:30 in the morning at this point so he decided to shake it off and start a normal morning. The next day he was in for a shock as his wife informed him that his daughter had awoken in the middle of the night "and saw a lot of bright flashing lights outside." This amazed him because he had told no one about the incident. Later, talking with his daughter about what she saw, she informed him that about 3:30 a.m. she woke up and saw "about eleven flashes of light" outside the window. She got frightened and ducked under the covers, then, peeking back out she no longer saw the lights but ran to tell her mom about what she had seen. So, here he had independent confirmation that something strange had taken place. From the time his daughter saw the flashes until the time he was back in the house there were two hours. Something happened to him during those two hours.[218]

There are many interesting things about this case. First is the wave-like flash that seemed to pass through him. Subsequently he sees a group of gray aliens standing behind him. It's as if these aliens had become pure energy and passed through him as waves of light before rematerializing in solid form behind him. This is of course speculation, but that's about all we can do with this one is speculate. And of course, the most awesome thing about this encounter is the tear in the sky preceded by a "thunderous sound." The craft literally disappear through this hole and then the sky closed up again. This reminds us of Chris's experience from before with the Spanish-speaking guide Peco. Peco tells him he is in another dimension and shows how this works by first showing a bed sheet and large objects causing a bend in the sheet. Then, he shows that by poking a hole in the sheet you can move into another dimension. Well, this case seems to be possible confirmation for this concept. Literally, it may be possible to rip a hole through the fabric of space-time.

Robert Waggoner experienced a tear in the fabric of reality that brought in another being, this time a human who came into his lucid dream. He became lucid and started walking around the dreamscape calling out to fellow lucid dreamer Ed Kellogg, saying "Ed Kellogg! Ed Kellogg come here!" He says, "Within thirty to forty seconds, as if stepping through a curtain tear in the air, out steps Ed Kellogg!" Waggoner relates that many other lucid dreamers also "mention entering the dream or having others enter their dream by creating a vertical or horizontal 'slit' in the dream screen."[219] So, I guess whether it's physical reality or dream reality things operate pretty much the same way.

It feels real!

We've seen many different inter-dimensional experiences in this chapter. I've argued for their reality. These people are not making up stories for shits and giggles, at least I hope not. The majority of them are sincere people who are having or have had extraordinary experiences. These experiences are very real to the people who have them. We saw how real Howard Storm's NDE felt, and to illustrate how real these experiences can be, take the words of Bonnie Hamilton who has extensive experience in alternate realities:

> "The experiences in the alternate reality became so life-like, that sometimes, I could not tell the difference from that reality and the waking world. The only true way for me to determine which world I was in was to take control of the environment, manipulating the energy to my own will. If I was able to instantly change a setting or fly through a wall, I knew I was in the alternate reality."[220]

This statement echoes the words of Robert Waggoner who makes the statement about a lucid dream:

> "The grass felt like real grass. My skin felt like real skin. If I truly focused on something, like the ground, I could actually see the individual blades of grass and grains of sand. When awake, we consider seeing and touching as largely physical activities, but in lucid dreaming, I began to see that seeing and touching were also mental activities and equally real-seeming when

consciously aware in the dream state."[221]

Similarly, an abductee dreamt about being outside and hearing a buzz-hum sound and a gray metal spaceship dropping down from the clouds. When it got close to her she felt a "tremendous, pushing, pressure" against her body. After losing consciousness and blacking out in the dream she awoke panting heavily, still able to hear the powerful sound that emanated from the craft. Speaking about this event, she says: "The dream seemed real, more real than I want to admit. I've never had a dream like that! Never. So clear and lucid."[222] It may have been a dream, but it certainly wasn't "dream-like." It was as real as any event in physical reality.

Mental Realities

These experiences may not be happening in this physical world, although we've seen that there is substantial possibility for crossover, including other dimensional beings coming into our physical time-space dimension and us moving into theirs. We've also seen numerous examples of things happening in the other dimension which crossover and show their effects in the physical. I agree with John Mack that we need to expand our definition of reality to encompass other dimensions and include more of our experience in the real category as opposed to the unreal.[223] We've come to define only the physical as real. Well, the physical is the reality our brains are attuned to most of the time and the one we experience most clearly. But dreams, NDEs, abductions, and out-of-body experiences all take our conscious mind away from physical reality for a moment and allow us to experience other, usually higher, dimensions of mind which can be experienced as being just as real as the physical.

A few cases from the annals of psychiatry will help to elucidate this reality of psychic, other-dimensional experiences. Carl Jung once had a catatonic patient who had "retreated into isolation" due to continued abuse and incest in her childhood. Her inner world was the world she knew best. The outer physical world was cruel, but in her inner world she found meaning and importance. After much persuasion, Jung got her to open up about this inner life she was experiencing. She told him she lived on the moon. On the moon she had been taken to a sublunar dwelling where women and children stayed. This was because a vampire lived in the mountains on the moon and he killed women and children. She decided to confront the vampire herself in order to destroy him. Wielding a knife she went to wait on a platform and watch for the vampire. After many nights she at last saw him coming towards the platform. He had many pairs of wings which completely covered his body. Curiously, she approached him seeing nothing but the feathers of his wings. Suddenly the vampire opened his wings and underneath she saw "a man of unearthly beauty." He captured her by enclosing her within his wings and flew off with her. She described the moon as "beautiful, and life there was rich in meaning." Once she got this story out and was accepted by Jung she was able to return to physical life. However, she later relapsed into catatonia due to her wish to be back on the moon. Jung again convinced her not to go back to the moon and she was eventually able to return to her native town, marry, and have several children without suffering a relapse.[224]

Obviously this case is rich in symbolic meaning. You can analyze it from a psychological standpoint all day long. More importantly, this woman's experience was real. In a telling interview, Jungian Psychologist Marie-Louise Von Franz relates what happened when she first met Jung:

> "[Jung] talked about a crazy girl and said she was on the moon, and talked about it as if it has been very real. And being rational I was indignant and said, 'She hasn't been on the moon,' and Jung says, 'Yes she has.' And I thought that cannot be, I said 'that satellite of the earth there which is uninhabited. She hasn't been there.' He just looked at me and said, 'She has been on the moon.' And I thought that old man is crazy or I am stupid. And then it certainly dawned on me that he meant that what happened psychically is absolutely real to the one to whom it happens. So I suddenly realized the reality of the psyche."[225]

Jung allowed his patient to express herself without any judgments or condescendence. He did not suggest that it was all in her head or that she was hallucinating. This was a real experience she was having in another dimension of mind. To her, it was as real, probably more real, than this world. Jung allowed her to see that this world was just as important and that she didn't need to keep living in this other dimension. Eventually, she was able to come back and integrate into a normal life. However, first it took someone who would listen to her and accept her experiences as real.

In a much similar case, a brilliant research scientist working for the government was referred to Dr. Robert Lindner for psychiatric evaluation after he became increasingly preoccupied with his life on another planet. The scientist, named Kirk Allen, was normal in every way except for his obsession with this alternate life. He claimed to have travelled to this other world psychically. He had compiled literally thousands of pages about his life in this distant galaxy on everything from the history of the empire he ruled there, to full-color maps of the planets, land masses, and cities which were within the galactic system of this other world, to specific aspects of this other world, such as "The Unique Brain Development of the Crystopeds of Srom Norbra X."

Dr. Lindner uncovered that Kirk had been an avid reader of science fiction and spent a lot of time in his youth "fantasizing about remote worlds." This stemmed from an unhappy and lonely childhood in which his father, a naval officer, "was assigned as governor of a remote Pacific island where they were the only white family." Adding to his troubles, "his mother abandoned him to a series of governesses, one of whom seduced him when he was eleven years old before running away with the husband of the island's only schoolteacher." Dr. Lindner decided that the only thing he could do for this man was to enter into his fantasy with him, "and to try to pry him from the psychosis from that position." In other words, he was going to try to accept, or at least pretend to, Kirk's adventures in non-ordinary reality as real and become a part of his inner world. Then, I suspect the psychiatrist was going to try to reason him out of it. That was the plan anyway. Dr. Lindner delved into the thousands of pages detailing life on this other world and became increasingly fascinated with it. If he found a gap in the record, or some missing piece of data, he would have Kirk psychically travel to the other world and report back about the missing data. Dr. Lindner soon "became caught in the game and often found himself anxiously awaiting the requested answers." As time went on though, Kirk began to lose interest in his fantasy life. He had lost the need to retreat into the world of the psyche and was ready to come back and live on Earth. However, since his psychiatrist was so interested in his journeys, he resorted to lying and making up data towards the end. When he finally confessed to Dr. Lindner that he had given up that alternate life, the doctor was at once happy with his triumph but also felt a wave of disappointment.[226] He remarks:

> "Until Kirk Allen came into my life I had never doubted my own stability. The aberrations of mind . . . were for others . . . It has been years since I saw Kirk Allen, but I think of him often, and of the days when we roamed the galaxies together."[227]

On clear summer nights, he even found himself sometimes looking up at the sky and smiling, asking to himself "How goes it with the Crystopeds? How are things in Seraneb?"[228]

Although Kirk later considered his adventures of the psyche foolish, while they were occurring these adventures were his reality. They weren't false aberrations of the mind, but very real inner, higher dimensional experiences. It was only by the acceptance of such realities on the part of his therapist that any help could come to him. He really had been to this other world, maybe not in this physical dimension but in a real dimension of the mind.

One wonders if this physical world is not the thought form of a higher mind who has created all of us and lives through us playing out a great drama that has spanned countless ages. Could loneliness be the driving force of such creation? Both Jung's patient and Lindner's retreated into the higher psychic dimensions because they were lonely, being abused and finding no companionship in this world. A need for love and companionship is the deepest human need. Maybe this is also the deepest need of the Source, who exists as the sole consciousness, the One. Would that not be a lonely existence as the one and only being? Would there not be a desire to create beings and realms that are at once a part of yourself, yet separate from you? Beings whom you could love and who could love you; beings who you could communicate with and live through; beings who could become creators of their own worlds and mythic dramas and share in all of creation. I think this is certainly possible.

Another experience that gives us a look into the reality of the psyche comes from Psychiatrist Stanislav Grof. It involves a psychotic patient named Flora who had tried all kinds of therapy, none of which worked. Flora had quite a history, but it boils down to the facts that she "had a criminal record, access to weapons, violent fantasies and impulses, and severe suicidal tendencies." It was decided that she should try out LSD therapy, which was in vogue at the time in the late 1960s. It was uncovered in the first two sessions that her childhood had included "alcoholism, violence, and incest in her family." She relived these major episodes under LSD and the direction of Grof. However, during the third session something remarkable happened. As Grof describes it:

> "Flora started to cry and complained that the painful cramps in her face were becoming unbearable. Before my eyes, the facial spasms were grotesquely accentuated, and her face froze into what can best be described as a mask of evil. She started talking in a deep, male voice, and everything about her was so different that I could not see much similarity between her present appearance and her former looks. Her eyes had an expression of indescribable malice reminiscent of the last scene of the movie *Rosemary's Baby*, which showed a close-up of the infant conceived by the devil. Her hands, which were now spastic and looked like claws, completed the picture. Then the energy that took control over her body and voice assumed a personified form and introduced itself as the Devil."[229]

"Oh, Fuck!" must have been what he was thinking, although he doesn't use those words. Literally it was as if she was possessed and, for all intents and purposes, she was. She changed into a completely different person with a palpable energy of evil and spoke in a different voice totally uncharacteristic of her own. Grof describes that the Devil, speaking through his patient, turned to him and warned him to leave her alone because she belonged to him. Explicit threats of blackmail were thrown against him and his colleagues if he continued therapy with her. This included personal knowledge about the private lives of some of the staff at the hospital that even Grof didn't know about. When Grof shared these revelations to the members of the staff whom they concerned, he said they were astounded because there is no way the patient could have known or obtained "such knowledge of those specific aspects of their private lives." Grof describes as he "experienced fear that had metaphysical dimensions." Oh, Fuck! is right. However, he kept his cool and refused to be swept up and ruled by this metaphysical being who took over his patients body. He proceeded to hold her cramped hands and look into her face while visualizing a white light surrounding the two of them. For two agonizing hours this went on until finally her hands relaxed and her face returned to normal. The session ended and she went on to an astonishing recovery. Grof says, "Flora lost her suicidal tendencies and developed a new appreciation for life. She gave up alcohol, heroin, and barbiturates and started zealously attending the meetings of a small religious group in Catonsville." Her facial cramps went away, she was released from the hospital and went on to become a taxi driver without ever having to return to the psychiatric hospital. Another interesting facet of this story is that she had no memory of her LSD session when she was possessed by the metaphysical entity. She remembered the first part of her session and the part following the possession, but had no memory of the time when the Devil was speaking through her. Since she was radiant and happy, Grof decided that there was no need to tell her about that part of her session and left it at that. Grof is still awed by the fact that this "dramatic therapeutic result," which is the most dramatic he's ever seen, "was not achieved by officially accepted respectable psychiatric treatment." He describes how it "resembled more a medieval exorcism or an intervention of a witchdoctor than a respectable rational therapeutic procedure based on discoveries of modern science."[230] It seems that science still has a long way to go in understanding reality, so this is not surprising to me. The ignorance of science to the ontological reality of other dimensions of mind and levels of being is the greatest ignorance of the modern world.

This last case demonstrates that we need to be careful here. Grof didn't give into the Devil's admonitions about what would happen to him if he continued therapy with the patient. He realized this was a real metaphysical, higher dimensional, entity he was dealing with, but also knew that he couldn't give in to the threats he was receiving or believe in them. We must never lose sight of our critical faculties when dealing with other dimensional beings. Just because the other dimensions and experiences in them are real doesn't mean we should accept everything we see in them or are told by the beings there. Just as you can bullshit your neighbor about how much sex you've had lately, you can bet the conscious beings in other dimensions can throw us a line or two of BS. In fact, I would speculate that this often happens.

Higher-dimensional beings are toying with us

Ufologist and journalist John Keel writing back in the 1970's gives us a message which we should all heed today:

"These chimeras and parahumans usually seem to be engaged in pointless exercises, but beneath the layer of nonsense there has always been a strain of propaganda and tactics identical to the tactics we now call psychological warfare – the repetition of half-truths until they are accepted as whole truths by much of the human population. The modern belief in extraterrestrial visitors springs not from the presentation of concrete evidence but from the repetition of the extraterrestrial 'line' through thousands of contactees over the past 30 years or so. All of our religious beliefs have a similar basis – prophets who have allegedly talked with supernatural beings have spread the beliefs to masses of people who have had no direct experience with the phenomenon but are willing to accept the word of those who have.

All over the world today there are lonely people laboriously writing massive books which no one will ever read. They are inspired by their contacts with parahumans and have taken part in long conversations about everything from the building of the pyramids and lost Atlantis to the great cataclysms we can expect at the end of this century. These people – and I have been directly in touch with many of them – sincerely believe that they, and they alone, have enjoyed a very special privilege: contact with God or Gabriel or Ashtar or Orthon. Who can say how many of the histories of the past were constructed in the very same way? How many important ideas were assimilated by the human race through this process?"[231]

Keel suggests a manipulation of our belief system on the part of the aliens, or parahumans as he calls them, toward some unknown goal. Jacque Vallee picked up on this too, stating that UFOs and alien contact "are the means through which man's concepts are being rearranged [. . .] it is human belief that is being controlled and conditioned."[232] He later notes that, "The observable change [in human beliefs] is an increased willingness to believe in extraterrestrial life."[233] Indeed, the extraterrestrial hypothesis has been indelibly ingrained in modern ufology. Folklorist and Ufologist Thomas Bullard made the comment that, "Since the early 1950s the extraterrestrial hypothesis has held much the same position in ufology as evolution theory in biology."[234] The places of origin of these aliens changes from Mars to Venus to way off in the Pleiades, but the extraterrestrial hypothesis does not go away. John Keel saw in this a kind of conspiracy, a deliberate sabotage of other ideas by the parahumans. He noted that investigators who had opted for an alternative explanation of UFOs and alien beings, such as being terrestrial in nature, "experienced more harassment, mail and phone problems, etc., than their colleagues who believe in outer-space vehicles."[235] Keel gives a few examples of tapes being mysteriously misplaced, overexposed and ruined, erased, or stolen and were never able to air on TV or radio containing the statements of investigators who opted for a different interpretation of the UFO phenomenon. In one instance a mysterious burglar broke into a radio station in France and stole the second pile of radio tapes that were still awaiting broadcast. The first pile of tapes had already been broadcast and contained the statements of "UFO witnesses and local French enthusiasts and officials," while the second pile featured interviews with more seasoned investigators who had opted for a different interpretation than the extraterrestrial hypothesis.[236]

These days the UFO narrative seems to be centered around the belief that some secret organization within the military or government, some shadow government, knows all about the aliens and is hiding this knowledge from the public. The story goes that the military has retrieved crashed disks and back-engineered the alien technology. That or they made secret deals with the aliens in exchange for their technology.[237] Modern abductions have morphed to keep up with these developments and now routinely feature military abductions, or MILAB for short. These military personnel are said to use advanced alien technology.[238] They work alongside aliens at secret military bases, but may only be involved with one or more alien races. They re-abduct abductees to extract information from them that the aliens are withholding.[239] They may also be involved in secret experimentations on humans and animals.[240]

What are we to make of this myth that has arisen? Human belief, I believe, feeds into the creation of reality in a continual feedback loop. These people are having real experiences of the nature I just described. But that doesn't mean it is a physical reality. It may occur entirely in another psychic higher dimensional space which then feeds back into physical reality in a constant interplay of real physical events that support the suppositions of the myth, which then feeds into the psychic narrative and experiences of abductees who experience a sort of lived mythology in other dimensions, which can sometimes be mistaken for real events in the physical world.

Higher dimensional entities are known for the creation of scenes that are ultimately illusory. As we've gone over, in higher dimensions what you experience is highly malleable to focused thought. A scene can be experienced as entirely realistic, yet be the mental projection of the person or of a higher dimensional entity. In one abduction encounter, the aliens created an elaborate conference room type imagine aboard the craft "complete with shag carpeting, mahogany paneling, and a large viewing screen." However when the abductee, Catherine, began to question the scenery she was told that this imagery was created to make her think it's a conference, so she would be in a serious state of mind and not make her "usual smart-ass remarks." Then, "the room was returned to its original state and Catherine was told to sit on a small, cold metal chair." The aliens then showed her beautiful scenes of nature followed by past lives she had supposedly lived.[241]

Another abductee was shown a big book by the aliens containing pictures of all of his past abduction experiences. He said, "All the pictures seem to have depth to them, like 3D pictures." He remarks that the alien who was showing him the book could touch the pictures and seemingly make them come alive. In one case, the alien touched the water in the picture and it changed, making waves.[242] This is similar to a case Psychotherapist Michael Newton reports where, this time in-between lives, a woman named Amy was in a library looking at "Life Books." When viewing pictures in the books she remarks, "It comes alive in three-dimensional color." Another time she says, "Okay. He flips to a page and I see myself onscreen in the village I just left. It isn't really a picture--it's so real--it's alive. I'm there." She remarks that she can actually be in the scene experiencing it or just viewing it as an observer.[243]

We also have a NDE that is very similar. Leo got hit by a car and then found himself out-of-body. He decided to go shooting through the cosmos on a little exploration tour, but was soon stopped by "an infinitely powerful and firm power" which grabbed him from behind and pulled him down. He was then staring at "a very vague face, in mid air." This being spoke "with incredible kindness and humor," asking him about what he was hauling behind his head. Leo looked to see "a small outgrowth" that appeared to be, "some kind of backups of my memories over my whole life, like icons, you just had to look at one to view the memory under the form of a small movie, however, by touching it I could also enter it, and I felt the emotion of the memory." Him and the being end up entering one of his memories together, one in which he had been very frightened while walking through a park at night about 20 years prior. Upon entering the memory, he was back in his 20 year younger body experiencing this memory and the fright he had then felt. However, it seems that he retained his current perspective as well, kind of like Duane who was "thrown into" his daughter and experienced all of her thoughts and feelings but was only a bystander in her world. The being who entered the memory with him is described as "a man wearing a white tunic, about 5'7" tall, black-eyed, a metis." He also reports seeing "tiny radiant white flashes on the back of his neck, on his shoulders." He describes how the being went off into the darkness to ascertain what was frightening him so bad, but upon returning exclaimed, "There's nothing there!"[244]

This is real life Harry Potter-like stuff. The only difference is that these are not fictional accounts, but real lived experiences. Experience in these other realms is highly dynamic and quite seemingly magical. Sometimes abductees will be shown scenes on television-like screens or even see life-like 3D holograms.[245] Other times they actually experience a constructed scene for their learning.[246] These scenes are varied but common themes emerge. One of the most common images shown to abductees is the future destruction of Earth caused by world-wide catastrophes, war, and maybe even alien attack.[247] One scenario holds that a new age will be ushered in and we will live in harmony with hybrid aliens who have been bred to populate the Earth after many people are killed in the coming catastrophes.[248] These hybrids have greatly expanded mental powers and psychic ability.

All sorts of knowledge can be given to abductees about the aliens and their purposes, where they are from, past lives the abductee has had, the future of the Earth, etc… It would be a mistake in my opinion to take all of this as literally true. All that can be said is that these people are having real experiences with alien entities who are trying to teach them and show them things. But, like Vallee and Keel point out, they may be telling us lies or half-truths to alter our belief system and make us believe a certain way, forcing upon us a new mythology to structure our lives and habits.

John Keel has first-hand experience with this control system perpetrated by aliens. In 1967 Keel noted a number of prophecies given to contactees that came true. Not only were UFO contactees reporting these prophecies, but trance mediums and automatic writers who were channeling spiritual entities were also coming up with near identical prophecies. Plane crashes, earthquakes, blackouts, a bridge collapse, bombings, and even the disappearance of a Prime Minister were all correctly prophesied accurately by the parahumans according to Keel. However, the big prophecies, like one that New York City would slide into the ocean due to a natural catastrophe, never happened. The aliens seemed to be toying with contactees and others involved in spiritual contact. They bait the contactees with "unerringly accurate" prophecies which couldn't be due to guesswork. Then they "introduce a joker into the deck." They have people fully convinced that some major catastrophe is going to come upon the world and it simply never happens.[249]

Making meaning of our manipulation

We may never know the full scope and purpose of this manipulation of our belief system. If we go back to the idea that a Source Mind manifests our physical world in a co-creation with our deep seated beliefs, desires, and expectations, then we could surmise that the purpose is to control our reality through a control of our beliefs. If they condition us by repeating the same ideas over and over again, then eventually more and more of society will believe it and that belief will become seated deeper within the structures of our minds. One wonders if then this subconscious thought form will eventually explode into actual physical reality and become real. In other words, the Source Mind will, in effect, manifest the physical in accordance with that overarching belief. If this is true, the aliens can control our given reality by controlling our beliefs. However, when dealing with things like major worldwide catastrophes or other things that affect large numbers of people, there is a complex interaction of many minds, some of which may have doubt or have opposing beliefs. Higher levels of mind could also block such a manifestation if it was not in the interest of the souls involved.

I have also considered the possibility that these messages could have a symbolic meaning. World-wide catastrophe need not be a physical reality. It could very well be symbolic of a breakup of the mind and its mental constructs. Specifically, old religious and materialistic concepts are being shaken by the new understandings of the New Age. This could be a difficult transition for many who have been indoctrinated over the years in traditional Newtonian views of the world as a materialistic "matter machine," or in traditional religious orthodoxy. Both of these systems of thought are today being undermined by New Age studies and beliefs coming from diverse areas, such as channeled literature, hypnotic regression, NDEs, UFO abductions, and OBEs. It does seem like we are being led into a literal "New Age" of beliefs, although this is being resisted on many levels including within academia. However, as I see it, this change is happening at a grassroots level, from the ground up. This revolution will not come from the religious or academic elite. They will vehemently oppose such a radical shift in thought. But it really doesn't matter because a new generation will grow up, as I have, instilled with these new progressive and mind expanding ideas that resonate deeply within the soul of man. In time, the old hierarchy of academic professors and religious authorities will die out, to be replaced by this new generation of open-minded individuals.

So, the symbology of global catastrophes could be a message of this breakup and overthrowing of outdated ways of looking at the world and of thinking. Furthermore, the new age in which hybrids are shown as this new race on Earth could very well be symbolic of the new human race, of humanities future evolution into more psychic beings in tune with nature and the cosmos. Our powers of consciousness will be enhanced, giving us a more intuitive awareness of things. The hybrids, as they are shown to abductees, are telepathic. Their mental abilities are greatly enhanced overall creating less of a reliance on the physical body, which could be why abductees sometimes see them as having frail bodies.[250] However, other abductees report that their bodies are strong and healthy like ours and can even be indistinguishable from a normal human being.[251]

Symbolically, the messages of global catastrophe followed by a new "hybrid" version of humanity living on a new Earth make perfect sense. If we look at it from an evolutionary standpoint, it points to the breakup and destruction of old concepts about reality and the human soul, followed by an age of greater awareness. Human evolution, in my opinion, is headed toward an expansion of consciousness with greater mental abilities, including what we now term paranormal, such as telepathy, telekinesis, out-of-body travel, and so on. In the next chapter we will come back to this evolutionary concept as we discuss metaphysics.

4

METAPHYSICS AND THE FUTURE

Comparing Worldviews

Let's examine two fundamentally different ways of looking at the world that are prominent in today's world. One view is touted by the scientific establishment, and when I say that I don't mean some secret cabal that's controlling science or knowledge, I just mean the mainstream academic scientists working at universities. The other view is supported by the "New Age" movement, which is such a broad term it's really hard to define. New age beliefs encompass all kinds of modern developments, such as the study of NDEs, UFO abductions, past-life regression, channeling, mediums and psychics, and the whole plethora of beliefs and ideas that have arisen out of those studies. Labels like scientific establishment or new ager don't really matter. What does matter is the underlying philosophies behind such systems of thought.

One system of thought holds that the Universe is like a giant machine ticking away through time to an eventual destruction. The world at large contains matter and energy that is entirely unconscious and undirected by any intelligent means. It operates on the basis of fixed physical laws, these laws being immutable and unchangeable. We just so happen to be in a universe that can support life, lucky by chance not by necessity. There could be other universes, untold numbers of them that don't support life. We just got lucky enough to be in one with physical laws that did allow for the formation of stars and planets like ours. Life arose on our planet by mere chance, random happenstance, and we're still not sure how it got started. But don't worry, someday we'll figure out how it happened via natural laws acting on random processes. Once life did get started, it evolved via random mutations and natural selection, or other natural undirected processes.

In this view, life is a cosmic accident and ultimately meaningless. You live one short 70 or so year life (if you're lucky). Then you die and cease to exist for the rest of eternity. Everything you learned in life, all the memories you obtained, and all of the joys and sorrows you experienced are gone forever, obliterated at the time of death with no chance of recovery. It was all for nothing. Generations continue on in this way, but ultimately nothing has meaning and all will be lost as the universe dies a slow death. After the universe dies or collapses back into a big crunch, we will be gone with no one to remember us, the knowledge of our existence wiped away.

This is not a pretty picture. You're born, you die, that's it. You're existence means nothing in the grand scheme of things. You are but an accident in an uncaring universe that is devoid of any intelligence or consciousness. We might as well commit mass suicide and save ourselves the trouble of continuing on through the generations only to be blotted out of existence anyway with nothing to gain from our achievements and strivings.

The other view is one that says the universe is guided by a supreme intelligent consciousness. It's no mistake that the universe is tuned so finely to be able to support life. Quite the contrary, this fine tuning of the laws of physics--so that, for instance, the force of gravity relative to the electric force and the strong and weak nuclear forces are set within a very narrow range which allows the formation of stars like ours and a stable life supporting universe--is the earmark of a divine intelligence.[1] Life is no accident either, in fact the underlying informational systems of life are too complex and highly specified to have possibly come about by chance. In the creation of life and in its subsequent evolution, an intelligence is demanded.

Human consciousness is a part of this vast underlying and preexisting Cosmic Consciousness. As such, life after death is assured because consciousness is fundamental, pre-existing any human body which acts as a temporary home and vehicle of experience. Memories are stored, not in material substrates, but within the fabric of consciousness itself in the form of indestructible waveforms. All knowledge, learning, and achievement as well as sorrow, setbacks, and misery are recorded for all time; a timeless record of experience contained within the ocean of

Cosmic Consciousness. Ultimately all finite experience is illusory, but by no means meaningless. This physical world and all other worlds and dimensions of conscious experience are actualizations of our potential, and by "our" I mean our collective Source Consciousness that we are all a part of and ultimately One with. We are here as conscious beings experiencing the world of our creation, not some unconscious accidental arrangement of matter. The world is guided by a higher Source Mind that manifests all matter and is the director of matter. Consciousness creates information, information which guides the flow of matter into the majestic creation that we see.

This is a pretty picture. All of your human experience is valuable and enriches yourself and the Source which you are a part of. Life is not limited to a single human life. You can live hundreds, thousands, an innumerable number of times if you like in many different bodies covering a vast array of experiences. You might be born in sub-Saharan Africa this go around and in the next life you might be born into an alcoholic family in northern Europe. The possibilities are endless. Each life is a chance to experience new things and learn from those experiences. Each life enriches the soul with experience and knowledge. After each life you carry those memories with you and continue your experience in other dimensions before coming back once again if the need arises. Each life has a purpose, tasks to be fulfilled, people to meet and influence, decisions to be made which determine how much you've learned and the direction your life course will take you. You create your experience in cooperation with other conscious beings and the Source; it is the experience you want. There are no limits to what we can experience because there are no limits to the infinite potential of the Source.

Mystical strands sometimes posit that we are like children of the Source, the One Infinite Consciousness. We are beings created by a kind of division of this One Clear Light, miniature units from this vast Collective Consciousness. We were created in order to love so that we are the object of the Source's divine Love. The Source allows us to create our own experience and helps us in that endeavor. We are never judged for our wrongdoings or transgressions, because ultimately there is no right or wrong, just experience. Ideas of right and wrong are relative concepts that guide our subjective view of experience.

We are here to create, experience, and envision ourselves and our world in whatever way we choose. It is our playground of experience. The

Source has set it up in accordance with our desires and is continually creating the world at every instant. We mostly forget about our power as the Source to create any possibility, but we can regain that power through knowledge and envision ourselves in a new light.

These two views of reality are diametrically opposed. One bleak and pointless, the other filled with possibilities and hope for a future, indeed infinite, existence. The reasons for accepting or rejecting a worldview should, of course, not be based entirely on the philosophical implications. However, it is important to study these implications to know just what we are dealing with; it's important to know what's at stake.

Why it's important

What's at stake is how we view and understand life and the universe, and the stakes are high. Take the story of Jesse Kilgore, who was a college student who committed suicide after reading Richard Dawkin's book *The God Delusion*.[2] Now, I'm not faulting Dawkins for this, nor am I implying that this is a normative case. However, this college student was religious and had a strong faith in God before he read Dawkin's book. Apparently, someone at his school challenged him to read it. After finishing, he related to friends and family that he had lost all of his faith. In effect, he had been persuaded by Dawkin's ideas. His committing suicide, I would argue, is simply a rational, logical decision based on Dawkin's view of the world (although Dawkins himself would probably disagree). If you don't believe in life after death or any higher intelligence, and if you believe that human life evolved as a meaningless accident in a meaningless universe, then logically there is no real reason to be here. What Jesse did was just to take Dawkin's view of the world and life to its logical conclusion, and made a rational decision based on that worldview to kill himself. If this seems abhorrent to you, then you need to carefully evaluate your beliefs. Is it a meaningless universe devoid of intelligence? Or is it a meaningful universe full of intelligence? Is there a God, or Source of existence of which we are a part, or is there not? The implications for life are important. If there is an intelligent Source to the universe and consciousness is fundamental and survives death, then life is meaningful. We have decided from a higher sphere of mind to come here and live in this world for our own experience and learning. We have decided to take part in this grand experience we call life, with all its ups and downs.

Indeed, we have created this world, and as our creation--it has meaning and purpose. So do all our adventures of consciousness in this dimension and in others.

The choice is yours

Besides the implications though, we should look for evidence to support our particular worldview. If there's no evidence to support it we should not accept it. Both of these worldviews can be supported by evidence. In our relative systems of thought we can accept the evidence that supports our worldview and reject evidence that is incompatible with it, or that points to another possibility. In my view, the weight of the evidence is in favor of a Cosmic Intelligence and continuation of life after death. From what I've read and learned over the years, this view makes more sense of the data than the view that it is all unguided matter and energy and the brain produces consciousness. I've discussed this evidence in this book. Again though, this is my subjective perspective. I'm not saying I'm right and the other side is wrong. The materialist scientist sees the world through the filter of knowledge that he has gained over the years. From his point of view, the evidence supports an unguided, unintelligent universe with humans as mere ephemeral biological machines that have no chance of surviving death.

No one side can prove to the other side their position. There are two sides to every coin, two nickels for every dime. No one is right and no one is wrong. We each have the free will to decide our beliefs and create the experience we want. If you want to live in a world devoid of meaning, destined to die and pass away without any remembrance, then you are free to live in that world. You can just ignore all of the evidence to the contrary or try your damndest to explain it away. But if you want to live in a world of meaning, where life never ends and death is nothing but a transition, then I welcome you to a much more magical and wonderful world.

When you think about yourself with the ability to think, feel emotions, write poetry, imagine, dream, and experience the multitude of experiences you have, the most illogical position is that this all came about by unintelligent processes. Indeed, it's so illogical as to be almost comical that anybody can take that stance. Unintelligence begets intelligence? An unconscious, unintelligent universe creates intelligent life and conscious beings? It does seem counter-intuitive, and I would argue impossible. I think you have to start with intelligence, with consciousness, to then get a world that supports and guides the evolution of intelligent conscious beings. Astrophysicist Bernard Haisch also is amazed that the majority of scientists still take the former view and try to justify it. He writes in his book, *The God Theory*:

> "I am constantly baffled by the fact that a majority of my colleagues seem to prefer a philosophical view of human beings as short-lived, chemically-driven machines that evolved by accident in a random, remote corner of the universe and whose existence is a pointless and utterly transient curiosity. Even when confronted with the proposition that these odd machines are only possible in a universe whose laws of physics are finely tuned to permit their existence, most of my colleagues fall back on an assumption that there must, therefore, exist a vast ensemble of other randomly distributed universes. The one we inhabit seems special only because we could not exist in any other to raise such questions in the first place. For some reason, the idea that an infinite number of random processes allows us to come into being as statistical flukes or quantum fluctuations has become the very touchstone of scientific rationality."[3]

Indeed, it's hard to see how this view that the majority of scientists take seems better or more likely than the opposite view that an intelligence underlies the formation of the universe. The evidence is all around them for life after death, the primacy of consciousness, and the intelligent evolution of life, but they just brush all that aside. It's the pinnacle of modern day scientific ignorance and irrationality.

Why "evil" is not a problem

One of the problems that needs to be dealt with, of course, is that of evil. It is a fundamental reason why people turn to atheism. However, if you understand manifest creation, then evil is not really a problem. We live in a world of light and dark, good and evil, big tits and small tits, etc. We can all imagine a world that is less polarized. Utopias have been envisioned where all negativity is erased and there is only love and goodness. Indeed, many afterlife depictions in NDEs reflect this kind of harmony. However, if all of creation was like this it would lack depth. If there is only good, then the good ceases to really mean anything or take on importance. As psychiatrist Stanislav Grof says, "The existence of the shadow side of creation enhances its light aspects by providing contrast and gives extraordinary richness and depth to the universal drama."[4] Without it, we would live in a one sided world that lacked depth.

However, some people still think that if there is a loving God, or Source, then reality should contain no evil. And of course, that is the kind of world we want to experience--one with no evil or suffering in it. But I beg to differ. I think we do desire to experience the negative sides of life along with the good. To prove my point, I will point to entertainment such as movies and video games. If our deepest desire is to experience a utopia, why do we create violent video games? Why do our movies contain just as much tragedy as love? If people really didn't want to experience these negative aspects of the world, the entertainment they consume should reflect those utopian desires. We should be happy watching a movie that contains all good acts and no evil or tragedy in the storyline. It should be a great joy to play a video game where all the characters are happy and live in harmony. We should reject and not want to watch any movie that contains evil and we should not desire to play a video game that contains violence. On some level we must enjoy these negative aspects of life, otherwise we wouldn't play violent video games or watch sad movies. Why should our entertainment not reflect our desires?

Although consciously we may desire only good to come into our lives, on some level we all have to admit that we have a yearning for the shadow side as well. Indeed, creation works by way of the interplay of opposites. Without opposing ideas and uncertainty, philosophers would be out of a job. Without disease we could also say bye bye to all of the doctors and scientists looking for cures and all of the Nobel Prize winners who have worked to advance our knowledge of medicine. When we eliminate oppressive regimes we eliminate also the heroic individuals, like Ghandi, who fought against them. If we eliminate all war and violence then our artwork, movies, music, and literature that were inspired by those themes disappear and our library, museum, movie, and CD collections would shrink accordingly.[5] So, you see, we lose as much good as we do evil every time we remove a negative aspect of creation.

We can shift the balance and create a more one-sided world with more good than bad, but do we want to? That's something we each have to decide for ourselves. I'm in favor of turning the tables and living in a more harmonious world, but I wouldn't want to completely eradicate evil. There needs to be a sufficient amount of depth to existence, some amount of pain and suffering to provide contrast and meaning to love and happiness. We need people with opposing views, things to fight against, and things to strive for. We need opportunities for growth, learning, and understanding. Only a world with both light and dark aspects can provide us with such opportunities.

One of the most interesting and mysterious findings I've come across regarding opposites is their underlying unity. As Psychoanalyst and past-life therapist Roger Woolger points out:

> "Almost invariably a victim's thoughts like 'How could he do this to me?' or 'I'll get back at him' produce violent images of causing that pain to another. Or else the torturer becomes deeply identified with his victim's agonies to the extent of secretly imagining how it hurts. So in the play of lives the victim turns persecutor or the torturer, in his constant infliction of pain, needs to suffer the very thing he inflicts."[6]

These emotions, thoughts and desires of revenge or wanting to feel the victim's pain get turned into actual experience in the play of lives. We create by thought, word, and action. Thought is the purest form of energy and fuels our words and actions. It also informs the Source of that which we desire to experience so that the world and our place in it can be structured accordingly. The only way out of this Karmic cycle is to release the underlying emotion and thought forms that keep us tied to it. Forgiveness, love and letting go are keys here.

Psychiatrist Stanislav Grof relates a personal story in this regard in his book, *When the Impossible Happens*. After immigrating from Czechoslovakia to the United States and establishing his professional life at Spring Grove State Hospital in Baltimore, Maryland, it was time for him to meet a mate. After many unsuccessful attempts he finally met Monica, who he had an instant deep attraction for and connection to. He describes how he fell in love with her quickly and they developed a passionate and unusually stormy relationship. Furthermore, he states:

> "Monica's brother Wolfgang hated me from the very first time we had met. He and Monica had an unusually intense relationship that seemed to have distinct incestuous features. Wolfgang was violently opposed to my relationship with

Monica and treated me like a rival."[7]

During this time in history, LSD was being tested for its psychotherapeutic potential. Grof, having done extensive research in this area and realizing the powerful psychological agent that LSD is, decided to volunteer for a high-dose LSD session at the hospital he worked at. At that time, it was open to professionals to have these sessions for training purposes. During the session it was his intention to unravel the complex dynamic that was going on in his relationship with Monica. As the session progressed, he found himself in a past life as the son of an aristocratic Egyptian family. While walking in a hall of an ancient Egyptian palace, his brother in that lifetime approached him. Grof relates:

> "As the figure came closer, I recognized that it was Wolfgang. He stopped about ten feet from me and looked at me with immense hatred. I realized that in this Egyptian incarnation Wolfgang, Monica, and I were siblings. I was the firstborn and, as such, I had married Monica and received many other privileges that came with that status. Wolfgang felt cheated and experienced agonizing jealousy and strong hatred toward me. I saw clearly that this was the basis of a destructive karmic pattern that then repeated itself in many variations throughout ages."[8]

This explains the instant connection and deep love he felt for Monica shortly after they met in his current lifetime, as he was married to her in the Egyptian lifetime. It also explains the "distinct incestuous features" of Monica's relationship to Wolfgang in this lifetime, as he had been her sibling before and had desired to marry her. Finally, it explains Wolfgang's instant hatred for Grof in the current lifetime, as Grof's relationship with Monica stirred up the unconscious memory of his hatred for Grof in the Egyptian lifetime for marrying Monica. It's just one big giant puzzle to which the past is the key to unlocking. We clearly see that Grof's current life experiences are in no way accidental; there is a purpose and reason for them.

While experiencing the intense hatred coming from the past life figure of Wolfgang, he decided to try and dissipate this hatred somehow. He telepathically communicated to Wolfgang that he had taken a powerful mind altering drug which allowed him to time travel and that he would like to do anything possible to dissipate this hatred Wolfgang had for him. He then stretched out his arms in an open position and telepathically relayed the message: "Here I am, this is all I have! Please, do anything you need to do to liberate us from this bondage, to set both of us free!" Next, Wolfgang accepted his offer and Grof experienced Wolfgang's hatred in the form of two intense rays of energy which burned his body and caused him great pain. Finally, after some time, the rays of energy lost their power and faded away.

The rays of energy represent the intense hatred and feelings Wolfgang had for him, which were now being released. Wolfgang was in a sense letting go of this bottled up energy. Skeptics might chalk something like this up to a psychological fantasy imagined by Grof. However, an intriguing synchronicity suggests otherwise. Shortly after his LSD session, Grof received a phone call from Wolfgang who wanted to discuss a problem he was having in a relationship with a woman. Grof writes:

> "He thought about discussing the issue with me, but had rejected the idea because of his strong negative feelings toward me. But then his attitude toward me suddenly changed radically. His hatred dissolved as if by magic, and he decided to call me and seek help. When I asked him when this had happened, I found out that it exactly coincided with the time when I had completed the reliving of the Egyptian sequence."[9]

It's one thing for Grof alone to experience psychologically the resolution of this ancient karmic pattern, but quite another for another player in the karmic pattern, who had no knowledge of what Grof was doing at the time, to experience the resolution of the same karmic pattern at the exact same time that Grof did. This suggests that something much deeper was going on beyond the confines of Grof's own psyche. It also suggests that Grof was indeed going back to the source of the karmic pattern that was playing itself out yet again in this life. Until the underlying emotional energy was cleared away, this pattern was bound to continue. But, after the dissipation of Wolfgang's underlying hatred, they could both be freed from this destructive pattern.

Woolger relates one story of a man who in one medieval life "took great sadistic pleasure in the torture and execution of witches." In another life he found himself on the receiving end as "the political victim of the Nazis." Specifically, he "is tortured to death for information he does not possess." He sees a similarity between his previous cruel self and the figure of the torturing Nazi. Realizing the potential for a spiraling cycle of vengeful lives, he opts instead to forgive his Nazi tormenter and end the cycle of violence and hatred. Thereby, he is released from the Karmic pattern.[10]

Lives may also alternate between a life of greed and one of giving away one's money generously, or between "callous disregard for human life" and "selfless devotion to others."[11] The possibilities are endless here, and of course we mostly live a life somewhere in the middle of these extremes. It all boils down to what we want to experience. When we are finally able to let go of the emotional connection to such events, have forgiveness, and no longer wish to experience them, then we can move on to different experiences. We could incarnate on other worlds, or in other dimensions. The possibilities for conscious experience are endless. We are sitting on a conscious ocean of possibilities just waiting to be actualized. I believe that the future holds great hope. As we become more consciously aware there is great potential for humanity to rise into new levels of awareness and develop greater powers of consciousness. Belief is the X factor here. If we are to expand our awareness beyond the physical and develop ourselves psychically, we need to believe in it. Belief is so important in determining not just how we see the world, but the actions we take and the things we try to accomplish. If we don't believe in the ability to be clairvoyant, telepathic, or telekinetic then we will never try to accomplish these feats. It's time to start believing in order to see. Evolution is taking us into these greater heights of consciousness. We must believe it in order to see, but once we do believe the possibilities are endless.

The future of conscious development

We see it in the expanded awareness of those who have other-dimensional experiences. People who go out-of-body or who become lucid in their dreams or who travel to the Light during a NDE or who interact with alien beings during an abduction all have one thing in common. They all see the greater potential of the human mind. Many come back changed as a result. Psychic Uri Gellar, who is known popularly for spoon bending using only his concentrated thought but who also has other reported psychic abilities such as telepathy, traces his powers back to a beam of light that came from the sky.[12]

After a close encounter with a UFO, one man found himself excessively tired for about two months. He also started having out-of-body experiences and showed changes in belief and perspective. Furthermore, he said he would write a book because "THEY" told him to.[13] A near-death experiencer (NDEr) named Stéphane had a NDE and a while afterwards "was seized with an irresistible desire to write about it." He wrote a 50 page document that he feels was "dictated to me." He didn't understand what he was writing until he had written it and went back to look over what he'd written. The subjects covered in the document included philosophy, poetry, life after death, spirituality, and scriptural revelations.[14] An abductee named Polly says that around age fourteen she had an obsession with finding out about "the workings of the universe." She says, "I felt I must understand the universe. It became a constant undercurrent of striving which persists even now."[15] Abductee Kim Carlsberg says that as a result of her contacts with aliens, she has "been left with unusual attributes, such as telepathy and hands-on healing abilities." It was consoling to her that many other abductees report the same changes.[16] NDErs, too, report these same kinds of changes. When asked if she had any psychic or non-ordinary abilities after her experience, Francine reported, "Yes Energy pours through my hands and I know exactly where to be on a person's body for healing."[17] Another NDEr, Cherie, reports that since her experience, "My degrees of telepathy, Clair essence, clairvoyance, clairsentient, etc. have all been heightened dramatically. I also feel the presence of many other dimensions at once which I had never previously experienced."[18] Recently, Grandmaster of NDE research, Dr. Jeffrey Long, noted that in his extensive online survey of NDE reports a whopping 45% of NDErs answered Yes to the question asking them if they had any psychic, paranormal or other special gifts as a result of their experience.[19] Former Grandmaster of NDE research Kenneth Ring said about his interviews with NDErs, "I could not help noticing the frequency with which psychic events were spontaneously reported by NDErs and how often these experiences were said to have occurred following the NDE."[20] In his own survey of NDErs, Ring reports that over half (58%) reported a significant increase in overall psychic ability.[21]

Something intriguing is going on in the world, and I'm not the first one to point this out. Writing around the turn of the twentieth century, Dr. Richard Maurice Bucke wrote an influential book in which he argued that human consciousness was due for an evolutionary leap into what he called "cosmic consciousness," or "the intuitional mind."[22] Intuition speaks to a direct knowing of things. Whereas the intellect is separate from the object which it analyzes, in the intuitional mind the separation of subject and object disappears and one enters into the object, becomes it, and knows it firsthand. This is strikingly similar to telepathy, a direct energy transference, or then again what I have called "conscious entanglement" where one's consciousness entangles with, or enters into, another person or object to know it directly. Telepathy is the most basic feature of nearly all other-dimensional experiences and one wonders if this capacity will not be developed here on Earth in this dimension. There are already studies, as we pointed out in the first chapter, suggesting that telepathy is a genuine faculty of the human mind.

In the course of human evolution, we may be moving toward a breakdown of the barriers between dimensions. The Earth may itself, and human consciousness along with it, transition into a higher level of mind. This will bring with it an illumination of the Oneness of all. At the same time psychic capacity will increase bringing increased powers of telepathy, clairvoyance, out-of-body travel, and finally telekinesis. In essence, we will have fewer restrictions and more power to create our own reality.

Kenneth Ring wrote about "an imaginal body" that would be used by future humans in a parallel realm, or dimension, beyond the confines of space and time.[23] These imaginal realms, I take it, correspond more or less to the higher levels of mind experienced by out-of-body explorers and lucid dreamers. These realms are more easily shaped and manipulated by one's consciousness. Ring suggests that over time these imaginal realms will stabilize and become our new reality. We will, in this sense, evolve out of the physical.

Future visions of the Earth have been reported that do match up to this kind of thinking. Robert Monroe speaks of visiting the Earth sometime after the year 3000 during one of his astral experiences. The Earth at this time has been restored to its natural ecological balance. He saw fewer people living on Earth. The people that were there could go in and out of their bodies at will, meaning they must have fully developed "imaginal" bodies to travel out-of-body and in other dimensions. There was no need for transportation as they could travel out-of-body and then enter a new physical body when they reached their destination. They also didn't need to eat and got their energy from the atmosphere, maybe through some sort of solar absorbance. They also have the ability to shape matter with their minds. They could literally take any substance, such as dirt, and mold it into anything they wanted with the power of thought.[24]

In another report of future Earth, Psychiatrist Brian Weiss took people under hypnosis to the future and reported many similar things as Monroe. One of his clients described going to the year 3200, which would roughly correspond to when Monroe visited. She also says the Earth is much greener with lush forests and seems restored. Also, she reports fewer people on Earth, as did Monroe. However, in her account everything seems more ethereal. She says people communicate telepathically at this time and have less dense bodies. She saw people living in small communities with a harmonic resonance with nature. Everything had a translucent quality and "a permeating light that connects everyone and everything in peace." She also saw a "liquid light" that pours into people and plants, possibly providing them nourishment.[25]

These are fantastic visions that may see like pure fantasy. However, these visions represent possibilities. We must act to make them realities. Many people who have other-dimensional experiences come to very similar conclusions and seem to be progressing toward ideas that are in line with the fulfillment of these future possibilities. Abductee Jane was given a dream lesson in which she was taught that the body was only a tool, only a shell of her conscious mind. She was taught that her soul could separate from her body before death. In her words, "I am a spiritual being only animating a shell. The body is nothing, the soul is all."[26] Abductee Leah Haley learned the same thing. She says, "I have learned my body is only a container for my soul and they cannot destroy that."[27] This echos the statements of NDEr Giselle, who says "I remember vividly that it was expected that my soul control my body, that the body is only the vehicle necessary for life on planet earth."[28]

We are One

The knowledge of Oneness with everyone and everything in the universe is also common among experiencers. Speaking from an alien perspective, abductee Eva said, "We are an offshoot of I or what you would equal to God."[29] Abductee Beth had an extra-dimensional experience in which she felt her brain was being taken out and put back in by the aliens. Afterwards, her mind was filled with new thoughts "about God and the unity of all life within that supreme source."[30] Abductee Peter "spoke of a 'great web' of connection, a 'consciousness of the whole . . . I am them, and they are me..."[31] Abductees are often given the knowledge that they and the aliens are One. Such statements as IRU URI are given to abductees, which literally means "I are you, you are I."[32] Kim Carlsberg was told "You are us." She said she had the "realization, a knowing we are all one . . . one consciousness, one mind, one being!"[33] I would interpret these statements as meaning we are all offshoots of one great Source Consciousness. NDErs also get this knowledge that everything is connected. NDEr Virginia Drake had a very profound revelation that's worth quoting:

> "I viewed my life and several events and realized that we are all one with the Universe so when I hurt someone I was really hurting myself and even more so I was hurting every soul in the Universe. I realized I was pure white light and each soul had a different hue, but I could see them. Many times other souls could not make the viewing so they would walk away from the light. Again not feeling worthy. God's goodness over doubt; that is what I was told, to stop doubting myself and know that I am the light of God. I also traveled through the Universe called the wheel of life, God or the consciousness of God was the center and we are all the spokes of the wheel. Felt what God felt and know what God knew and it is not of this world of man but different world all together."[34]

This essential Oneness and connection to a greater Source is the ultimate revelation that is occurring on a broad scale today. Mystical experiences are becoming more and more common through peoples extraordinary experiences. The knowledge is that we are one with a great Source Consciousness that is experienced as Light, which is all knowing, all powerful, and is All. One gets the idea that Consciousness is Light, possibly in both a literal and metaphoric sense. It is intelligent, sentient, aware light with the ability to form and control matter/energy.

I believe through other-dimensional experiences humanity is being prepared for the future evolution of consciousness. Indeed, this evolution is happening right now. However, it's not as if everyone will be telepathic tomorrow. People aren't ready on a broad enough scale for that. Eventually, as more and more people have these experiences the wider culture will accept such things as natural. But, the tide of scientific reasoning also needs to come along and accept consciousness as fundamental to reality. We need not only a cultural shift, but also a shift in our institutions that teach society what to believe. Without that, there will be great resistance to any change.

As it is now, science is in the business of telling people that any other experience besides the physical is not real. Therefore, most people who have these kinds of experiences stay quiet about them. They don't share their experience with others for fear of being labeled crazy. That negative attitude towards other-dimensional experiences needs to change.

The only time is NOW

There are various teachings about the nature of the universe that are coming through extra-ordinary experiences. I will touch on a couple here. NDEr Glenda saw the universe as one giant interdimensional grid with "various planes crossing and intersecting." It was as if all time and place was just energy vibrating at different speeds.[35] Abductee Bonnie Jean Hamilton was informed "that many different dimensions existed simultaneously, side by side."[36] NDEr Cherie got the impression that "the universe consists of different dimensions occurring at different levels of what we call time or speed. Some are happening at the same time, some are in the past and some are in the future."[37] Comic book writer Alan Moore had an experience of being in an altered state of consciouness and speaking with "what seemed to be the second-century Roman snake god Glycon." He was shown "that all of time was happening at once. Linear time was purely a construction of the conscious mind..."[38]

What we have here is knowledge that all dimensions, and indeed all of time, exists in an eternal NOW. We move through time linearly because that's the way our minds construct experience. From the highest level of mind—Source Consciousness—we could see all time as a single whole and know all things past, present, and future. From our perspective and current state of consciousness though, we experience moving through time moment by moment. Things happen slowly and we are constantly making decisions about what to do. However, just as all of our past experiences and lives already exist, so too do all of our future decisions and lives already exist because there really is no time; only an eternal NOW. This doesn't abdicate free will as some might think. Even though all time exists NOW, you still live your life and make decisions, learn and grow. It's just that all of those decisions are actually already made, or have been made, because all time already exists.

So, all dimensions and all time are open for conscious exploration and exist in the ever present NOW. A recent movie, Men in Black 3, shows this theme in a character known as Griffin who can see all possibilities and calculate what the probable future(s) is. It could be that all possibilities do exist as actual lived realities, but we are only aware of one of them--the one time dimension stream we are currently weaving our way through. It could also be that all possibilities exist in potential, as unmanifest possibilities. As we go through life, we manifest--or actualize--some possibilities to the exclusion of others. However, all events that happened in the past or that will happen in the future already exist NOW, we're just not aware of them.

Moving Forward

As I mentioned before, people are being prepared for the shifting evolution of consciousness. Bonnie Hamilton received psychic training from "the star people" including energy manipulation using the mind.[39] Other abductees have received similar psychic training or have otherwise gained an increased psychic ability due to their abductions.[40] As stated before, NDErs also report more psychic phenomena after their experiences. Also, abductees and NDErs report an increased sensitivity towards the Earth and a concern for its ecology.[41] They also report a shift away from valuing material things to a valuation of things spiritual.[42]

Evolution in this regard will continue ever so slowly with more and more people experiencing the truly extraordinary. As soon as the larger culture and scientific community becomes accepting of them, evolution can really take a giant step forward. I cannot say how this future evolution will unfold, only that we are in the midst of it. Henri Bergson was right when he said the universe was "a machine for the making of gods."[43] We are gods and can create entire worlds of which we are the master of. In fact, we have created this one at a higher level of mind, and can ascend back to that level through conscious evolution. We can begin our evolution with the making of our very own imaginal worlds and out-of-body explorations into those worlds. In time, as more and more people become consciously aware, we will be able to use our minds to recreate the physical in our desired image. We will have the same power over the physical as we do over the imaginal.

Alas! Reality can be what we want it to be. We can take reality by the balls and say, "You're my bitch now!" With that proclamation we will make reality conform to our will and say "Fuck You" to anyone who stands in our way. This egotistic thinking needs to be forgotten. We exist in human bodies with a very limited consciousness as of present. I wouldn't want to be given full responsibility for creating reality in my present state. My knowledge is much too limited, my perspective insanely biased. I think I'm smart, yet have read only a tiny sliver of the millions of books that have been written, have studied a mere grain of sand of all the subjects available for study, have been to a fraction of the countries in the world. In my current state I am no more the master of the world than I am the master of my passions.

It is not I who coordinates this world or defines its laws. That would be far too big a job for any human being. Yet I know that I am a part of the process, that my life has meaning, and that ultimately it is I who am responsible for the entire cosmos. It is "I" in the form of the great "I AM," the Source Mind of the universe. At the highest level I am identical with the Source. You are too, we all are. It is the Source who forms and has the ultimate control over reality. It is us, yet it is not us in our present state.

Being connected to the Source, we do have power to shape the world. If the Source is us, wouldn't the Source, after all, be listening to us? Every thought and every desire being a kind of wish. Then we have to ask, how deep is that wish? Is there any opposing belief that we might have? We can all think of thousands of examples where reality didn't bend to our beliefs or expectations. At a certain level of mind, the world is at our complete control but as we ourselves exist now, this cannot be said. Higher levels of mind control most of reality, leading to claims that the world is objective and is apart from ourselves. But the world is created from within, the information that our minds use to construct the world emanates from within the deeper levels of mind. What we see is a projection.

Evolution is destined to propel us into ever higher spheres of mind, giving us ever greater knowledge, understanding, and power over reality. Even now, we can access those levels. With a sufficient conviction and belief that has no resistance at the higher levels of mind, we can change our reality right now. By using our imagination, we can tap into the subconscious mind and imagine ourselves in a new way. By focusing on that image and asking repeatedly, the power of our thought will condense and become sufficient to move mountains. Ultimately we must trust that we are one with the Source and that Source has our best interests at heart. We must tell the Source through our minds, through our beliefs, through our imaginations, what we want and let go, trusting that this higher level of mind will work with us to provide us with what we want. We must focus on what we want, knowing that anything is possible and trusting in the universe, all the while working towards our goals and doing what we can to further ourselves. Dream yourself into being and never doubt or be discouraged because you know, you know it's possible. Dedicate yourself to something and be persistent. Communicate with the higher spheres of mind through your thought, knowing that there is a universe that cares and is listening. Ask for answers and then wait for the universe to provide those answers. Imagine yourself as you want to be and believe in the image, continually telling the Source, "This is what I want." Don't doubt the power of your mind. In the end, the world as it is matters much less than the world as we imagine it to be.

CONCLUSION

Bone breakage healing instantly, UFOs disappearing and reappearing in a flash or ripping holes in the fabric of space-time, people traveling outside of their bodies to distant planets and dimensions, the information systems and complex inner workings of the smallest cell, the complex interplay of belief and the operation of physical reality, the minds access to information outside the purview of the senses, and the movement of matter by way of the mind are all fundamental mysteries. We will never understand these miraculous happenings in our world without acknowledging that reality is a play of consciousness. Consciousness creates reality and has power over it.

The evidence I've presented in this book is both compelling and fascinating. Surely, if you want you can try to explain it away and hang on to a pre-existing belief system. Or you might find other ways to interpret it than I have. That is perfectly fine. We are each boundlessly free to form our own belief systems and examine those data which conform to them, and explain away any data that doesn't. That is the way any belief system works. I, for one, do my best to try and not exclude data. In fact, I would argue that the more data a theory excludes, the weaker and more tenuous it is. And indeed what data could be excluded from a belief system that envisions consciousness as the creator of reality, with multiple dimensions and infinite possibilities of experience within those dimensions. Quite simply, what you experience, whether in this dimension or another is real. It is a creation of consciousness. Even a hallucination not seen by others is real to the percipient, part of their mind and the higher dimensions of the psyche. It may even have an ontological existence apart from the percipient, an existence in an alternate dimension of reality which the percipient happens to be tuned into.

One tactic scientists often use to ignore data is to call it anecdotal, meaning that it is a reported experience that did not occur in a laboratory or under controlled conditions. I don't agree with ignoring evidence because it's anecdotal. Repeated experiences of a certain kind across vast numbers of people suffice to establish the reality of a phenomenon, such as telepathy or precognition. Laboratory experiments are a mere formality, proving what we already know to be true by repeated direct experience. Just to take a simple example, dropping a heavy object on your toe will cause pain and sometimes result in swelling. If I get 10,000 reports of people who have dropped heavy objects on their toes and experienced pain, then I can pretty well establish the theory that dropping heavy things on your toe causes pain. A laboratory experiment may formally prove it, but it's just a formality. With that said, a laboratory experiment under controlled conditions is beneficial for exploring technicalities of the experience, such as how heavy the object has to be before it causes pain, or from what height it must be dropped.

Now some things, like the existence of subatomic particles or the higgs boson, absolutely require controlled laboratory experiments to establish their reality. There is no other way to observe such things. But most human experiences do not require laboratory experiments to demonstrate their truth. What is required is repeated experience of the same type of phenomenon. So, if I have 10,000 NDE reports, or 10,000 UFO abduction reports, with distinct commonalities and features, then I know it is real and don't need the experience to be demonstrated in a laboratory. Not that these experiences could be confirmed in a laboratory, as there is no laboratory that can monitor experiences in another dimension, but you know what I mean. Now, this line of reasoning does have some snags. For instance, say I have 10,000 reports of people who say they've seen the Loc Ness Monster. Well, there may be natural explanations for some sightings and active imaginations or fraudulent stories may make up a significant portion of the rest. So, I cannot conclude that there is a real, physical Loc Ness Monster just based on the fact that I have 10,000 sighting reports. The reports need to be carefully sifted through and analyzed from multiple perspectives. With an extra-dimensional experience like the NDE, we need to also keep a critical eye out for reporting bias or exaggeration. For instance, a NDEr may see a being of light and think, "that must be Jesus." The being may even take on a form and appearance that conforms with the experiencer's expectations of what Jesus should look like. However, the being may not be Jesus at all, but some other conscious entity. Keep in mind that in higher dimensions you can change your appearance and take on different forms. Often times beings in the afterlife will come to us in a form which we find comfortable or familiar and we will experience things appropriate for our level of consciousness. This can explain many cultural differences in the reports. In any case, there is always an underlying reality. In the case of the Loch Ness Monster, that underlying reality may be an oddly shaped tree log floating in the water at dawn. In the case of Jesus encountered during NDEs, the underlying reality is a being of light. Now, I'm not trying to assert that there is actually no Loch Ness Monster, or that Jesus himself doesn't actually appear to some NDErs. In both cases, I don't know. I'm just saying we need to keep a critical eye when sifting through reports. This doesn't mean that we need to try and explain away everything people see during these experiences. For instance, you could try to explain away all NDE or abduction reports as imagination. Here, we have to look for commonalities of reports. If enough people have the experience, reporting it as a real lived experience, with details that match up from report to report then it makes more sense to explain it based on actual experience rather than imagination. Imagination should be highly individualized, whereas a real experience should show more commonalities among reports. When the reports match up, and are described as real experiences, we need to posit that the experiences are real. Even with the Loch Ness Monster, if I have a significant number of reports of people who have had no contact with each other reporting the same kind of Monster with the same kind of features that I can't explain as a natural phenomenon, then I would posit an actual existence for this creature. It may not be physically real however. They may all be tapping into a higher psychic dimension where it exists.

With this in mind, I would like to call for a science of conscious experience. This will be a science of direct, repeated human experience. It involves collecting reports of peoples experiences with a certain phenomenon, say out-of-body experiences, and analyzing those reports for commonalities and differences. Not just that, but we can examine the knowledge about reality that comes from the experience. After analyzing a sufficient number of cases, theories and hypotheses can be formulated and debated. Any type of anomalous experience can be analyzed this way. There are already projects underway which allow for such a science. For instance, The Near Death Experience Research Foundation (NDERF) currently has well over 2000 near death experiences listed on their website in full text for anyone to read.[1] This is a mass of data and a very important contribution. There is also a sister website for people to report experiences of other sorts, like out-of-body experiences. I feel projects like these need to be stepped up and more centers of data collection should be set up. I would encourage the data to be freely available on the internet for the benefit of researchers. The NDERF serves as an exemplary model. On the site, people can fill out an online survey describing their experience in as many words as they choose and answer survey questions about the experience. This type of survey collection will enable researchers to read through reports of peoples experiences, which should all be freely available online, to look for commonalities and theorize about the data. I believe the most pressing need in this regard is a website devoted to alien abduction, or alien contact, experiences where people can report in detail their abduction memories and answer questions directed towards that kind of experience. That's one of the reasons I decided to make my own website devoted to gathering accounts of paranormal happenings. I have surveys directed toward many different categories of anomalous experience, including alien abduction, telepathy, and telekinesis. So, I encourage readers who have experienced something paranormal to go to my website (www.anomalousexperience.com) and fill out the survey including a complete description of the experience.

There is a role for traditional laboratory science in this regard as well. I know I derided laboratory experiments as unnecessary in most cases, but in all truth, proving experiences via highly controlled conditions is a good thing. Especially, it helps to have that kind of evidence when trying to convince others that the phenomenon is real. It is the strongest kind of evidence, and as such is valuable. Also, I mentioned that technicalities can be explored this way. The problem is that any kind of research into these anomalous phenomena is automatically ridiculed and labeled pseudoscience. Quite often it is ignored. This is highly unfortunate, but what can you do? Not much. We just have to keep experimenting and eventually the mentality of the greater scientific world will hopefully shift. Indeed, as the trend of society shifts toward a higher belief in the anomalous, science must follow or be left behind. So, I would like to propose some suggestions for research.

In regards to out-of-body experiences, experienced individuals able to induce OBEs willfully and often need to be found and brought into a sleep laboratory. The experiment I will describe involves two OBErs. They are to have no prior contact with each other and no history of any contact. They will be housed in separate rooms. A formal greeting between the two participants should be allowed, but closely monitored. This is so they at least know who the other person is, what they look like, and their name. Also, it can help in establishing a friendly rapport between participants. So they should be brought together once for a, "Hey my name's Dave. Good to see you." "Hi, I'm Jerry. Nice to meet you." "So, where are you from Jerry?" "I'm from Wisconsin, and you?" "Oh, I'm from Toronto. I love the Packers though." "Yeah, I forgot to bring my cheese head. I've been to Toronto once, love the Maple Leafs." "You better, haha." [The researcher buts in] "Ok, well that's enough of a greeting. We'll take you to your separate rooms now and get started with the experiment." After this initial meeting, there should be absolutely no contact between the two OBErs. They should be kept at the laboratory for several nights and instructed to try and have an OBE each night and meet the other experimental subject at a specified location. They will be instructed that when they successfully meet they should each, in turn, tell the other a specific memory they have, relaying detailed information about some past event in their life. The memory should be short, confined to one or two sentences, since a long detailed memory would probably be too hard for a person to remember after coming back to their body. However, it should contain specific details, such as the age when the event occurred. Something like, "when I was 13, I got my first gun and shot a pheasant," should do. They are to choose prior to the OBE which memory to discuss, but they are not to inform anyone of this memory, including the researchers.

Then they are to decide together, while out-of-body, to go to another specific location (like the parking lot outside) and take note of specifically what they see. This other location will be decided during their OBE and they can pick any location on Earth or in another dimension of their choosing, but they must decide and go there together. Then they will each come back to their bodies. Upon awakening they should have access to a recording device which they can immediately dictate their experience into. They can also write it down, every detail that they remember. The separate dictations will then be analyzed by the experimenters and the participants interviewed separately about what they experienced, specifically what memory they told to the other, what memory the other told them, what subsequent location they both travelled to and every detail they remember of that location. So, there are really two variables here that can be checked. One is the memory and the other is the second location they went to together while out-of-body and what they saw there.

There are many factors that could confound an experiment like this, such as one of the OBErs prematurely reentering their body. However, this is a much more interesting experiment than the standard of placing a 5-digit number in a location that cannot be seen unless floating near the ceiling and having the person have an OBE and report the number. Boring experiments are fine, and much cheaper to perform. However, the more interesting the experiment, the better. I think the motivation of the participants in the experiment I described would be much higher than if they were simply to look at a number and report it back to the researcher. I might even propose a hypothesis: The more interesting the experiments are to the participants, the better the results you will obtain. Let's see if this holds true!

If a researcher is bold enough, they can replicate the experiments of earlier researchers with trance mediums. For this experiment a good trance medium should be found who can produce psychokinetic effects in the trance state. Controls can be applied to make sure the medium does not physically interact with the objects being levitated. Also, objects in the room can be wired up and monitored by machinery in another room. That way if any force is applied to the object, it can be measured. I would also encourage other tests of psychokinesis with people trying to produce the phenomenon from a normal state of consciousness. But please, no more boring experiments involving moving a circle of lights in a certain direction. Spice it up a little and try for more of a macro-PK effect. Playfair's experiment may serve as a useful guide in this regard.

In regards to NDEs, it's too highly unethical to induce them in the laboratory. However, work such as Cardiologist Pim Van Lommel's should continue. In hospitals around the world, immediately or soon after a person is revived from a cardiac arrest, they should be asked if they experienced any subjective experience during their period of unconsciousness. If they say yes, a detailed description of the experience should be asked for. If they report leaving their bodies and experiencing events in the hospital, attempted validation from hospital staff or other individuals involved in their perception should be undertaken as soon as possible. Notes should be taken as to the EEG readings and the time of unconsciousness relative to the reported experiences of out-of-body perception. This will help establish if the out-of-body perception was indeed at a time when their EEG readings indicated that they should not have been conscious or aware of the environment.

These kinds of studies will help validate the reality of the phenomenon and establish clear scientific grounds for believing in the existence of consciousness apart from the physical body. Other types of experiences, such as alien abductions, unfortunately cannot be studied this way because the experiences seem to be dictated by higher intelligences and happen mostly in other dimensions inaccessible to modern science. So, the science of consciousness as I have formulated it will have to study those and other experiences that can't be reproduced on demand. We have much to learn about paranormal phenomena. That's why centers for collecting reports need to be continually set up and the information freely available for evaluation by researchers online. Detailed reports and surveys need to be collected about each kind of experience. Databases, such as provided by NDERF, will help us learn much more about such experiences.

The modern worldview of the universe as a purely physical system with no inherent meaning or purpose has not always been held. The ancients felt themselves to be part of the surrounding world. In those days, the world was alive with meaning and purpose. This was an inner *felt* experience. Every rock, every stone, every star in the sky was alive and held an integral place in God's creation. Nature was a great mystery that was not looked at from an objective position apart, but experienced as a living creation of the mind of God.

As science has progressed, we have progressively separated ourselves from the world, studying "inanimate" matter devoid of a living spirit. Ironically science has come full circle, back to a living, conscious universe which our consciousness actively participates in. In biology we know there must be an intelligence at work in every cell. Our DNA, proteins, and protein machines all show exquisite design that could only come about through the actions of an intelligent agent. If there's an intelligence at such a small level of life, then it's safe to suggest that this intelligence must underlie the universe itself.

Quantum physics has directly confronted our participation in reality, with consciousness directly linked to the creation of physical particles themselves at the subatomic level. Our conscious decision to gain information about, say, the spin of an electron, actually creates that particle out of a hypothetical "probability distribution," or "wave function" which cannot be located in space and time as we know it. Mind creates matter. There's really no simpler way to put it. Mind is fundamental, material reality an epiphenomenon. And on top of that incredible finding, we have to pile on fact after fact about how our minds somehow also play a role in *how* reality is created and acts. I believe a higher level of mind, Source Consciousness, controls the underlying aspects of how we all collectively see and experience the world. In other words, the Source controls the rule set by which we experience, and sets the laws of physics as we know them. But, I also believe that we participate in this process by in-forming the Source through our beliefs, expectations, emotions, and desires (the contents of our consciousness really) about that which we want to experience. We are not necessarily conscious of this process, but can become conscious of it and dream ourselves into being, so to speak. For this to work well we need a focused mind, a certain goal from which we cannot be deterred. Doubt is the plague that sets us back. If we are to be our own Authors, as Jeffrey Kripal would say, we must allow ourselves to believe the impossible.[2] There are no limits.

I invite you to live a life of meaning, wonder, awe, purpose, and divine Being. Feel it, breathe it, be a part of it. Rejoice in your underlying nature as a child of the Source, a beautiful, magnificent, radiant creation of the one divine Mind. You are part of the Source and you are One with it. At this level of reality we all have separate ego consciousnesses which view others, the world, and ourselves as distinct from one another. But underlying all of that, there is a collective Source consciousness where all things and beings become One. It's just a deeper level of mind. As we move from the physical level to that of higher dimensions, our separateness is still evident but begins to break down as we communicate telepathically and experience things more intimately. In higher dimensions we are much more aware of our participation in the creation of reality, as our thoughts manifest much more quickly and with greater ease. Reality itself is one big maze of dimensions and universes where the creative force is *thought* itself. Intelligent, aware consciousness underlies it all.   We used to think that this Earth was too vast to explore fully. Before airplanes and billions of people who could go just about anywhere, this world was a big place and not many people traveled very far. There were still vast untapped areas to explore. Now, we've been all over the Earth and have found incredible things, including exotic life forms, mysterious caves, and precious stones. These days we need a new adventure. It is time to get that excitement again that comes with wide open vistas ripe for exploration. Well, we got that vista. It's called multidimensional reality, and it's ripe for exploration. What lands lie in the deep reaches of our minds? What exotic alien life forms can we meet on other planets and in other dimensions? What more great discoveries await us? Let the imagination reign!

APPENDIX

On Random Mutation and Natural Selection

Random mutation and natural selection certainly does occur, and can have very noticeable and sometimes beneficial effects. This is not in question and we will look at some examples of what random mutation can do shortly. What is in question is if random mutation/natural selection can have the kind of effect that scientists say it can, namely the creation of new forms of life from pre-existing ones through successive beneficial mutations of the DNA. I intend to show that there is strong evidence, both scientific and logical, for thinking that it cannot. It is my intention to show that an intelligence is necessarily guiding the process of evolution. The blind man without a stick to guide him is lost. He needs his stick to guide him, and evolution needs its intelligence to guide it.

First, we should understand a little bit about how random mutation operates. Michael Behe, of Lehigh University, provides a good assessment of how random mutation works in his book *The Edge of Evolution*. Random mutation occurs when the cell's DNA replication machinery makes a mistake during coping. It can do this in many ways, including switching one nucleotide, or letter, with another, deleting one or more nucleotides, adding one or more nucleotides, flipping a section of nucleotides, doubling a set of nucleotides by copying them twice, or even doubling the entire genome by copying the entire sequence of DNA twice.[1]

According to Behe, random mutations most often degrade the DNA code. An example is the mutation that creates sickle cell hemoglobin. Hemoglobin is the protein found in red blood cells that carries oxygen from the lungs to all of the tissues of the body. In sickle cell hemoglobin, a single amino acid is substituted for another in the protein structure of hemoglobin. This distorts the structure of the hemoglobin molecule, creating misshapen red blood cells. Although normal red blood cells have a donut shape, sickle cells have "bizarre shapes, including crescents and sickles." Now, this is a harmful mutation because it causes the hemoglobin to act like a magnet and stick to other hemoglobin molecules, which "congeals into a gelatinous mess inside each red blood cell." This jamming together of hemoglobin seriously reduces the flexibility of the red blood cell and may cause the cells to get stuck in tiny capillaries, where the bloodstream narrows.[2]

This simple example is meant to prove a major point about the complexity and coherence of biological systems. Just one amino acid change caused major structural damage to a wonderfully constructed molecule. Based on this, the specificity of the arrangement of amino acids in the proteins that make up hemoglobin seems remarkable. Just changing one of the hundreds of amino acids that make up hemoglobin causes a degradation of the protein as a whole. This shows that proteins are constructed in very specific ways to allow them to function properly.

However, this change leading to sickle cell hemoglobin happened to be selected by natural selection because it gave resistance to malaria. The malaria parasite, which invades red blood cells, cannot operate for a sufficient enough time to feed and reproduce in the misshapen red blood cells. This is because they gel together and are quickly eliminated by the spleen.[3] Therefore, although degrading function, it is beneficial in one sense. So, it is an example of an undirected mutation that is then selected by environmental factors.

Sometimes random changes in an amino acid sequence don't hurt the protein that bad, and can even slightly modify it in a way that might be wholly advantageous. And that leads us into our next example of Darwinian style evolution. Hold onto your seats for this one. This next experiment we will look at is the granddaddy of all evolution experiments.

The experiment in question was and still is being performed by Richard Lenski and colleagues at Michigan State University. Lenski has performed the most comprehensive "lab evolution" ever conducted. The experiment is really ingenious. It involves the bacterium *E-coli*. What Lenski did was to take some E-coli bacteria from a single source and place the bacteria in 12 separate flasks. Since the bacteria all came from the same source, they started out more or less genetically identical. Inside the flasks was a nutrient broth that included glucose as the main food source. The flasks were placed in a 'shaking incubator' where they were kept warm and shaken to distribute the bacteria evenly throughout the solution. Furthermore, the flasks for each of the 12 lines of bacterial evolution were changed every day. Every day, precisely one-hundredth of the volume of the old flask was withdrawn and put into a new flask with a fresh supply of glucose-rich solution.[4] This experiment, started in 1988, is still ongoing today. Can you imagine that, changing the flasks for all twelve lines of 'evolving' bacteria every day for over 20 years! Bravo, I say.

As Richard Dawkins correctly points out, DNA mutations are rare, but even if we assume a low rate of mutation, such as one mutation per billion bacterial reproductions, since bacteria multiply so quickly there are many chances for Darwinian-style evolution to take place. So, what were the magnificent results that Dawkins calls "a beautiful demonstration of evolution in action"?[5] Did the bacteria grow new structures, such as eyes, legs, or fins? Did the bacteria change body plan over time to become more like another organism? The answer to both of these questions is a big No. Most of the mutations the bacteria underwent were degenerative, leading to a loss of function.[6] One result was that the bacteria increased in body size. Each of the twelve lines of evolving bacteria increased in size, although not uniformly since each line did it at different rates and ended up leveling off at different cell volumes.[7] The fact that bacteria grew in size is hardly surprising or significant. But that's not all that happened...

After approximately 33,000 generations of growing bacteria (trillions upon trillions of organisms), in one of the lines the population density shot up like a rocket. In fact, after this new population density leveled off it was about 6 times higher than it had been before. There were now 6 times more bacteria thriving in the same space as before.[8] How did this happen?

What happened was that the bacteria developed the ability to utilize citrate, which was another nutrient in the broth which *E-coli* bacteria normally cannot utilize in the presence of oxygen, not because they lack the digestive mechanisms to digest the substance, but only because they lack an enzyme needed to draw citrate into the cell through the membrane. As Behe responds:

> "Now, wild E-coli already has a number of enzymes that
> normally use citrate and can digest it (it's not some exotic
> chemical the bacterium has never seen before). However, the
> wild bacterium lacks an enzyme called a "citrate permease"

which can transport citrate from outside the cell through the cell's membrane into its interior. So all the bacterium needed to do to use citrate was to find a way to get it into the cell. The rest of the machinery for its metabolism was already there."[9]

The researchers know this ability to get citrate into the cell would have required more than one mutation. That's because 30,000 generations was enough time for every gene in the genome of the bacterium to have mutated at least once. Therefore, if it was a single mutation we would expect it to show up in all twelve lines.[10] Instead of a single mutation accounting for the change, it probably required a whopping two mutations. It was shown by some ingenious testing that after generation 20,000, the bacteria were 'primed' by a first mutation so as to be able to take advantage of the second mutation that occurred around generation 33,000.[11] It seems that these 2 mutations together modified one of the bacteria's enzymes just enough so as to be able to allow it to transport citrate into the cell in the presence of oxygen. As Behe explains:

> "Other workers (cited by Lenski) in the past several decades have also identified mutant E. coli that could use citrate as a food source. In one instance the mutation wasn't tracked down. (2) In another instance a protein coded by a gene called citT, which normally transports citrate in the absence of oxygen, was overexpressed. (3) The overexpressed protein allowed E. coli to grow on citrate in the presence of oxygen. It seems likely that Lenski's mutant will turn out to be either this gene or another of the bacterium's citrate-using genes, tweaked a bit to allow it to transport citrate in the presence of oxygen. (He hasn't yet tracked down the mutation.)"[12]

So, the E-coli was already in possession of a protein that could transport citrate in the absence of oxygen. All that needed to be done was to tweak this protein a little so that it could transport citrate with oxygen present. The researchers have now tracked down the specific mutations that allowed the bacteria to get citrate in the presence of oxygen into the cell. No surprise, they found that we are merely dealing with a duplication mutation. As Behe describes in his latest blog on the matter:

> "The gene for the citrate transporter, citT, that works in the

absence of oxygen is directly upstream from the genes for two other proteins that have promoters that are active in the presence of oxygen. A duplication of a segment of this region serendipitously placed the *citT* gene next to one of these promoters, so the *citT* gene could then be expressed in the presence of oxygen."[13]

This duplication was later refined with multiple duplications of the mutant gene region. Other than this, all that was need was another mutation elsewhere which they haven't quite tracked down, but possibly could be a mutation that simply deactivated, or disabled, a certain other gene. In the final analysis, we are *not* dealing with a complex new structure or novel protein being created. All that's going on is modifying already existing complex genes. Shuffling things around, overexpressing a gene, and disabling another gene is not creating any novel DNA code that might build, for instance, a brand new protein or novel structure within the cell. This slight tweaking is only useful for a limited set of problems. If the bacteria would have also needed new cellular structures to be able to digest the citrate, then random mutation would be left struggling for air. In any case, this is a case of multiple random mutations that confer a survival advantage to the bacteria in question.

We will look at one more example of random mutation and natural selection in action, but I don't want to leave this example without looking once more at the number of organisms involved, or the time frame. I want to stress the fact that it took 30,000+ generations and trillions of organisms just for a beneficial 'double mutation' to show up by random chance. And after all those generations, nothing new was actually created--no new body plans arose, no new complex proteins were created, nor did any new cellular structures emerge.

For our next example of Darwinian style evolution, let's take a dive into the ocean. Notothenioid fish can live in the Antarctic ocean because they possess a protein that acts like antifreeze. To describe the evolution of this protein, I will quote from Behe:

"In 1997 a group of scientists at the University of Illinois sequenced the gene for an antifreeze protein from Antarctic fish. They were startled to discover so-called control regions to the left and the right of the portion of the gene that coded for the antifreeze protein that were very similar to control regions for another protein, a digestive enzyme. Both portions had a certain nine-letter sequence, but in the antifreeze gene the nine-nucleotide region was repeated many times. This gave the protein a simple sequence that consisted of three amino acids repeated many times over.

   The scientists proposed that the antifreeze protein evolved in a Darwinian fashion, by random mutations and natural selection, beginning with a duplicate copy of the digestive-enzyme gene. A probable scenario goes something like the following: The first copy of that gene simply continued its normal job. But by chance, in one of the fish in the ancient Antarctic regions, the cell's machinery stuttered when copying the second, extra gene. That stutter gave the mutant fish several copies of the nine-nucleotide region. The altered protein serendipitously protected the fish a bit from ice crystals, and so its progeny became more numerous in the frigid ocean.

   In one of the fish descendants of the original lucky mutant, presumably, the copying machinery stuttered again, adding even more nine-nucleotide repeats and further improving the antifreeze protein. (Tandemly repeated sequences in DNA are particularly prone to being copied extra times.) The progeny of that second mutant were even more fit–they could survive in water that was marginally colder–so they quickly dominated the population. Then a deletion mutation removed the original coding region, perhaps making the antifreeze protein more stable. One or two more mutations, each of which improved it, and we've reached the modern version of the protein."[14]

The case of the antifreeze protein in Notothenioid fish shows both the power and limitations of evolution by random mutation. We see a number of simple steps whereby a region of DNA is accidentally copied over and over again. This just so happened to protect the fish from freezing in cold water so that it could thrive in the Antarctic. But notice the simplicity of this mutation. This is not the path that will be able to produce complex sequences of amino acids that will fold into 3-dimensional structures (as most proteins are) to produce complex molecular machinery. As Behe asserts:

   "...the antifreeze protein in Antarctic fish is not really a discrete structure comparable to, say, hemoglobin. Hemoglobin and almost all other proteins are coded by single genes that produce proteins of definite length. They resemble precisely engineered dams. But the antifreeze protein is coded by multiple genes of different lengths, all of which produce amino acid chains that get chopped into smaller fragments of differing lengths–very much like the junk in my gutter. In fact, the Antarctic protein appears not to have any definite structure. Its amino acid chain is floppy and unfolded, unlike the very precisely folded shapes of most proteins (such as hemoglobin)."[15]

Behe goes on to say that the ability to bind ice has also been adapted to by other proteins and that, "the antifreeze protein discovered in Antarctic fish is not so much a molecular machine as it is a blood additive."[16] Another analogy is that it's like the lubricant needed for the molecular machines to operate. It is not sophisticated, it is not complex, and it does not interact with other proteins like you would see in molecular machines. It doesn't even have a folded 3-dimensional structure like most proteins.

This simple process of copying, pasting, and deleting may be beneficial on some occasions, but it is not the type of process that will produce novel complex code, or DNA sequencing, that is required to perform most of the cells duties. In fact, most often it will be detrimental to the functioning of the cell, as we saw with randomly mutating hemoglobin. As Behe says later on in his book:

> "We see that random mutation wreaks havoc on a genome. Even when it 'helps,' it breaks things much more easily than it makes things and acts incoherently rather than focusing on building integrated molecular systems. Random mutation does not account for the 'mind-boggling' systems discovered in the cell."[17]

Random mutation can also have an effect by manipulating control regions that act as switches to control the expression of genes. For example, "the different sizes and shapes of dogs, the patterns of coloration of insect wings, and more can very likely be attributed to Darwinian processes affecting gene switches."[18] In other words, intra-species variation, such as the different sizes and shapes of dogs or the different sizes and shapes of finch beaks, may very well be accounted for by random variations in areas of DNA that control the expression of genes.

This is what you might call micro-evolution, or variation within a species, which is much different than macro-evolution that is evidenced in the fossil record. While micro-evolution is all about modifications to existing proteins and structures, macro-evolution is in the business of creating new proteins, cell types, and structures altogether. Consider that:

> "Genes require specified arrangements of nucleotide bases; proteins require specified arrangements of amino acids; new cell types require specified arrangements of proteins and systems of proteins; new body plans require specialized arrangements of cell types and organs. Organisms not only contain information-rich components (such as proteins and genes), but they comprise information-rich arrangements of those components and the subsystems that comprise them."[19]

Very simple logic can take us to the conclusion that life could not have evolved from a single cell to all of the various forms of life we see today from the perspective of random mutation acting on natural selection. We must start with the knowledge that natural selection cannot select anything before it gives an organism a functional advantage. Now, follow my logic carefully. Before natural selection can select a functional protein, that functional protein must be properly coded for within DNA. However, to hit on this code by chance, as we have already assessed in the first chapter of this book, is extremely unlikely. Many specifically sequenced proteins working together to create a molecular machine is extremely unlikely raised to the 10th power. Arranging many molecular machines into a coherent system to perform the functions of a specific type of cell is extremely unlikely raised to the 20th power. Going even further, a group of new cell types arranged in a specific way to produce an organ or structure is extremely unlikely raised to the 30th power. This, my friends, is not just beyond statistical probability, it is beyond statistical imagination. Of course, this is not exact math, but you get the point. The evolution of life requires the evolution (genetic coding) of new proteins, cell types, and structures. Life simply did not evolve via random mutation and natural selection.

Natural selection acting on random mutations does have its place in evolution, but it operates in a very limited sphere. It can modify existing systems, mostly detrimentally but sometimes beneficially. But it cannot take the coherent multiple steps required for the evolution of new proteins, molecular machines, cell types, and ultimately life forms.

NOTES

Chapter 1

1. Carter, *Science and Psychic Phenomena,* pgs. 82-83
2. Ibid., pg. 103
3. Ibid., pg. 102
4. Beauregard, *Brain Wars,* pg. 143
5. Inglis, *Natural & Supernatural,* pg. 135
6. Marquis de Puységur, Mémoires *pour servir à l'histoire et à l'établissement du magnétisme animal,* pg. 49
7. For instance, see Inglis, *Natural & Supernatural,* pgs. 348-49; Playfair, *If This Be Magic,* pgs. 144-146
8. Vallee, *Dimensions,* pg. 224
9. Astronomer Guillermo Gonzalez was denied tenure at Iowa State University, not for making claims about UFOs, but for making claims about a similar "untouchable" subject in academia: Intelligent Design. He wrote a book called *The Privileged Planet* claiming that the universe is intelligently designed. See the documentary starring Ben Stein entitled *Expelled: No Intelligence Allowed,* 2008.
10. Bullard, *The Myth and Mystery of UFOs,* pg. 6
11. Ibid., pg. 65
12. Ibid., pg. 66
13. Vallee, *UFOs: The Psychic Solution,* pg. 58
14. Ibid., pg. 59
15. Vallee, *Confrontations,* pg. 38
16. Vallee, *Dimensions,* pg. 234
17. Carter, *Science and Psychic Phenomena,* pg. 1
18. If you're interested in theories that attempt to explain consciousness, I recommend reading: Chalmers, David J., *The Character of Consciousness.* New York: Oxford University Press, 2010.

19. Neiman, Daniel. (2010). "A New View of Consciousness and Reality". [Online Article, last accessed on August 3rd, 2012] http://www.world-mysteries.com/daniel_neiman.htm.

20. Ring, *The Omega Project,* pgs. 99-100

21. Lommel, *Consciousness Beyond Life,* pg. 161

22. Ibid., pg. 162

23. Murphy, *The Future of the Body,* pg. 243

24. Lewin, R. (12 December 1980). "Is Your Brain Really Necessary?" *Science* 210: 1232-1234.

25. Lommel, *Consciousness Beyond Life,* pgs. 20-21

26. Smit, R. H. (2008). "Corroboration of the Dentures Anecdote Involving Veridical Perception in a Near-Death Experience" *Journal of Near-Death Studies*, 27(1), pg. 58

27. Carter, *Science and The Near-Death Experience,* pg. 164

28. For a great overview of different aspects of the NDE, see my article: Neiman, Daniel. (2010). "The Near Death 'Experience'". [Online Article, last accessed on August 3rd, 2012] http://www.nderf.org/nde_general_info2.htm.

29. Carter, *Science and The Near-Death Experience,* chapters 10 and 11

30. For examples, see: Long, *Evidence of the Afterlife,* pgs. 108-115

31. For examples, see: Ring, *Heading Toward Omega,* pgs. 57-67; Neiman, Daniel. (2010). "The Near Death 'Experience'". [Online Article, last accessed on August 3rd, 2012] http://www.nderf.org/nde_general_info2.htm.

32. For examples of enhanced perception during an NDE, see: Brumblay, R. J. (2003). Hyperdimensional Perspectives in Out-of-Body and Near-Death Experiences. *Journal of Near-Death Studies, 21(4),* 213-215; Long, *Evidence of the Afterlife,* pg. 90; Neiman, Daniel. (2010). "The Near Death 'Experience'". [Online Article, last accessed on August 3rd, 2012] http://www.nderf.org/nde_general_info2.htm.

33. Near Death Experience Research Foundation. *Mary's NDE.* Accessed on August 3, 2012. http://www.nderf.org/NDERF/NDE_Experiences/mary's_NDE.htm.

34. James, *Memories and Studies,* pgs. 78, 82; Inglis, *Natural & Supernatural,* pgs. 378-379; Wallace, *Miracles and Modern Spiritualism,* chapter 10

35. Kelly, *The Human Antenna,* pgs. 80-81

36. For more examples, see: Inglis, *Science and Parascience,* pgs. 50-51, 55-57, 61, 71, 197-200; Grosso, *Experiencing the Next World Now,* pgs. 67, 71-72, 77-78, 89-90, 98-100.

37. For examples, see: Kripal, *Authors of the Impossible,* pgs. 52-54; Inglis, *Natural & Supernatural,* pgs. 387-399.

38. Wallace, *Miracles and Modern Spiritualism,* chapter 10

39. Ibid., pgs. 107-112, 219

40. Playfair, *If This be Magic,* pg. 169

41. Wallace, *Contributions to the Theory of Natural Selection,* pgs. 359-60

42. Wallace, *Miracles and Modern Spiritualism,* pgs. vi-vii

43. Ibid., pgs. 146-148

44. James, *Memories and Studies,* pg. 64

45. Wallace, *Miracles and Modern Spiritualism,* pg. 152

46. Grof, *When the Impossible Happens,* pg. 326

47. Ibid., 329

48. Carter, *Science and Psychic Phenomena,* pg. 106

49. Ibid., pg. 27

50. Ibid., pg. 28

51. Ibid., pg. 34

52. Ibid., pgs. 28-29

53. Ibid., pg. 29

54. Ibid., pg. 32

55. Ibid., pgs. 32-33

56. Ibid., pg. 33. The article in question was: Marvin Zelen, Paul Kurtz, and George Abell, "Is There a Mars Effect?" *The Humanist* 37(6, November/December 1977), pp. 36-39

57. LeGrice, *The Archetypal Cosmos,* pg. 64

58. Ibid., pg. 64

59. Typical horoscope astrology you read about in the paper is in my opinion not very precise or scientific. I mean, in theory, astrology can be practiced and is routinely practiced on a very scientific basis with well laid out systems of interpretation based on mathematical relationships between the planets. Therefore, if there's evidence to back up its claims, as there appears to be with the "Mars effect" then, being a very scientific endeavor, it should be easier for scientists to embrace it as true science as opposed to pseudoscience.

60. Sternberg, Richard. "How My Views on Evolution Evolved". [Online PDF, last accessed on August 4, 2012] http://www.richardsternberg.com/pdf/sternintellbio08.pdf. pg. 5

61. Ibid., pg. 6

62. Ibid., pgs. 6-7

63. Ibid., pg. 7

64. Ibid., pgs. 7-8

65. Dawkins, *The Greatest Show on Earth,* pgs. 27-28

66. Ibid., pgs. 62-64. Also, see: Darwin, *On the Origin of Species,* chapter IV

67. *Expelled: No Intelligence Allowed.* Dir. Nathan Frankowski. Premise, 2008. Film.

68. Haeckel, *The Wonders of Life,* pg. 130

69. See the appendix for information about the limits of natural selection and random mutation.

70. Denton, *Evolution,* pgs. 328-329

71. Meyer introduces this term. See: Meyer, *Signature in the Cell,* pgs. 105-110

72. Meyer, Stephen C., (2004) "The Origins of Biological Information and the Higher Taxonomic Categories". *Proceedings of the Biological Society of Washington,* 117(2): 213-239 [Available online here: http://www.discovery.org/a/2177]; Meyer, S. C., Ross, M., Nelson, P., and Chien, P. "The Cambrian Explosion: Biology's Big Bang." In *Darwinism, Design, and Education*. Ed. John Angus Campbell and Steven C. Meyer, East Lancing, MI: Michigan State University Press, 2004. pgs. 340, 350. You can also find this article online here: http://www.darwinismanddesign.com/excerpts.php

73. Campbell and Meyer, *Darwinism, Design and Public Education,* pg. 324

74. Ibid., pgs. 324-325

75. Meyer, Stephen C., (2004) "The Origins of Biological Information and the Higher Taxonomic Categories". *Proceedings of the Biological Society of Washington,* 117(2): 213-239 [Available online here: http://www.discovery.org/a/2177]

76. Meyer, Stephen C., "Is There a Signature in the Cell?" The Royal Horseguards Hotel, London. 17 November 2011. Lecture. [Available on Youtube: http://www.youtube.com/watch?v=NbluTDb1Nfs] Start

watching at about 55:00

77. Johnson, *Programming of Life,* pg. 35

78. Meyer, *Signature in the Cell,* pgs. 242-244

79. Johnson, *Programming of Life,* pg. 25

80. For a wonderful video demonstration of this process, view the discovery institute's video "Journey Inside the Cell." Available here: http://www.youtube.com/watch?v=1fiJupfbSpg

81. Johnson, *Programming of Life,* pg. 26

82. These are just a few functions I'm pulling from a list of 10 different functions that have been found for the "non-coding" regions of DNA Meyer lists in his book. Meyer, *Signature in the Cell,* pg. 407

83. Meyer, *Signature in the Cell,* pg. 407

84. Johnson, *Programming of Life,* pg. 26

85. Ibid., pg. 27

86. Woodward and Gills, *The Mysterious Epigenome,* pgs. 69-70

87. Ibid., pg. 76

88. Noory, George. (Host). *Coast to Coast AM.* (July 28, 2009). http://www.coasttocoastam.com/show/2009/07/28

89. O'Connell, Claire, "Passing the baton of life - from Schrödinger to Venter". *New Scientist,* July 13, 2012. [Available from: http://www.newscientist.com/blogs/culturelab/2012/07/passing-the-baton-of-life---from-schrodinger-to-venter.html]

90. Meyer, *Signature in the Cell,* pg. 92

91. Ibid., pg. 211

92. Ibid., pg. 210; Granted this is only one calculation based on a 150 amino acid sequence. More calculations should be done on sequences of varying lengths to determine if it always truly is this difficult to find a stable protein folding sequence in the space of possible amino acid arrangements. However, based on what we know about the specified complexity of DNA and proteins I suspect this kind of low probability to hold for all proteins regardless of how many amino acids go into their construction.

93. Now, the argument has been put forth, most notably by Richard Dawkins, that you could start with just one protein and then modify it little by little, or amino acid by amino acid, until it turns into another protein quite different from the original. (Dawkins, *The Greatest Show on Earth*, page 241.) This would be akin to modifying my last sentence one letter at a time until it turned into a completely different coherent and

meaningful sentence. You may be able to anticipate the problem already. To change the sentence letter by letter, or even two letters at a time, would take that sentence through a whole host of meaningless sequences until it finally arrived at the new meaningful sentence, whatever that may be. And most likely you never would arrive at that new sentence even if give vast amounts of time. Indeed, if randomly mutating sentences into other sentences that then fit together to create an integrated meaningful text was so easy, authors would have a much easier time writing their novels. The problem turns out to be even worse for proteins. This is because if you change too many of the amino acids in a protein, it will not only degrade function, but the amino-acid sequence that constitutes the protein will cease to fold into a 3-dimensional shape altogether. Therefore, one protein cannot morph into another protein with a completely novel function. If you start changing the amino acid sequence of a protein, function quickly degrades, and the process soon leads to amino acid sequences that fail to fold into a stable structure at all. (Campbell and Meyer, *Darwinism, Design and Public Education,* pg. 373) Therefore, they should be weeded out by natural selection long before they are mutated enough to acquire new functionality. Dawkins, however, *imagines* that proteins can change their shape little by little to successively approximate a completely different shape necessary to perform a completely different function. As stated above, this is of course, a purely imaginary line of reasoning. It does not reflect reality.

94. Johnson, *Programming of Life,* pg. 54

95. Meyer, *Signature in the Cell,* pg. 346

96. Random mutations however do occur and have a place. Random mutations, though, far from generating new complex information in DNA serve to alter the already information rich code which may in some cases provide an advantage to the organism which will be selected by natural selection, although the general rule is that these random mutations degrade function. See Appendix 1 for more information about what random mutation does.

97. Meyer, Stephen, Sternberg, Richard, Shermer, Michael, and Prothero, Donald, "Debate on Origins of Life." [Available from: http://www.discovery.org/v/1711] Start listening at about 13:00

98. Of course there are other modern twists on Evolutionary theory, such as "evo-devo" which focuses on regulatory proteins and gene switches. Gene switches are very short DNA regions which regulatory

proteins bind to in order to switch on or off a genetic program. Since the "switch" areas of DNA are relatively short sequences, it is hypothesized that you wouldn't need very many random mutations to create a switch area and be able to activate a genetic program, such as a program for building an eye, limb, wing, or even a protein. Evolution could then scoot along much faster by just turning on the right genetic programs to help create, for example, a novel appendage. (Behe, *The Edge of Evolution,* 183-4) However, explaining how sequences of genes get turned on or off is interesting and good science, but it doesn't help us understand the "hard problem" of evolution. How did the information in the genetic programs get there? Just because you've figured out that regulatory proteins bind to switch areas of the DNA to activate or deactivate genes doesn't tell us anything about how those activated genes got their information. Where does the information for building an eye in an organism come from? That's what needs to be explained and that's what no current evolutionary theory can explain.

99. Meyer, *Signature in the Cell,* pg. 496

100. Ibid., pg. 497

101. Meyer, Stephen C., (2004) "The Origins of Biological Information and the Higher Taxonomic Categories". *Proceedings of the Biological Society of Washington,* 117(2): 213-239 [Available online here: http://www.discovery.org/a/2177]

102. Meyer, *Signature in the Cell,* pg. 497

103. Ibid., pg. 407

104. "New Findings Challenge Established Views on Human Genome: ENCODE Research Consortium Uncovers Surprises Related to Organization and Function of Human Genetic Blueprint," NIH News Release, June 13, 2007, http://www.genome.gov/25521554

105. Woodward and Gills, *The Mysterious Epigenome,* pg. 20; Encode Project Consortium, "Identification and analysis of functional elements in 1% of the human genome by the ENCODE pilot project" *Nature,* 447 (14 June 2007), pg. 803 [Available Online: http://www.genome.gov/Pages/Research/ENCODE/nature05874.pdf]

106. Encode Project Consortium, "An Integrated Encyclopedia of DNA Elements in the Human Genome." *Nature, 489* (6 September 2012), pgs. 57-74 [Available Online: http://www.nature.com/nature/journal/v489/n7414/pdf/nature11247.pdf]; Luskin, Casey, "Junk No More: ENCODE Project *Nature* Paper Finds

'Biochemical Functions for 80% of the Genome'". *Evolution News and Views,* Last accessed on September 10, 2012:
http://www.evolutionnews.org/2012/09/junk_no_more_en_1064001.html

107. Hunter, Amy, "How Your Appendix Works". *How Stuff Works,* Last accessed on August 7, 2012:
http://science.howstuffworks.com/environmental/life/human-biology/appendix3.htm

108. "What is the function of the human appendix? Did it once have a purpose that has since been lost?". *Scientific American,* 21 October 1999, Last accessed on August 7, 2012:
http://www.scientificamerican.com/article.cfm?id=what-is-the-function-of-t

109. Ibid

110. Bell, Art (Host), *Coast to Coast AM,* "Art Bell: Somewhere in Time". April 23, 2011 (Originally aired on October 18, 2001),
http://www.coasttocoastam.com/show/2011/04/23/art

111. Grof, *When the Impossible Happens,* pgs. 80-82

112. Hagelin, John S., Rainforth, Maxwell V., et al. "Effects of Group Practice of the Transcendental Meditation Program on Preventing Violent Crime in Washington, DC: Results of the National Demonstration Project, June–July 1993". Last accessed on August 7th 2012.
http://www.mum.edu/m_effect/dc_md.html

113. Behe, *The Edge of Evolution,* pg. 261

114. Ibid., pg. 262

115. Behe, *Darwin's Black Box,* pg. 39

116. Miller, Ken, "The Collapse of Intelligent Design: Will the Next Monkey Trial be in Ohio?" Lecture at Case Western University.
http://www.youtube.com/watch?v=JVRsWAjvQSg

117. Ibid., start watching at 45:20

118. Behe, *The Edge of Evolution,* pg. 267

119. Ibid., pgs. 162-3

120. One objection to positing an intelligent designer is that it's not falsifiable. How could we prove it's not the designer? To reject the design hypothesis one would need to show a step by step unguided process through which new functional code is inserted into the DNA and through which protein machines are assembled piece by piece. No one has yet been able to do this. We have falsified Darwin's theory by showing that it

is an inadequate causal mechanism for the generation of complex information rich genetic code. (See appendix one)

121. For a wonderful video demonstration of this process, view the discovery institute's video "Journey Inside the Cell." Available here: http://www.youtube.com/watch?v=1fiJupfbSpg

122. What can be inferred from the fossil record is that evolution did happen. The mistake is to assume that it happened via an undirected natural process.

123. M., Jonathan, "Nice Try! A Review of Alan Rogers's *The Evidence for Evolution*". *Evolution News and Views.* April 27, 2012. Last accessed on August 8, 2012.
http://www.evolutionnews.org/2012/04/a_review_of_ala058641.html

124. Sometimes a scientist will get a hair up his ass and design tricky ways to show that random mutation and natural selection can evolve complex life forms. You can watch such "evolution simulations" on youtube (http://www.youtube.com/watch?v=b1rHS3ROllU) One involves evolving "block creatures," or little artificial life forms made out of blocks, that evolve to perform a certain task more and more efficiently. The task might be the ability to swim faster or to follow a red light. Certain "laws" are programmed into the simulation that stipulate how the bodies of the creatures are formed (via blocks) and how the blocks are connected via joints which can bend and twist. The blocks have sensors that sense the angle of the joints, and this information is used by an artificial nervous system to tell the blocks when to move. Depending on how the blocks are connected, they can move (or swim) together faster or slower and can move in different ways. A computer breeds these artificial block creatures, randomly mutating them in each successive generation. If the random mutation helps the block creatures achieve their goal, for example swimming faster, then that mutation is saved. Over time, you do see these simulated creatures getting better and better at the task. Ok, so what's the flaw? The problem is that these simulations vastly simplify the task of evolution. Look at what they are using, blocks. These are simple blocks with no complexity. Compare this simple block with an actual cell consisting of hundreds of proteins and complex protein machinery all interacting together. In the above described simulation sure the blocks can be different sizes and move in different ways, but they're not constructed in any complex way. This makes the task of evolution simple. Just like in Darwin's day, if cells were really just homogenous blobs of

protoplasm then evolution might in fact be easy. But they're not. They require complex protein machinery to do the jobs of the cell, like taking in nutrients, digesting those nutrients, eliminating waste, unwinding and copying strands of DNA to make proteins, moving around, and on and on. To build a new type of cell with a new function is not like changing the size or arrangement of simple blocks. You have to have new precisely shaped protein parts that fit together into new types of cellular machinery that in turn coordinate their activities with vast numbers of other protein machinery. And as I've explored in this first chapter, to even build one simple protein requires specified code in the DNA molecule.

To get closer to simulating what real evolution would require, they would need to take that block creature, increase its size so that it's hundreds of blocks in length. Then it would need to fold into a specific 3-dimensional shape (like a real protein) and still be able to perform some function *that's dependent upon having that precise shape*. Then you would need to randomly mutate that block creature (like adding blocks, removing them, changing the size of the blocks) until you get 30 different block creatures each with a different 3-dimensional shape. These various block creatures would then need to fit together with each other in a precise manner (based on their shapes) and be able to work as a whole (like a protein machine) to perform some function. Then in the same manner you would need to make 20 other "block machines" that each performed a different function. And not just that, but to simulate a cell three or four machines would have to work in tandem to perform some complex operation that requires many steps, like a multi-step factory process or the multi-step process of protein synthesis. Finally, you have to coordinate all of the machineries actions so as not to interfere with one another, but to work as an integrated whole.

And here's the kicker: you cannot program the simulation with information about how all of these protein machines should be coordinated together, nor which specific job each created machine will do (assuming you could actually get as far as creating one block machine). You can also not specify which of the multiple block machines should come together and work like an assembly line factory to perform some complex operation. But, of course, you could tell the program that it is possible for many block machines to work together and that they should try to do this. And, of course, you can preprogram specific functions that need to be performed. (It would be nice if these functions were similar to actual functions performed in a cell) But which block creature/block machine(s) perform them cannot be stipulated in the program. The block creatures/machines have to figure out themselves which task they are best suited for and how to coordinate their actions with the actions of all the other block creatures/machines.   So, just to recap, you can program into the simulation how the block creatures are formed, how they can be randomly mutated, how these creatures could come together to form block machines, the fact that multiple machines can work together to perform a complex task, and an array of functions that need to be performed. The block creatures/machines have to figure out the rest, including what tasks to perform, how to work together to perform tasks, and how to coordinate themselves together to do all of the tasks without interfering with one another.

As I see it, to even build one block machine is going to be extremely hard because you would have to find 30 different shapes which fit together precisely, and we're talking about block creatures that are 3-dimensional and contain hundreds of blocks. So even getting that far would be pretty amazing. Compounded on top of this problem is the fact that not only do 30 different block creatures have to come together to work as one machine, but that this machine should be able to perform some task. You might get 30 block creatures to fit together, but it won't be able to perform one of the tasks. And then an even bigger hurdle is the coordination problem. What machine will perform what task? How will they not interfere with each other? Again, you can't program this information in.

Now, run this simulation and see if you don't end up with one big cluster fuck, the mess of which is worse than my sisters old bedroom. Cluster Fuck--Big One--Mark my words.

125. Meyer, Stephen, Sternberg, Richard, Shermer, Michael, and Prothero, Donald, "Debate on Origins of Life." [Available from: http://www.discovery.org/v/1711] Start listening at about 40:22

126. Wiseman, Richard, "'Heads I Win, Tails You Lose': How Parapsychologists Nullify Null Results". *Skeptical Inquirer* 34(1), January/February 2010. http://www.csicop.org/si/show/heads_i_win_tails_you_loser_how_pa rapsychologists_nullify_null_results

127. Radin, *The Conscious Universe,* pg. 81

128. Chris Carter wrote an excellent article documenting the

different ways skeptics try to explain away the data. I especially like his analysis of Richard Wiseman and Julie Milton's 1999 meta-analysis where they blatantly ignored sample size when doing their meta-analysis of ganzfeld studies. See: Carter, Chris, (2010). "'Heads I Lose, Tails You Win', Or, How Richard Wiseman Nullifies Positive Results, and What to Do about It: A Response to Wiseman's (2010) Critique of Parapsychology". *Journal for the Society of Psychical Research* 74: 156-167. Available Online here:
http://www.sheldrake.org/D&C/controversies/Carter_Wiseman.pdf

129. Murphy, *The Future of the Body,* pg. 376

130. Kripal, *Authors of the Impossible,* pg. 14

Chapter 2

1. Beauregard, *Brain Wars,* pg. 38
2. Kirsch, *The Emperor's New Drugs,* pg. 9
3. Ibid., pg. 10
4. Ibid., pg. 11
5. Ibid., pg. 12
6. Ibid., pg. 13
7. Ibid., pg. 14
8. Ibid., pg. 15
9. Ibid., pgs. 28-30
10. Ibid., pg. 31
11. Ibid., pg. 33
12. Ibid., pgs. 83-87
13. Ibid., pgs. 88-89
14. Ibid., pg. 91
15. Ibid., pg. 97
16. Ibid., pgs. 99-100
17. Playfair, *If This Be Magic,* pg. 24
18. Kirsch, *The Emperor's New Drugs,* pg. 104
19. Playfair, *If This Be Magic,* pg. 25
20. Kirsch, *The Emperor's New Drugs,* pgs. 104-105
21. Beauregard, *Brain Wars,* pg. 26
22. Ibid., pg. 30
23. Ibid., pg. 30
24. Ibid., pg. 29

25. Kirsch, *The Emperor's New Drugs,* pg. 113; Beauregard, *Brain Wars,* pg. 29

26. Kirsch, *The Emperor's New Drugs,* pg. 114

27. Ibid., pg. 114

28. Ibid., pg. 111

29. Ibid., pg. 112

30. Ibid., pg. 112

31. Benson, *Timeless Healing,* pg. 34

32. Beauregard, *Brain Wars,* pg. 17

33. Ibid., pg. 19

34. Ibid., pg. 19

35. Vallee, *UFOs: The Psychic Solution,* pg. 165

36. Ibid., pg. 164

37. Ibid., pg. 166

38. Ibid., pgs. 166-168

39. Lipton, *The Biology of Belief,* pg. 93

40. Beauregard, *Brain Wars,* pg. 109

41. Lipton, *The Biology of Belief,* pg. 93

42. Beauregard, *Brain Wars,* pg. 110

43. Playfair, *If This Be Magic,* pg. 13

44. Lipton, *The Biology of Belief,* pg. 94

45. New Living Translation of the Christian Holy Bible, Matthew 21:21

46. Kirsch, *The Emperor's New Drugs,* pg. 110

47. Ibid., pg. 111

48. Playfair, *If This Be Magic,* pg. 242

49. Ibid., pgs. 242-243

50. Lipton, *The Biology of Belief,* pgs. 95-96

51. Kalweit, *Shamans, Healers, and Medicine Men,* pg. 74

52. Ibid., pg. 75

53. Grof, *When the Impossible Happens,* pgs. 196-197

54. Talbot, *The Holographic Universe,* pg. 134

55. Wallace, *Miracles and Modern Spiritualism,* pg. 128

56. Talbot, *The Holographic Universe,* pg. 142; Inglis, *Natural & Supernatural,* pgs. 174-175

57. Talbot, *The Holographic Universe,* pg. 141

58. Kripal, *Authors of the Impossible,* pg. 235

59. Ibid., pg. 236

60. Ibid., pg. 237

61. Inglis, *Natural & Supernatural,* pg. 176

62. Ibid., pg. 177

63. Ibid., pg. 174

64. Grosso, *Experiencing the Next World Now,* pg. 49

65. For some examples see: Inglis, *Natural & Supernatural,* pgs. 148-149, 188, 208-209

66. Ibid., pg. 234

67. Grof, *When the Impossible Happens,* pg. 300

68. Ibid., pg. 110

69. Grof, *The Holotropic Mind,* pgs. 111-112

70. Huxley, *The Doors of Perception,* pgs. 22-23

71. Lommel, *Consciousness Beyond Life,* pg. 265

72. For a great presentation of the double slit experiment, that showed the wave/particle duality, and its interpretation, I highly recommend physicist Tom Campbell's lectures on youtube (Channel twcjr44). For instance, see: "Tom Campbell: Calgary Theory only (Sat) 1/3" Lecture at the University of Calgary, Alberta Canada. September 23,24,25, 2011. http://www.youtube.com/watch?v=2Nlbro2MNBs&list=PLEB923BB17E5849A3. Start watching at about 37:35

73. Personal email communication with physicist Aric Hackebill, May 24, 2012.

74. Carter, *Science and Psychic Phenomena,* pg. 76

75. Radin, *The Conscious Universe,* pg. 151

76. Inglis, *Natural & Supernatural,* pgs. 216-217

77. Ibid., pgs. 249-251

78. Inglis, *Natural & Supernatural,* pgs. 432, 395, 434-435; Inglis, *Science and Parascience,* pgs. 106-107

79. Inglis, *Natural & Supernatural,* pg. 434

80. Ibid., pg. 432

81. Ibid., pg. 401

82. Ibid., pgs. 223, 225, 226-227

83. Inglis, *Natural & Supernatural,* pgs. 271-272; Inglis, *Science and Parascience,* pgs. 224-225

84. Inglis, *Natural & Supernatural,* pgs. 267, 285

85. Playfair, *If This Be Magic,* pg. 182

86. Ibid., pg. 185

87. Inglis, *Natural & Supernatural,* pg. 208

88. Ibid., pg. 203

89. Ibid., pg. 204

90. Playfair, *If This Be Magic,* pg. 192

91. Ibid., pg. 193

92. Ibid., pgs. 196-197

93. http://site.uri-geller.com/what_scientists_say_about_uri_geller

94. Mishlove, *The PK Man,* pgs. 22-23

95. Playfair, *If This Be Magic,* pg. 184

96. Kripal, *Mutants and Mystics,* pgs. 181-182

97. Ibid., pg. 154

98. Kripal, *Authors of the Impossible,* pg. 208

99. Rosenblum and Kuttner, *Quantum Enigma,* pg. 201

100. Grof, *LSD Doorway to the Numinous,* pgs. 46-47

101. Ibid., pgs. 49-51

102. Bryan, *Close Encounters of the Fourth Kind,* pgs. 270-271

103. Keel, *The Cosmic Question,* pg. 125

104. Modi, *Remarkable Healings,* pgs. 321-323

105. Ibid., pgs. 302-333

106. Weiss, *Many Lives, Many Masters,* pg. 27

107. Ibid., pg. 35

108. Ibid., pg. 54-57

109. "Experiencer - Ariel School UFO Encounter - Ruwa Zimbabwe" TV documentary. http://www.youtube.com/watch?v=XCF0BfSnYls

110. Mack, *Abduction,* pgs. 3-4

111. Ibid., pgs. 420-422

112. Mack, John E. "Messengers From the Unseen." *Oberlin Alumni Magazine,* 98(2), Fall 2002, pg. 25 [Available online: http://makemagicproductions.com/media/mack_2002_OberlinAlumniMag.pdf]

113. Ibid., pg. 26

114. "Michael Newton Interview Part 1 of 5". *The One on One Interview Series,* Gateway Television Series: http://www.youtube.com/watch?v=c5zsuKG3fzc

115. Kripal, *Authors of the Impossible,* pg. 222

116. Haisch, *The God Theory,* pgs. 28-29

Chapter 3

1. McKnight, *Cosmic Journeys,* pg. 169
2. Out of Body Experience Research Foundation. *Steve SOBE 2615.* Accessed on August 11, 2012. http://www.oberf.org/steve_sobe.htm.
3. Out of Body Experience Research Foundation. *Katherine B SOBE 2598.* Accessed on August 11, 2012. http://www.oberf.org/katherine_b_sobe.htm.
4. Carlsberg, *Beyond My Wildest Dreams,* pg. 134
5. Monroe, *Journeys Out of the Body,* pg. 24
6. Ibid., pg. 22
7. Mack, *Abduction,* pg. 348
8. Ibid., pg. 354
9. Moody, *Reunions,* pg. 44
10. Ibid., pg. 66
11. Ibid., pg. 102
12. Ibid., pg. 116
13. Ibid., pg. 76
14. Konkolesky, *Experiencer,* pg. 29
15. Ibid., pg. 30
16. Vallee, *Passport to Magonia,* pg. 110
17. Strassman, *DMT: The Spirit Molecule,* pg. 178
18. Ibid., pg. 213
19. Ibid., pg. 214
20. Vieira, *Projections of the Consciousness,* pgs. 115, 144
21. Ibid., pg. 115
22. Mack, *Passport to the Cosmos,* pg. 81
23. Ibid., pg. 82
24. Mack, *Abduction,* pgs. 168-169
25. Ibid., pg. 297
26. Sparks, *The Keepers,* pgs. 177-178
27. Monroe, *Journeys Out of the Body,* pg. 158
28. Ibid., pg. 158
29. Turner, *Taken,* pg. 118
30. Haley, *Lost Was the Key,* pg. 102
31. Mack, *Abduction,* pg. 98
32. Ibid., pg. 183
33. Carlsberg, *Beyond My Wildest Dreams,* pgs. 175-176
34. Monroe, *Journeys Out of the Body,* pg. 159
35. Mack, *Abduction,* pg. 147

36. Hamilton, *Invitation to the Self,* pg. 98

37. Ibid., pg. 99

38. Fowler, *The Watchers,* pgs. 96-97

39. Lorenzen, *Flying Saucer Occupants,* pgs. 23-24

40. Fowler, *The Watchers,* pgs. 104-105

41. Ibid., pgs. 106-107

42. Sparks, *The Keepers,* pg. 18

43. Carter, *Science and The Near-Death Experience,* pg. 167

44. Sparks, *The Keepers,* pgs. 112-113

45. Ibid., pgs. 113-115

46. Clear, *Reaching for Reality,* pg. 109

47. Carlsberg, *Beyond My Wildest Dreams,* pgs. 220-221

48. Mack, *Passport to the Cosmos,* pgs. 188-189

49. Ibid., pgs. 189-190

50. Weidner, Jay, dir. *Infinity: The Ultimate Trip.. Journey Beyond Death.* Sacred Mysteries Productions, 2009. Film.

51. Kripal, *Mutants and Mystics,* pgs. 260-262

52. Vieira, *Projections of the Consciousness,* pg. 73

53. Ibid., pg. 41

54. Waggoner, *Lucid Dreaming,* pg. 29

55. Lommel, *Consciousness Beyond Life,* pg. 140; Near Death Experience Research Foundation. *Mary's NDE.* Accessed on August 3, 2012. http://www.nderf.org/NDERF/NDE_Experiences/mary's_NDE.htm.

56. Fowler, *The Watchers,* pgs. 291, 295

57. Ibid., pg. 124

58. Ibid., pgs. 125, 129

59. Turner, *Taken,* pg. 11

60. Hopkins, *Science, UFO Invisibility and Transgenic Beings,* pg. 408; Fowler, *The Watchers,* pg. 340

61. Turner, *Taken,* pg. 149

62. Near Death Experience Research Foundation. *Chris D's 794.* Accessed on August 3, 2012. http://www.nderf.org/NDERF/NDE_Experiences/chris_d's_nde.htm

63. Near Death Experience Research Foundation. *Duane's NDE.* Accessed on August 3, 2012. http://www.nderf.org/NDERF/NDE_Experiences/Duane's%20NDE.htm

64. Near Death Experience Research Foundation. *Natalie S NDE 6246.* Accessed on August 3, 2012.

http://www.nderf.org/NDERF/NDE_Experiences/natalie_s_nde.htm

65. Near Death Experience Research Foundation. *Earl M NDE 6197.* Accessed on August 3, 2012. http://www.nderf.org/NDERF/NDE_Experiences/earl_m_nde.htm

66. Monroe, *Far Journeys,* pg. 92

67. Near Death Experience Research Foundation. *Earl M NDE 6197.* Accessed on August 3, 2012. http://www.nderf.org/NDERF/NDE_Experiences/earl_m_nde.htm; Near Death Experience Research Foundation. *Hector A Uncle NDE 5413.* Accessed on August 3, 2012. http://www.nderf.org/NDERF/NDE_Experiences/hector_a_uncle_nde.htm; Vieira, *Projections of the Consciousness,* pg. 191

68. Monroe, *Journeys Out of the Body,* pg. 184

69. Moody, *Reunions,* pg. 80

70. Mack, *Abduction,* pg. 162

71. Carlsberg, *Beyond My Wildest Dreams,* pg. 246

72. Kripal, *Mutants and Mystics,* pgs. 206

73. Lommel, *Consciousness Beyond Life,* pg. 245

74. Ibid., pg. 244

75. Ibid., pg. 265

76. Playfair, *If This Be Magic,* pg. 155

77. Waggoner, *Lucid Dreaming,* pg. 181

78. Near Death Experience Research Foundation. *Duane's NDE.* Accessed on August 3, 2012. http://www.nderf.org/NDERF/NDE_Experiences/Duane's%20NDE.htm

79. Laszlo, *The Connectivity Hypothesis,* pgs. 9-10

80. Grof, *The Holotropic Mind,* pgs. 95-96

81. Grof, *LSD Doorway to the Numinous,* pg. 187

82. Waggoner, *Lucid Dreaming,* pg. 28

83. Ibid., pg. 10

84. Ibid., pg. 115

85. Ibid., pg. 48

86. Ibid., pg. 49

87. Ibid., pg. 127

88. Ibid., pg. 142

89. Ibid., pg. 141

90. Ibid., pg. 147

91. Ibid., pgs. 56-57

92. Ibid., pgs. 57-58
93. Ibid., pgs. 112-114
94. Magnus, *Astral Projection and the Nature of Reality,* pg. 228
95. Ibid., pg. 249
96. Ibid., pgs. 203-204
97. Ibid., pg. 108
98. Monroe, *Journeys Out of the Body,* pg. 240
99. Vieira, *Projections of the Consciousness,* pgs. 180-185
100. Waggoner, *Lucid Dreaming,* pg. 147
101. Hamilton, *Invitation to the Self,* pg. 194
102. Waggoner, *Lucid Dreaming,* pg. 31
103. Vieira, *Projections of the Consciousness,* pg. 163
104. Magnus, *Astral Projection and the Nature of Reality,* pg. 245
105. Vieira, *Projections of the Consciousness,* pgs. 213-215
106. Monroe, *Journeys Out of the Body,* pgs. 260-261
107. Ibid., pg. 261
108. Ibid., pg. 262
109. Monroe, *Far Journeys,* pgs. 174-175
110. Ibid., pg. 177
111. Ibid., pg. 162
112. Ibid., pgs. 162-170
113. Mack, *Abduction,* pg. 107
114. Carlsberg, *Beyond My Wildest Dreams,* pgs. 162-164
115. Strassman, *DMT: The Spirit Molecule,* pg. 206
116. Fowler, *The Watchers,* pg. 119
117. Monroe, *Journeys Out of the Body,* pg. 74
118. Ibid., pg. 75
119. Magnus, *Astral Projection and the Nature of Reality,* pgs. 64-65
120. Ibid., pg. 68
121. Ibid., pg. 64
122. Ibid., pg. 274
123. Monroe, *Journeys Out of the Body,* pg. 141
124. Hamilton, *Invitation to the Self,* pgs. 63-64
125. Ibid., pg. 102
126. Vieira, *Projections of the Consciousness,* pg. 67
127. Waggoner, *Lucid Dreaming,* pg. 36
128. Vieira, *Projections of the Consciousness,* pg. 67
129. Waggoner, *Lucid Dreaming,* pg. 219

130. Bruce, *Astral Dynamics,* pgs. 232-233

131. Carlsberg, *Beyond My Wildest Dreams,* pg. 243

132. Ibid., pg. 244

133. Ibid., pgs. 245-248

134. Ibid., pg. 249

135. Talbot, *The Holographic Universe,* pgs. 180-181

136. Keel, *The Mothman Prophecies,* pgs. 5-6

137. Hanks, *Magic, Mysticism & The Molecule.* pgs. 123-124

138. Hamilton, *Invitation to the Self,* pg. 166

139. Haley, *Lost Was the Key,* pgs. 145-147; Wilson, *I Forgot What I Wasn't Supposed to Remember,* pgs. 155-159, 172-174; Turner, *Taken,* pgs. 14-15

140. Turner, *Taken,* pg. 43

141. Ibid., pg. 101

142. Hamilton, *Invitation to the Self,* pgs. 168-169

143. Ibid., pg. 170

144. Praagh, *Ghosts Among Us,* pg. 76

145. Kellogg, E. W., "Mutual Lucid Dream Event." *Dream Time,* 14(2), (1997), pgs. 32-34
Available Online:
http://www.asdreams.org/telepathy/kellogg_1997_mutual_lucid_dream_event.htm

146. Newton, *Journey of Souls,* pgs. 254-256

147. Ibid., pg. 256

148. Playfair, *If This Be Magic,* pg. 143

149. Ibid., pg. 143

150. Inglis, *Natural & Supernatural,* pg. 174

151. Mack, *Abduction,* pg. 158

152. Ibid., pg. 159

153. Ibid., pg. 161

154. Ibid., pg. 276

155. Fowler, *The Watchers,* pg. 181

156. Magnus, *Astral Projection and the Nature of Reality,* pg. 265

157. Strassman, *DMT: The Spirit Molecule,* pgs. 208-209

158. Ibid., pgs. 243-244

159. Ibid., pg. 188

160. Waggoner, *Lucid Dreaming,* pgs. 240-241

161. Monroe, *Journeys Out of the Body,* pg. 114

162. Vieira, *Projections of the Consciousness,* pgs. 152-153

163. Near Death Experience Research Foundation. *Bill W's NDE.* Accessed on August 3, 2012.
http://www.nderf.org/NDERF/NDE_Experiences/bill_w's_nde.htm

164. Oakford, *Journey Through The World of Spirit,* pg. 45-55

165. Ring, *Heading Toward Omega,* pg. 73

166. Near Death Experience Research Foundation. *Nancy T NDE 6240.* Accessed on August 3, 2012.
http://www.nderf.org/NDERF/NDE_Experiences/nancy_t_nde_6240.htm

167. Near Death Experience Research Foundation. *Jean R NDE 6166.* Accessed on August 3, 2012.
http://www.nderf.org/NDERF/NDE_Experiences/jean_r_nde_6166.htm

168. Near Death Experience Research Foundation. *Cynthia H NDE 5071.* Accessed on August 3, 2012.
http://www.nderf.org/NDERF/NDE_Experiences/cynthia_h_nde_5071.htm

169. Monroe, *Far Journeys,* pg. 196

170. Near Death Experience Research Foundation. *Glenda G Possible NDE 2601OBE.* Accessed on August 3, 2012.
http://www.nderf.org/NDERF/NDE_Experiences/glenda_g_possible_nde.htm

171. Near Death Experience Research Foundation. *Garth P Probable NDE EO32512.* Accessed on August 3, 2012.
http://www.nderf.org/NDERF/NDE_Experiences/garth_p_probable_nde.htm

172. Near Death Experience Research Foundation. *Glenn F NDE 6144.* Accessed on August 3, 2012.
http://www.nderf.org/NDERF/NDE_Experiences/glenn_f_nde.htm

173. Vieira, *Projections of the Consciousness,* pgs. 179-185

174. Praagh, *Ghosts Among Us,* pg. 161

175. McKnight, *Cosmic Journeys,* pgs. 262-266

176. Ibid., pg. 267

177. Praagh, *Ghosts Among Us,* pgs. 48-51

178. Near Death Experience Research Foundation. *Sarah's NDE.* Accessed on August 3, 2012.
http://www.nderf.org/NDERF/NDE_Experiences/Sarah_nde.htm

179. Storm, *My Descent Into Death,* pg. 4

180. Ibid., pg. 8

181. Ibid., pg. 6

182. Ibid., pg. 9

183. Ibid., pgs. 10-11

184. Ibid., pg. 15

185. Ibid., pgs. 16-17

186. Ibid., pg. 20

187. Ibid., pg. 25

188. Ibid., pg. 27

189. Taylor, *Dream Work,* pg. 215

190. Murphy, *The Future of the Body,* pg. 235; Murphy quotes from an article in the Lancet: Moody, R. L. 1946. "Bodily Changes During Abreaction." *Lancet* (Dec. 28), pgs. 934-935

191. Konkolesky, *Experiencer,* pg. 33

192. Wilson, *I Forgot What I Wasn't Supposed to Remember,* pgs. 171-172

193. Turner, *Taken,* pg. 58

194. Hopkins, *Intruders,* pgs. 56, 162; Fowler, *UFO Testament,* pgs. 391, 413-418

195. Turner, *Taken,* pg. 51

196. Ibid., pgs. 20, 82, 92

197. Clear, *Reaching for Reality,* pg. 175

198. Carlsberg, *Beyond My Wildest Dreams,* pg. 120

199. Mack, *Passport to the Cosmos,* pgs. 210-212

200. Ibid., pgs. 212-213

201. Vallee, *Confrontations,* pgs. 114-116

202. Ibid., pg. 116

203. Sparks, *The Keepers,* pgs. 13-14

204. Ibid., pgs. 14-16

205. Keel, *The Cosmic Question,* pg. 142

206. Mack, *Abduction,* pg. 268

207. Ibid., pg. 269

208. Ibid., pg. 282

209. Clear, *Reaching for Reality,* pg. 176

210. Sparks, *The Keepers,* pg. 158

211. Hamilton, *Invitation to the Self,* pg. 237

212. Fowler, *The Watchers II,* pg. 109

213. Ibid., pg. 137

214. Praagh, *Unfinished Business,* pg. 103

215. Vallee, *UFOs: The Psychic Solution,* pgs. 150-154

216. Dean, *True Police Stories of the Strange & Unexplained,* pgs. 217-218

217. Ibid., pg. 219

218. Ibid., pgs. 219-220

219. Waggoner, *Lucid Dreaming,* pg. 224

220. Hamilton, *Invitation to the Self,* pg. 224

221. Waggoner, *Lucid Dreaming,* pg. 10

222. Turner, *Taken,* pg. 83

223. Mack, John E. "Messengers From the Unseen." *Oberlin Alumni Magazine,* 98(2), Fall 2002, pgs. 26-29 [Available online: http://makemagicproductions.com/media/mack_2002_OberlinAlumniMag.pdf]

224. Jung, *Memories, Dreams, Reflections,* pgs. 128-130

225. "Carl Jung - The Wisdom of the Dream - A Life of Dreams Part 1 of 3". PBS Documentary Series. http://www.youtube.com/watch?v=Us7XofxPX48. For the part I quote watch from 10:55-12:07

226. Vallee, *Revelations,* pgs. 117-121

227. Ibid., pg. 121

228. ibid., pg. 121

229. Grof, *When the Impossible Happens,* pg. 291

230. Ibid., pgs. 288-294

231. Keel, *The Cosmic Question,* pgs. 189-190

232. Vallee, *UFOs: The Psychic Solution,* pg. 204

233. Ibid., pg. 211

234. Bullard, *The Myth and Mystery of UFOs,* pg. 125

235. Keel, *The Cosmic Question,* pg. 158

236. Ibid., pgs. 158-160

237. Bullard, *The Myth and Mystery of UFOs,* pgs. 90-91, 96

238. For instance, see: Wilson, *I Forgot What I Wasn't Supposed to Remember,* pgs. 83-84

239. For examples, see: Wilson, *I Forgot What I Wasn't Supposed to Remember,* pgs. 72-73, 153-54; Turner, *Taken,* pgs. 100-104; Haley, *Lost Was the Key,* pg. 146

240. For examples, see: Hamilton, *Invitation to the Self,* pgs. 120-121; Wilson, *I Forgot What I Wasn't Supposed to Remember,* pgs. 104-105, 155-164

241. Mack, *Abduction,* pgs. 170-171

242. Clear, *Reaching for Reality,* pgs. 157-158

243. Newton, *Destiny of Souls,* pgs. 158-160

244. Near Death Experience Research Foundation. *Leo P's NDE 1117.* Accessed on August 3, 2012. http://www.nderf.org/NDERF/NDE_Experiences/leo_p's_nde.htm

245. For examples, see: Mack, *Abduction,* pg. 231; Clear, *Reaching for Reality,* pg. 98

246. For examples, see: Carlsberg, *Beyond My Wildest Dreams,* pgs. 85, 180, 187, 231-233

247. Turner, *Taken,* pgs. 38-39, 53; Hamilton, *Invitation to the Self,* pg. 150; Mack, *Abduction,* pg. 323; Wilson, *I Forgot What I Wasn't Supposed to Remember,* pgs. 221-222

248. Mack, *Abduction,* pgs. 324-325, 327-328; Wilson, *I Forgot What I Wasn't Supposed to Remember,* pgs. 215-218

249. Keel, *Operation Trojan Horse,* pgs. 244-248

250. For examples, see: Mack, *Abduction,* pg. 327; Carlsberg, *Beyond My Wildest Dreams,* pgs. 208-210

251. For examples, see: Wilson, *I Forgot What I Wasn't Supposed to Remember,* pg. 211; Hamilton, *Invitation to the Self,* pg. 50; Carlsberg, *Beyond My Wildest Dreams,* pg. 229

Chapter 4

1. For examples of how precisely fine-tuned these laws are, see: Guillermo and Richards, *The Privileged Planet,* pgs. 201-204; Haisch, *The Purpose-Guided Universe,* pgs. 70-74

2. Unruh, Bob. "Dad Links Son's Suicide to 'The God Delusion'". *World Net Daily.* Posted on November 20, 2008. http://www.wnd.com/2008/11/81459/

3. Haisch, *The God Theory,* pg. 131

4. Grof, *The Cosmic Game,* pg. 114

5. This is adapted from Grof's version of the same concept: Ibid., pgs. 115-116

6. Woolger, *Other Lives, Other Selves,* pgs. 201-202

7. Grof, *When the Impossible Happens,* pg. 143

8. Ibid., pg. 144

9. Ibid., pg. 147

10. Woolger, *Other Lives, Other Selves,* pg. 220

11. Ibid., pg. 218

12. Vallee, *UFOs: The Psychic Solution,* pg. 35

13. Ibid., pgs. 42-43

14. Near Death Experience Research Foundation. *Stéphane R NDE 5406.* Accessed on August 3, 2012. http://www.nderf.org/NDERF/stephane_r_nde.htm

15. Turner, *Taken,* pg. 25

16. Carlsberg, *Beyond My Wildest Dreams,* pg. 113

17. Near Death Experience Research Foundation. *Francine W Probable NDE 6277.* Accessed on August 3, 2012. http://www.nderf.org/NDERF/NDE_Experiences/francine_w_probable_n de.htm

18. Near Death Experience Research Foundation. *Cherie B NDE EO30112.* Accessed on August 3, 2012. http://www.nderf.org/NDERF/NDE_Experiences/cherie_b_nde.htm

19. Long, *Evidence of the Afterlife,* pg. 189

20. Ring, *Heading Toward Omega,* pg. 166

21. Ibid., pg. 172

22. Bucke, *Cosmic Consciousness,* pg. 13

23. Ring, *The Omega Project,* pg. 240

24. Monroe, *Far Journeys,* pgs. 206-215

25. Weiss, *Same Soul, Many Bodies,* pgs. 210-211

26. Turner, *Taken,* pg. 87

27. Haley, *Lost Was the Key,* pg. 158

28. Near Death Experience Research Foundation. *Giselle RV NDE 4859.* Accessed on August 3, 2012. http://www.nderf.org/NDERF/NDE_Experiences/giselle_rv_nde.htm

29. Mack, *Abduction,* pg. 251

30. Turner, *Taken,* pg. 63

31. Mack, *Abduction,* pg. 317

32. Turner, *Taken,* pg. 52

33. Carlsberg, *Beyond My Wildest Dreams,* pg. 82

34. Near Death Experience Research Foundation. *Virginia D NDE 4591.* Accessed on August 3, 2012. http://www.nderf.org/NDERF/NDE_Experiences/virginia_d_nde.htm

35. Near Death Experience Research Foundation. *Glenda G Possible NDE 2601OBE.* Accessed on August 3, 2012.

http://www.nderf.org/NDERF/NDE_Experiences/glenda_g_possible_nde.htm

36. Hamilton, *Invitation to the Self,* pg. 142

37. Near Death Experience Research Foundation. *Cherie B NDE EO30112.* Accessed on August 3, 2012.
http://www.nderf.org/NDERF/NDE_Experiences/cherie_b_nde.htm

38. Babcock, Jay. "Magic is Afoot: A Conversation With Alan Moore About the Arts and the Occult". *Arthur,* No. 4, May 2003.
http://www.arthurmag.com/2007/05/10/1815/

39. Hamilton, *Invitation to the Self,* pg. 77

40. For examples, see: Mack, *Abduction,* pgs. 13, 108, 168, 234; Turner, *Taken,* pg.109

41. Ring, *The Omega Project,* pgs. 179-182; Mack, *Abduction,* pgs. 90, 160, 398

42. Ring, *The Omega Project,* pgs. 175-176, 280; Bullard, *The Myth and Mystery of UFOs,* pg. 214

43. Bergson, *The Two Sources of Morality and Religion,* pg. 275

Conclusion

1. http://www.nderf.org/

2. Kripal invites his readers to become their own authors at the end of his book: Kripal, *Mutants and Mystics,* pg. 334

Appendix

1. Behe, *The Edge of Evolution,* pgs. 66-67

2. Ibid., pgs. 21-22

3. Ibid., pg. 25

4. Dawkins, *The Greatest Show on Earth,* pg. 118

5. Ibid., pg. 117

6. Behe, *The Edge of Evolution,* pg. 142

7. Dawkins, *The Greatest Show on Earth,* pgs. 122-123

8. Ibid., pgs. 126-127

9. Behe, M. J. (2008, June 6). "Multiple Mutations Needed for E-Coli." Blog posting. Retrieved from:
http://behe.uncommondescent.com/2008/06/multiple-mutations-needed-for-e-coli/

10. Dawkins, *The Greatest Show on Earth,* pg. 128

11. Ibid., pg. 130

12. Behe, M. J. (2008, June 6). "Multiple Mutations Needed for E-Coli." Blog posting. Retrieved from: http://behe.uncommondescent.com/2008/06/multiple-mutations-needed-for-e-coli/

13. Behe, M. J. (2012, November 13). "Rose-Colored Glasses: Lenski, Citrate, and BioLogos." *Evolution News and Views,* Last accessed on November 17, 2012: http://www.evolutionnews.org/2012/11/rose-colored_gl066361.html

14. Behe, *The Edge of Evolution,* pgs. 79-80

15. Ibid., pg. 81

16. Ibid., pg. 82

17. Ibid., pg. 164

18. Ibid., pg. 201

19. Meyer, S. C., Ross, M., Nelson, P., and Chien, P. "The Cambrian Explosion: Biology's Big Bang." In *Darwinism, Design, and Education.* Ed. John Angus Campbell and Steven C. Meyer, East Lancing, MI: Michigan State University Press, 2004. Page 382. You can also find this article online here: http://www.darwinismanddesign.com/excerpts.php

SELECTED BIBLIOGRAPHY

Beauregard, Mario, *Brain Wars.* New York: HarperOne, 2012.

Behe, Michael J., *Darwin's Black Box.* New York: Free Press, 2006. (Originally published in 1996)

Behe, Michael J., *The Edge of Evolution.* New York: Free Press, 2007.

Benson, Herbert, *Timeless Healing.* New York: Fireside, 1996.

Bergson, Henri, *The Two Sources of Morality and Religion.* London: MacMillan, 1935.

Bruce, Robert, *Astral Dynamics.* Charlottesville: Hampton Roads, 2009.

Bryan, C.D.B., *Close Encounters of the Fourth Kind.* New York: Penguin/Arkana, 1996.

Bucke, Richard M., *Cosmic Consciousness.* Philadelphia: Innes & Sons, 1905.

Bullard, Thomas, *The Myth and Mystery of UFOs.* Lawrence: University Press of Kansas, 2010.

Carter, Chris, *Science and Psychic Phenomena.* Rochester: Inner Traditions, 2012. (Originally published in 2007 under a different title)

Carter, Chris, *Science and The Near-Death Experience.* Rochester: Inner Traditions, 2010.

Campbell, John A., and Meyer, Stephen C., eds. *Darwinism, Design and Public Education.* East Lansing: Michigan State University Press, 2003.

Carlsberg, Kim, *Beyond My Wildest Dreams: Diary of a UFO Abductee.* Santa Fe: Bear & Company, 1995.

Clear, Constance, *Reaching for Reality: Seven Incredible True Stories of Alien Abduction.* San Antonio: Consciousness Now, 1999.

Darwin, Charles, *On the Origin of Species.* London: John Murray, 1859.

Dawkins, Richard, *The Greatest Show on Earth: The Evidence for Evolution.* New York: Free Press, 2009.

Dean, Ingrid P., *True Police Stories of the Strange & Unexplained.* Woodbury: Llewellyn, 2011.

Denton, Michael, *Evolution: A Theory in Crisis.* Chevy Chase: Adler & Adler, 3rd edn, 1986.

Fowler, Raymond E., *The Watchers.* New York: Bantam, 1990.

Fowler, Raymond E., *The Watchers II.* Newberg: Wild Flower Press, 1995.

Fowler, Raymond E., *UFO Testament: Anatomy of an Abductee.* Lincoln: iUniverse, 2002.

Grof, Stanislav, *LSD Doorway to the Numinous.* Rochester: Park Street Press, 2009. (Originally published in 1975 under the title *Realms of the Human Unconscious*)

Grof, Stanislav, *The Cosmic Game.* New York: State University of New York Press, 1998.

Grof, Stanislav, *The Holotropic Mind.* San Francisco: HarperSanFrancisco, 1993.

Grof, Stanislav, *When the Impossible Happens.* Boulder: Sounds True,

2006.

Grosso, Michael, *Experiencing the Next World Now*. New York: Paraview Pocket Books, 2004.

Guillermo, Gonzalez, and Richards, Jay W., *The Privileged Planet*. Washington DC: Regnery, 2004.

Haeckel, Ernst, *The Wonders of Life.* Translated by Joseph McCabe. London: Harper & Brothers, 1905.

Haisch, Bernard, *The God Theory*. SanFrancisco: Red Wheel/Weiser, 2006.

Haisch, Bernard, *The Purpose-Guided Universe*. Franklin Lakes: New Page, 2010.

Haley, Leah A., *Lost Was the Key.* Murfreesboro: Greanleaf Publications, 1993.

Hamilton, Bonnie J., *Invitation to the Self: Journey with the Star People.* Morrisville: Lulu, 2011.

Hanks, Micah A., *Magic, Mysticism & The Molecule.* CreateSpace, 2010.

Hopkins, Budd, *Intruders.* New York: Random House, 1987.

Hopkins, Budd, and Rainey, Carol, *Science, UFO Invisibility and Transgenic Beings.* New York: Atria, 2003.

Huxley, Aldous, *The Doors of Perception & Heaven and Hell.* New York: Harper Perennial, 2004. (Originally published as separate titles in 1954 and 1956 respectively)

Inglis, Brian, *Natural & Supernatural: A History of the Paranormal From the Earliest Times to 1914.* Guildford: White Crow Books, 2012. (Originally published in 1977)

Inglis, Brian, *Science and Parascience: A History of the Paranormal, 1914-*

1939. London: Hodder and Stoughton, 1984.

James, William, *Memories and Studies.* Rockville: Arc Manor, 2008.

Johnson, Donald E., *Programming of Life.* Sylacauga: Big Mac Publishers, 2010.

Jung, Carl G., *Memories, Dreams, Reflections.* New York: Vintage Books, 1989.

Kalweit, Holger, *Shamans, Healers, and Medicine Men.* Boston: Shambhala, 1992.

Keel, John A., *Operation Trojan Horse.* Lilburn: IllumiNet Press, 1996. (Originally published in 1970)

Keel, John A., *The Cosmic Question.* London: Granada, 1978.

Keel, John A., *The Mothman Prophecies.* New York: Tor Books, 2002. (Originally published in 1975)

Kelly, Robin, *The Human Antenna.* Santa Rosa: Energy Psychology Press, 2007.

Kirsch, Irving, *The Emperor's New Drugs.* New York: Basic Books, 2010.

Konkolesky, William J., *Experiencer: Raised in Two Worlds.* Morrisville: Lulu, 2009.

Kripal, Jeffrey J., *Authors of the Impossible,* Chicago: University of Chicago Press, 2010.

Kripal, Jeffrey J., *Mutants and Mystics: Science Fiction, Superhero Comics, and the Paranormal.* Chicago: University of Chicago Press, 2011.

Laszlo, Ervin, *The Connectivity Hypothesis.* New York: State University of New York Press, 2003.

LeGrice, Keiron, *The Archetypal Cosmos.* Edinburgh: Floris Books, 2010.

Lipton, Bruce H., *The Biology of Belief: Unleashing the Power of Consciousness, Matter & Miracles.* New York: Hay House, 14th edn, 2011. (Originally published in 2005)

Lommel, Pim Van, *Consciousness Beyond Life: The Science of the Near-Death Experience.* New York: HarperOne, 2010.

Long, Jeffrey, *Evidence of the Afterlife.* New York: HarperOne, 2010.

Lorenzen, Coral and Lorenzen, Jim, *Flying Saucer Occupants.* New York: Signet, 1967.

Mack, John E., *Abduction.* New York: Charles Scribner's Sons, 1994.

Mack, John E., *Passport to the Cosmos: Human Transformation and Alien Encounters.* New York: Three Rivers Press, 1999.

Magnus, John, *Astral Projection and The Nature of Reality.* Charlottesville: Hampton Roads, 2005.

McKnight, Rosalind A., *Cosmic Journeys.* Charlottesville: Hampton Roads, 1999.

Meyer, Stephen C., *Signature in the Cell: DNA and the Evidence for Intelligent Design.* New York: HarperOne, 2009.

Mishlove, Jeffrey, *The PK Man: A True Story of Mind Over Matter.* Charlottesville: Hampton Roads, 2000.

Modi, Shakuntala, *Remarkable Healings.* Charlottesville: Hampton Roads, 1997.

Monroe, Robert A., *Far Journeys.* New York: Broadway Books, 2001. (Originally published in 1985)

Monroe, Robert A., *Journeys Out of the Body.* New York: Broadway Books,

2001. (Originally published in 1971)

Moody, Raymond, *Reunions: Visionary Encounters With Departed Loved Ones.* New York: Ivy Books, 1993.

Murphy, Michael, *The Future of the Body.* New York: Tarcher/Putnam, 1992.

Newton, Michael, *Destiny of Souls.* Woodbury: Llewellyn, 2006.

Newton, Michael, *Journey of Souls.* Woodbury: Llewellyn, 5th edn, 2006.

Oakford, David L., *Journey Through The World of Spirit: God, Gaia, and Guardian Angels.* Foresthill: Reality Entertainment, 2007.

Playfair, Guy Lyon, *If This Be Magic: The Forgotten Power of Hypnotism.* Guildford: White Crow Books, 2011. (Originally published in 1985)

Praagh, James V., *Ghosts Among Us.* New York: HarperOne, 2008.

Praagh, James V., *Unfinished Business.* New York: HarperOne, 2009.

Puységur, Marquis de, *Mémoires pour servir à l'histoire et à l'établissement du magnétisme animal.* Paris: Cellot, 2nd edn, 1809.

Radin, Dean, *The Conscious Universe.* New York: HarperOne, 1997.

Ring, Kenneth, *Heading Toward Omega: In Search of the Meaning of the Near-Death Experience.* New York: William Morrow and Company, 1984.

Ring, Kenneth, *The Omega Project: Near-Death Experiences, UFO Encounters, and Mind at Large.* New York: William Morrow and Company, 1992.

Rosenblum, Bruce, and Kuttner, Fred, *Quantum Enigma: Physics Encounters Consciousness.* New York: Oxford University Press, 2006.

Sparks, Jim, *The Keepers: An Alien Message for the Human Race.*

Columbus: Wild Flower Press, 2nd edn, 2008.

Storm, Howard, *My Descent Into Death.* New York: Doubleday, 2005.

Strassman, Rick, *DMT: The Spirit Molecule.* Rochester: Park Street Press, 2001.

Talbot, Michael, *The Holographic Universe.* New York: Harper Perennial, 1991.

Taylor, Jeremy, *Dream Work: Techniques for Discovering the Creative Power in Dreams.* New York: Paulist Press, 1983.

Turner, Karla, *Taken: Inside the Alien-Human Agenda.* Tallahassee: Rose Printing Company, 1994. [http://www.jeffpolachek.com/kt-books]

Vallee, Jacques, *Confrontations: A Scientist's Search for Alien Contact.* San Antonio: Anomalist Books, 2008. (Originally published in 1990)

Vallee, Jacques, *Dimensions: A Casebook of Alien Contact.* San Antonio: Anomalist Books, 2008. (Originally published in 1988)

Vallee, Jacques, *Passport to Magonia: On UFOs, Folklore, and Parallel Worlds.* Chicago: McGraw-Hill/Contemporary, 1993. (Originally published in 1969)

Vallee, Jacques, *Revelations: Alien Contact and Human Deception.* San Antonio: Anomalist Books, 2008. (Originally published in 1991)

Vallee, Jacques, *UFOs: The Psychic Solution.* Frogmore, U.K.: Panther, 1977. (Originally published in 1975 by E.P. Dutton & Co under the title *The Invisible College*)

Vieira, Waldo, *Projections of the Consciousness: A Diary of Out-of-Body Experiences.* New York: International Academy of Consciousness, 3rd edn, 2007.

Waggoner, Robert, *Lucid Dreaming: Gateway to the Inner Self.* Needham:

Moment Point Press, 2009.

Wallace, Alfred R., *Contributions to the Theory of Natural Selection: A Series of Essays.* London: Macmillan, 1870.

Wallace, Alfred R., *Miracles and Modern Spiritualism.* London: George Redway, 3rd edn, 1896.

Weiss, Brian L., *Many Lives, Many Masters.* New York: Fireside, 1988.

Weiss, Brian L., *Same Soul, Many Bodies.* New York: Free Press, 2004.

Wilson, Kay, *I Forgot What I Wasn't Supposed to Remember.* Electronic PDF, 2011.
http://www.alienjigsaw.com/The_Books/I_Forgot_What_I_Wasn't_Suppo
sed_to_Remember.pdf

Woodward, Thomas E. and Gills, James P., *The Mysterious Epigenome: What Lies Beyond DNA.* Grand Rapids: Kregel, 2012.

Woolger, Roger J., *Other Lives, Other Selves.* New York: Bantam, 1988.

ABOUT THE AUTHOR

Daniel Neiman holds a Bachelor's Degree from the University of Nebraska at Lincoln. He is an independent researcher with a focus on altered states of consciousness and life after death. He currently lives in Seoul, South Korea where he teaches English, researches and writes. The author's website is www.anomalousexperience.com and his email address is danneiman@gmail.com

www.ingramcontent.com/pod-product-compliance
Lightning Source LLC
LaVergne TN
LVHW051459080426
835509LV00017B/1819